When You Come Home

A Novel

Matthew D. Meadors

WHEN YOU COME HOME

© 2007 by Matthew D. Meadors

Cover design by DzinDNA, Mark Combs

International Standard Book Number: 978-0-615-26442-4

Printed in the United States of America

"This fictional novel reflects the true-to-life emotional and logistical rollercoaster of international adoption. I am amazed and pleased to report that this compelling story caused even an adoption professional to burn the midnight oil! My attention was captured on the very first page."

Susanna Will

Director of Development

Dillon International, Inc.

Tulsa, Oklahoma

For more information on international adoption visit Dillon's website at www.dillonadopt.com.

To Martha, Coutney and Cassidy Yin Meadors, my girls.

Martha, you're the beautiful wife I don't deserve but am so thankful I have. You are living proof that God renews his grace each day – for I see it alive in you every day. Thanks for believing in this knuckle head!

Courtney, the day you were born I thought I couldn't be prouder. Boy was I wrong! Believe in yourself like I believe in you and you'll do great things for the Lord.

Yin Yin, God's plan is perfect, and we learned that when we found you in China. You'll never know how much I admire you. You are a conqueror!

I love you all – moreler!

Mom, Dad, Joseph and Soul'd Out. I hope you'll accept a sincere "Thanks!" I can't begin to tell you what you mean to me. Mark, your designs are the bomb!

Jesus, my Lord and Savior, I dedicate this to you. What would we be without the cross? You are awesome!

Chapter 1

"Katie?" There was no answer from behind the bathroom door so Aaron Phelps turned and paced his bedroom. *What could be taking so long?*

He stalked over to the west side, pulled back one panel of the light green, tabbed curtains that hung over the large bank of windows and looked out across the two acre lot he and his wife, Katherine, owned on the western edge of Tulsa county. He bit his lip as he watched a hawk circling high above the hills to the west. It was a cold, gray day in early December and he could feel the effect of it on the frosty window panes. The hills, barren of foliage during this time of year, seemed dark and foreboding.

It was just a few weeks before Christmas, and Katie had been waiting for this special moment to give him "his Christmas gift." Aaron wasn't so sure he wanted such a gift. He didn't know if he was ready for it. He wasn't certain he'd ever be ready. But he knew how much this meant to his wife, and he didn't want to disappoint her so he had agreed to try, though secretly the idea caused him to shudder with apprehension.

Aaron sighed as he turned from the windows and resumed his pacing, repeating the path he had been traveling for over twenty minutes now. He arced around the foot of the bed to the closed bathroom door on the east side of the room. Then he paused in front of the door, but heard little, so he turned back toward the windows.

He stopped again at the window and peeked out. The hawk was no longer within eyesight, leaving just the empty hills, so he retraced his steps toward the bathroom door, dragging his hand along the top rail of the oak footboard on their bed. This time he stopped in front of the bathroom door and tapped on it.

"Come on, Katie, it's been over twenty minutes. I know it doesn't take that long," Aaron whispered. Twenty minutes was ample time to take a home pregnancy test, and he was certain Katie would have exploded from the bathroom had the test shown the slightest hint of a positive sign.

Aaron felt like his emotions were trapped in a blender. He was sad for Katie, and maybe for himself too. Yet, he felt guilt because he knew that somewhere deep within him there was a sense of relief that he wasn't going to be a father.

He pressed the side of his face against the door. "Hey, babe, it's gonna be alright," he said, knowing that the hollow words brought her little, if any, comfort.

Finally the door opened to reveal Katie's deep blue eyes filled with tears. Aaron felt his heart breaking for her. Her hands hung at her side, and her shoulders bobbed with quiet sobs. Aaron took the test from her right hand and looked at it – no pink line revealing the anticipated news.

He tucked the stick into the back pocket of his jeans and wrapped her up in his strong arms. Heartbroken, Katie buried her face in his chest and began to cry. They stood this way for several minutes. Aaron didn't try to stop her crying. Instead he loved her – the only thing he could do, struggling with her pain, and waging his own private battle as well.

With her head still buried in his chest, Aaron could hear Katie's muffled speech between her gasps as she fought to steady her breathing. "I'm sorry."

Aaron kissed the top of her head. "Me too," he said as he ran his fingers through her dark brown hair.

"I don't know what to do," she said, her breath starting to come more regularly.

"Me neither," he replied, "but then again, when do I ever?"

Katie gathered herself with a shiver, and pulled away from Aaron just enough to look at him. "We could think about seeing a doctor," she said between sniffles.

"Or we could just keep trying." Aaron smiled as he looked at her. Even now, red and puffy, her eyes shone.

"That's what you said last time."

"Well, if at first you don't succeed . . ."

Katie smiled back at him. "I'm sure you're willing to do whatever it takes."

Aaron put his right hand over his heart. "There's no limit to the sacrifices I'll make for you, my love."

"Mmm hmmm, I'm sure."

*　　*　　*

She hid behind a dumpster, in the shadows of a steel plant across the alley from the large two-story building. It was just before dawn so it was still mostly dark, yet her large eyes darted all around and she clamped her jaws together trying to quell the rising nerves that were causing her teeth to chatter. The building looked plain, unadorned and somewhat rundown from the outside. Its once white façade was now dirty from years of steeping in the grime and pollution of Chongqing, the largest, most populated city in the People's Republic of China. Her heart sank with the suspicion that it wasn't any better on the inside. The thick cardboard box lay on the front steps, vulnerable. From within the sanctuary of the shadows she surveyed her surroundings. At this time in the morning there was very little movement on the streets around the building. She had spent the previous four mornings in surveillance – watching the comings and goings of the people who lived and worked there. She felt certain she knew their routine, and that the same person, an older, kind looking woman whom she'd come to think of as "auntie" would soon emerge from inside as she made her morning rounds.

She had convinced herself she was doing the right thing. After all, this was better than coming home from the rice fields to find that the "problem" had been disposed of by her parents or grandparents, perhaps discarded into the nearby Yangtze River.

She had planned and rehearsed this moment over and over in her mind. She would leave the package on the porch and escape. But, reality was taking its toll. She knew she shouldn't stay – to stay and be caught would mean certain imprisonment, and quite possibly death. But she couldn't force herself to leave either. Every part of her being longed to retrieve the box with its most precious contents and run far away.

The young woman fought back tears. The State's policies combined with life's circumstances had forced her to this point, where she was now about to betray every instinct within her. Yet she couldn't help but wonder: What kind of a person would do what she was doing? Could she really become just another shameful, nameless statistic? Her short, choppy breaths created puffs of steam in the frigid morning air. She held her breath as an old man on a bicycle wobbled by on the dirty, cracked sidewalk running in front of the building. He gave the box little more than a passing glance as he rolled past it. She gathered her tattered grey coat around her shoulders. In a city of fifteen million people, she felt isolated and alone – abandoned by her god. Fear and desperation surged within her.

Then it happened, right on time. The front lights to the building flickered on. The row of bare bulbs cast dim swaths of light across its front. Tears blurred her vision. Breathless, she stared at the front door from within the cover of shadow. The kindly old "auntie" stepped through the door with broom in hand. She stopped in front of the box and stared down at it, then snapped her head up and surveyed the area, searching for someone.

The girl withdrew further within the shadows and squatted down behind the dumpster, hiding from the searching gaze. It felt as if she were imploding. She couldn't breathe, and her legs began to tremble underneath her. Paralyzed with fear, she watched the old woman look back down at the box for several seconds before leaning the broom against the wall, then bending over and carefully picking the box up with both hands. As the old grandma rose, she scanned the area again with a sad, knowing expression, and then turned to take the package into the building.

The young girl clinched her teeth, and put her hands over her mouth, a muffled sob escaping her lips. The old woman stopped short at the door and turned, searching once again. The woman peered straight in her direction, seemingly without seeing her. She memorized every line in her old, wrinkled face – the eyes looked sad. She held her breath, trembling now, out of control. Then, just like that, the old woman turned and walked into the building, carrying away the precious gift she would never see again.

With both hands still covering her mouth, the young, heartbroken mother clenched her eyes tight and threw her head back. Her stomach convulsed and she dropped to her knees, doubled over in pain. She reached out to the door, arms stretching, grasping for the old woman, the box – her heart torn from her and carried away. Tears streamed down her cheeks in torrents. She had never before known such despair and anguish. How could she ever be delivered from this memory? Her life would never be complete again. She wished she could die.

*   *   *

Katie dipped a toe into the bath to test the water, found it satisfactory, then stepped in, and eased down into the tub. Her head hurt, just like it always did when she cried too hard. But her heart hurt more. She needed to relax, and spend time alone with God. She ached for His comfort and reassurance. Several lighted candles flickered at the other end of the big claw foot tub Aaron had installed in their master bathroom a year earlier. Their shadows floated in a peaceful dance across the ceiling. She lay back, sliding down to the point where just her head was above the bubbles. The hot tub soothed her body, and she felt the tension begin to dissipate amid the bubbles.

Lord, Father God, you know my heart. Search me and tell me if I'm mistaken. What's wrong with wanting a baby?

She felt the pangs in her heart. They were unlike any other she had ever known in her twenty-nine years of life. She worried about Aaron. He was always so supportive, and so open about everything in their lives. They had such a wonderful relationship. They could talk about anything and she felt so secure in his arms. He was her knight in shining armor.

Yet on this subject he seemed so withdrawn and sullen. For the first time she had mentioned seeing a doctor to him, and had received the response she anticipated and dreaded. He had just blown her off. *What is going on with him, Lord?*

Katie reached over the side of the tub and retrieved her cup of hot tea from a small side table. Holding it in both hands, she sipped from the cup.

No, she suddenly concluded, wanting a baby couldn't be wrong. What could be more natural? *But what if it's not God's will for us to have one?* They had been trying for over two years now. Each failure served only to feed her pain, and make her desire for a child that much stronger. Except for the knowledge of her pain, Aaron seemed relatively unaffected by the disappointment each passing month brought. The more frustrated and upset Katie became, the more nonchalant he became.

I swear, if he says something about winning one for the Gipper, I'll slug him!

Katie watched the shadows from the candles dance on the ceiling. One flickering shadow seemed to merge into the other, much like the passing of time. She swirled the bath water, making lazy circles in the foam with her right index finger.

You know my heart's desire, Father. You told us you would give us what we want if we ask in Jesus' name. I'm asking now, Lord. Grant me this gift, and give me a baby to love. Help Aaron. I love him so much, God, and I know that he loves me too. Touch his heart, or show me where I can help him. Make us one in this, Father. I need him. I feel lost and alone, and I can't make it through this – whatever this is – without him.

Setting the cup back down, she turned the hot water on with the toes of her foot. She could see the steam rising from the bath. Turning the water back off, she slid down completely below the surface of the bathwater, cocooned within its warmth. She didn't know how many more times she could bounce back from defeat, but she would keep trying.

God, I know you have a plan. Give me this gift, or take the desire from me. But either way, let your will be done.

She pushed herself back up from the water. As her head broke the surface, the words from Romans chapter eight rushed over her, as if someone were whispering them in her ear: "We've been made more than conquerors, through the blood of Jesus Christ."

Thank you, Father, for the hope I have in you.

* * *

Wu Chien gave the frail baby a sponge bath. She wasn't sure, but she thought this was maybe the twentieth, or was it the thirtieth, baby to come to the orphanage this year. At any rate, it didn't matter. Whatever the number, it was too high. It upset her to think of all the baby girls who were abandoned each year in China, her beloved homeland. She believed it displeased Yesu even more. God's only Son, died for all so that none might be turned away. Yet here in the Middle Kingdom Yesu's youngest children were being abandoned, or worse, every day.

Times like this occasionally caused her to struggle with her faith. How could a God that loves His people let them come to such desperate circumstances? Parents had to abandon their children for fear of punishment from their own government, or because they were too poor to feed and support them. And why must she live out her Christian faith in secret for fear of punishment from the government? Yet every time she had such doubts, she was reminded of Romans chapter eight, verse twenty-eight: "All things work together for those who are in Christ Jesus."

The baby squirmed as she caressed her neck, behind her ears, and on her shoulders. She thought she had seen a young woman hiding in the shadows of the alley, but she wasn't sure. She didn't want to know. Nor did she want to face the choice of turning someone in to the authorities, or risk accusations of aiding and abetting.

She leaned over and whispered in the baby's ear. "I pray to my Yesu for your mama. He will be near to her."

I know my Yesu would forgive her if she was to ask, but will she ever be able to forgive herself?

She carefully lifted the baby to an upright position and supported her while she washed her back. Humming a soft song, Chien watched the child relax, soothed by her sounds.

Did her mother sing her this lullaby?

Chien was sixty-five years old, and had been working in this orphanage in Chongqing for about fifteen years. In that time, she'd seen many babies come and go. Some had been adopted from people in other countries. As much as she hated to see all of these beautiful little girls leaving their homeland, she thanked God that He was providing homes for them. She worried much less about those babies than she did the ones who had grown up in the orphanage and then were turned out to fend for themselves when they were eighteen. She had also seen some babies die from illnesses that weren't treated properly due to insufficient resources. There were plenty of times that the babies in this orphanage had known hunger. The adopted babies were going to prosperous countries like Switzerland, England, or, best of all, America, but she shuddered to imagine what fate might have awaited some of the babies who were never adopted, and "graduated" from the orphanage.

Wu Chien had been married for nearly thirty years before her husband died sixteen years ago. Their only child, a boy, died when he was thirteen. She had been without any of her own family for sixteen years. The workers and the children were her surrogate family now. Despite her advancing age she was needed and useful here. She liked that. She and her husband had both come to know Christ as savior twenty-five years ago from a missionary that came to their village. She had served with zeal in the underground churches until her husband died. Now, this orphanage was her mission field, and she set about the business of introducing the babies to Yesu.

Wu Chien picked up an old, thin towel and dried the baby. She leaned down to smell of her. She loved to smell babies after they had been bathed. She whispered in the baby's ear. "My Yesu has placed me here to care for you, and all of the other little ones. I promise you I will be faithful to His calling for me."

It wasn't easy, her job. She had to try to care for, and mother the children without growing overly attached. This child seemed special, though. She would have to fight attaching to this one. For some reason, the instinct to mother her and give her special attention seemed more intense. She was worried though. The child seemed to have something wrong with her. Her breathing was sometimes irregular and short, as if she were struggling for air. As she put the layers of clothing onto the baby, she studied her. Maybe this one would be able to see a doctor. Even better, maybe this one could be adopted by a family from America where she could go and receive treatment from American doctors, and live in a prosperity Chien herself had never known.

She kissed the baby on the head. "You are a good baby, mei mei. I pray for wonderful things for you."

Chapter 2

At exactly 4:30 in the afternoon on Friday Aaron tapped on the office door of James Patterson, pastor of Crossroads Community Church. Patterson had his back to Aaron, looking at his computer screen. Turning around, he stood and smiled. "Come on in, shut the door."

"Thank you," Aaron said as he stepped into the office and did as asked. Aaron and Katie had only been members of the church for about two years, but in that time Aaron had grown quite fond of "Pastor James," as he called him. He wasn't sure exactly why he was here, other than groping for an answer to the mixed feelings he had about being a father. He fought with guilt for not telling Katie what he was doing; his movements were awkward and hesitant as a result.

To Aaron's relief, James eased his nerves, at least a little, by walking around the desk and shaking Aaron's hand. His grip was solid, but gentle. He was slightly shorter and leaner than Aaron, but still athletic looking. Wire rimmed glasses covered his brown eyes and he sported khaki pants and a blue knit pullover shirt. He directed Aaron to two side chairs on the wall opposite of his big oak desk, leaving a small table between them. "Have a seat. Can I get you anything?"

"No, no thank you," Aaron said as he took his seat and looked around at the pastor's office. The office was modest, but nice. The walls were painted a warm olive color, and various pictures, plaques, and framed documents hung on three of them. The windows had rattan shades that were raised three quarters of the way up with eggplant colored valances over their top. Matching wingback chairs fronted the pastor's desk, and the wall behind the desk was lined top-to-bottom with custom made oak bookshelves. The shelves were almost stuffed to their capacity with various sized books and binders.

"All those books make you anymore God-like?" Aaron asked, hoping his nerves would settle some more.

James smiled "I'm certain they haven't, but I can usually count on them to show me how far I still have to go."

"Any suggestions?"

"From the books? A few. Of course God's word is still the ultimate source."

"I suppose so," Aaron said as he fidgeted in the chair.

Pastor James had taken a seat in the other side chair and positioned himself where they could look at each other easily. Leaning towards Aaron, he zeroed in on him in a pleasant, natural manner that put Aaron a little more at ease.

"What can I do for you, Aaron?"

Aaron sighed and stretched his neck muscles. "Good question. I'm not really sure myself."

The pastor nodded his head. "I understand. It can be difficult to open up, or even know where to start, but we've got to start someplace. Is there something troubling you?"

Aaron pulled at the knot in his red silk tie before speaking. "Katie and I have been trying to have a baby, but we're having trouble," he finally blurted out. He ducked his head in embarrassment and shock at his own words. "She wants to see a specialist, a fertility doctor."

"Sounds like a logical next step."

"Yeah, maybe." Aaron could feel his breath coming a little shorter now that he had started. "But I guess the biggest problem is that I'm not even sure I want to have a kid in the first place, much less take our problems to some doctor I've never met."

James maintained his steady gaze on Aaron as he sat back in his chair. As far as Aaron could tell, he could've just told him the sky was blue for the lack of reaction.

"That would be a problem wouldn't it," the pastor replied, "but I understand. Fatherhood can be a scary proposition."

Aaron drummed his fingers on the arm of his chair and looked back at Patterson. "Terrifying, that's what I'd call it."

"Why so?"

"Oh, I don't know," Aaron said as he looked away. "It just is. I don't know if I'm ready. I don't know if we can afford it. Sometimes I wonder how responsible I am about myself and my actions, let alone being responsible for another person."

James took off his glasses and exhaled on them, then wiped them off with his shirt. Putting them back on, he looked at Aaron, but the look wasn't judgmental, or mean. It was more as if he were studying Aaron, sizing him up, while he formed his next thoughts.

Aaron had always had authority issues, but the pastor didn't bring those out in him. Instead, Aaron felt very comfortable in his presence. So he waited as patiently as possible.

Finally James clasped his hands together as though he'd affirmed something important. "It's quite a daunting proposition, isn't it?" he said. "And rest assured, you can never really afford it, yet somehow the Lord always provides and helps you make ends meet. But if you and Katie are truly called to be parents then the Lord will provide you with the love, wisdom, perseverance and patience to handle the task if you just ask Him. But here's a question for you to ask yourself first. Knowing this, then if God is the Lord of your life, and in Him all things are possible, what are you *really* afraid of?"

Aaron broke into a half-hearted smile. "Why don't you just quit beating around the bush and cut straight to the chase?"

"I'm not a licensed counselor or therapist. I'm not trained in 'shrink-talk'. I'm speaking to you as your pastor, and as a friend. The only way I know to attack a problem is head-on. Frankly, your reticence surprises me. You certainly don't strike me as the timid type."

"I guess I'm not when it comes to certain things. But when it comes to applying words to my feelings, that's a whole different story."

"So, here we are. I can't make you talk about this, and yet I can't offer any help if you don't."

Aaron stood and walked to a window that looked out on a small courtyard between two of the church buildings. He wanted a good stiff drink, and he wasn't even a drinker anymore. Maybe a big shot of bourbon would make him numb enough to spill his guts. He could feel the pastor's gaze resting on his back. He knew he was wasting his time, and he didn't want to do that.

Still facing the window, but no longer really looking at anything, Aaron sighed. With all the courage he could muster, he said "I don't want to have a baby because I'm scared." In the large office, his voice sounded pinched off and tiny.

"Why are you scared?"

"I don't know, I just am, I guess."

"You guess? I'm sure if you dig a little deeper you can figure it out."

Aaron turned and faced the pastor. Sitting down on the windowsill he pointed a defiant chin at him. He didn't like being scared. It made him angry. "What kind of counseling is this? 'Physician heal thyself'?"

The pastor folded his hands in his lap and smiled easily back at Aaron. "I prefer to call it letting the Holy Spirit reveal the truth."

Aaron nodded his head at the pastor and looked down, ashamed that he had reacted with such anger toward him.

"Now, why are you so scared?"

Still looking down he mumbled, "I don't know how to be a dad."
Aaron sighed and his shoulders drooped, as if his last ounce of fight were
oozing from him at that moment. "I don't know how to be a dad because I
never had one."

"Your biological father?"

"Is gone. I never knew him. He left the day after I was born. Told
my mother he was too young to be tied down to a family." Aaron snorted in
disgust. "He said he needed his freedom."

Aaron could feel the weight of his emotions and words pressing
down on him. He wanted to run, but felt like his feet were stuck in cement
blocks.

"Must have been tough growing up without a father?"

"Had its moments, that's for sure," Aaron said. "Mom tried the best
she could. Often worked two jobs. I was alone a lot."

"Where's your mother now?" James asked.

Aaron ducked his head. He still regretted that his mom was never
able to see how the Lord had turned his life around. "Home."

"Where's home?"

"With the Lord. She died in a car accident six months after I
graduated high school."

"I'm sorry, I didn't know."

"It's okay."

"Your mother was a Christian?"

"Yes, very faithful. The finest woman I ever knew – until Katie."
Aaron paused. All of a sudden he felt as though his legs couldn't hold him
up any longer. He walked back to his chair and plopped onto it, slumping
below its back. The office was very still but his head was spinning. The
memory of the disappointment he must have brought to his mother seared
through his heart like a hot knife. "She had taken me to Sunday school and

church for as long as I could remember. It hurt her to see the direction my life went once I reached high school, but she never condemned me. Her love was unfailing. She never met Katie. I'm sure she would have loved her though."

James nodded his head, seemingly to himself. "Back to your teenage years. What did you do with all that loneliness?"

"Played sports mostly. As I got older I started fighting other boys more and more."

"Did you win?"

Aaron shrugged. "I guess – most of the time. I'd fight anybody though, so I ran into a few that got the best of me."

James didn't move. His whole countenance had changed as his focus narrowed in on the discussion. "Why do you suppose that is? Why did you fight so much?"

Aaron stood up and walked towards the pastor's desk. He knew he was restless, but he couldn't help himself. As he neared the desk, he stopped and looked back over his shoulder at James, who nodded his head in one slight motion. Aaron walked behind the desk and gazed up at the books in the bookshelves. "I don't know. I guess it was to prove who was the toughest."

"What else do you think you were proving?"

Aaron had never really thought much about those days. When he had come to know the Lord in college he had put them behind him. But now the realization dawned on Aaron and he turned around to look at the wise pastor. "I guess I was trying to prove I was a man."

James nodded his head again. "Many a boy has confused physical prowess with manliness. You didn't have a father figure to show you the way so you did the best you could."

Aaron crossed his arms over his chest. "So what does that have to do with me and Katie, and babies?"

"Aaron, I don't know what you were like in college. I imagine you were a good kid, just confused. But I do know that He is making you into a fine man. Don't you think He can make you a good father as well? The Lord can use you for any purpose He has, as long as you are willing and faithful."

"I would think he needs something to work with first."

The pastor shook his head. "You know better than that. You must believe that God can make you what he wants you to be."

Aaron felt that spark of anger fire off in his stomach again. "That's funny, I prayed for years that God would give me a dad and he never did. In return, he took my mom as well."

"I can't even attempt to explain why things happen, Aaron," James said. "All I can tell you is what you should already know. God has a purpose for your life here and now. He can work that purpose through any and all circumstances. Have you told Katherine?"

"Which part?"

"All of it."

Aaron cleared his hoarse throat. "No I haven't, not all of it. She knows I grew up without a dad, and that my mom died, of course. But she doesn't know any of the rest."

"So she doesn't know you're here?"

Aaron bristled that the pastor could make that assumption – and be right about it. "That's correct."

"You've got to level with her, Aaron. Tell her your fears and worries. I'm sure she'll understand."

"I don't know if I can. I want to talk to her, I try to, but the only things I can think of to say sound so pathetic. Like me." Aaron clenched his fists. "I just don't know if I have the strength to admit my weaknesses to her."

James smiled at this. "Ah, the male ego. I struggle with one myself."

Aaron grinned at the pastor. "What? I thought you were perfect."

"Just go talk to my wife. Wouldn't need God's grace if I were." The pastor looked at his watch and shook his head. "I'm sorry, Aaron, but I've got another appointment." He stood and put his arm around Aaron's shoulder and started walking to the door with him.

"Think about what we've talked about – about what I've said to you. You're carrying a lot of baggage. Rejected by your father, guilt from how you were living when your mother died. Talk to Katie about these things. Remember your vows to her. Love, honor, and cherish. Part of honoring her is to be open and honest. I would be willing to wager you just might find that she is quite a strong woman. I have found her to be a wonderful person, myself."

"Yup, she's just as wonderful in private as well. I definitely married up."

As they reached the door James opened it and stepped to one side. "Most of us have. Do you care to come back and pursue this more? I really think you should."

"I'm not sure, but I'll let you know," Aaron said as he shook the pastor's hand. "Thanks for your time."

"I'm always here, but I cannot stress enough that you need to work on this. Give it to the Lord. Get more help. As a matter of fact, a Christian therapist would be better than me. Like I told you, I can only speak to you as a friend. However, I can refer you to one if you would like?"

"Thanks, but I'd just as soon stick with you," Aaron said.

"Okay then, suit yourself. Feel free to come to me anytime."

Aaron smiled at James. "Thanks, I will." He left the church building and fought to keep from staggering across the asphalt parking lot to his Dodge pickup truck. He felt dizzy and breathless from the intensity of the discussion. He stopped at the truck and gulped in as much of the cold air as he could.

Maybe he was still more screwed up than he cared to admit. He knew he needed to tell Katie, but he didn't know if he could. *Lord, I need your help. Without You, I don't even know where to begin*

*   *   *

Katie walked through Woodland Hills Mall in south Tulsa trying to dodge the many Christmas shoppers who were hustling through it, obviously on a mission to get in, get the goods, and get out. Aaron had left a message on her voice mail at work that he would be home late so she had taken this opportunity to pick up another gift or two, and just get away from her present worries and troubles.

While she couldn't drag Aaron to the mall during the Christmas season with a team of Clydesdales, she enjoyed it at this time of year. The windows in the various shops were always glowing with lights and the twenty foot Christmas tree that greeted shoppers when they entered through the main doors was always spectacular. She had stopped at a bookstore and picked up the latest Alcorn novel for Aaron, then hit Dillard's where she found some nice, silky pajamas that her dad had asked her to get for her mother.

Up ahead she spotted a Starbuck's and the image of a caramel latte sprang to mind. On her way there she passed a Lane Bryant store and stopped to window shop. She could see her reflection in the mirror, and she didn't like what she saw. It looked like the reflection of a woman who was destined to be a desperate old woman without kids. Janie, her sister, would probably have three or four, and she could be dear, sweet Auntie Katie. She would pinch her nieces' and nephews' cheeks while they humored her, understanding that she had gone slightly bonkers trying to have a child of her own.

She sighed and moved on, anticipating the smooth, sweet taste of the "fru-fru coffee," as Aaron called it. As she neared the coffee shop she saw a large play area for children right behind it.

They're haunting me.

She ordered a small caramel latte and paid for it then took it and sat down just outside the play area. She didn't realize she'd been drawn that direction until she found a seat behind two mothers who were sitting inside the nice, oak colored half-walls that surrounded the play area.

The floor of the play area appeared to be made of a padded material with a bright, colorful carpet covering it. There were various plastic animals that the kids climbed on and over. There was also a plastic fort-like area with a round tunnel that connected two areas and a small slide at one end. Children seemed to be swarming in and around it like bees in a hive.

There was a small dollop of whipped cream floating on top of Katie's coffee, and she used the plastic stirrer to scoop a portion of it into her mouth, and then mixed the rest of it into her latte.

Every nationality seemed to be represented among the dozens of kids packed into the four hundred square foot play area. Katie watched a little black boy and white girl bump into each other, then fall down laughing as they rolled into another little Asian girl. Their joy seemed innocent and perfect, and maybe a little contagious, as Katie found herself smiling at them. Soon she was lost in a dream world of little fingers and toes, Johnson's baby shampoo and dirty diapers.

She was snapped out of her dream world though, when she noticed someone staring at her out of the corner of her eye. That someone was a small girl with curly blond hair and bright blue eyes. Katie smiled at her, and she smiled back.

"I'm Kinsey," the little girl said.

Katie turned to face her. "Hi Kinsey, I'm Katie. How old are you?"

"I'm four years old," she said, holding up three fingers and looking confused.

Katie looked around for an adult. "Where's your mommy?"

"She's over there," Kinsey said, pointing her tiny finger at the Dairy Queen Katie and Aaron always visited when she made him come to the mall with her.

Katie saw a bigger, older version of Kinsey walking away from the DQ carrying an ice cream cone, looking around the play area. She seemed on the verge of frantic, so Katie waved to her. She noticed Katie's wave then spotted her child next to Katie and began heading their direction.

"Where's your kid?" the little girl asked.

"Uh, I don't have any kids," Katie said, trying to hide the sadness in her voice.

"Why not?"

"That's a good question, sweetie."

Kinsey's mother reached them and smiled humorlessly at Katie before sitting down next to her daughter.

"Kinsey Marie, you know better than to sneak off from me like that. I should just throw this ice cream away. You scared me to death!"

Kinsey flashed her most angelic smile at her mother. "I'm sorry, Mommy," she said reaching for the cone.

Her mother looked at Katie. "I'm sorry about this," she said. "You know how kids are."

Katie nodded and smiled.

I wish.

Chapter 3

The baby squirmed and whimpered as the doctor examined her. The director of the orphanage had allowed Wu Chien to name the baby – a rare honor for a caretaker in an orphanage. She named her Yu Lin, after her own mother and she called her Lin-Lin. It had been three days since she had found her on the front steps. They had called the doctor that same day, but he was unable to visit until now. He examined her eyes, ears, nose and throat. All checked out well. The baby was somewhat underweight and frail looking. But that, unfortunately, wasn't an uncommon condition for abandoned babies. Chien watched intently as the doctor listened to her chest and heart. Bent over the baby, he frowned, repositioned the stethoscope and listened again. This time he shook his head and mumbled something so soft that she couldn't make it out.

"What is it?" Chien asked.

"I thought I heard something while I was listening to her heart," he said, "like a murmur, but I didn't hear it again."

"So, what does that mean?"

"It means," the doctor said, "that we wait and see."

"Shouldn't we run tests?"

"We need to monitor this child and see what happens first. Maybe we can avoid the extra expenses for tests that might not be necessary. Understand?"

Chien didn't like the doctor's answer, but she nodded her head anyway. "Do you know how old she is?" she asked.

"I estimate that she's eight days old."

"That means she was five days old when we found her, and her birthday would be December 1."

"Approximately, yes."

"Anything else?"

"No, nothing really. But you need to keep an eye on her and call me if you notice anything out of the ordinary. I'm concerned about what I heard."

Chien nodded her head at the doctor. "Thank you," she said in reply. "I will."

"I must be going," the doctor said, as he gathered his belongings.

Chien stood. "I'll see you out."

"No need, I know the way."

Chien watched the doctor leave then turned back to Lin Lin. "Hear that, *mei mei*? I need to watch you extra special," she said as she picked the child up and cradled her in her arms. "My Yesu is the best watcher of them all. His eyes never leave His children."

She wondered why the Lord had brought them together. Why this child was so different. What did Yesu have in store for this child? She could only hope it was something good. Maybe she could find a family. But she feared something was dreadfully wrong and that it may be hard for Lin to attract a family. Chien smiled down at the sweet face of this little orphan. The baby didn't even know she was an orphan, or what that meant. Lin Lin's eyes closed as she began to drift off to sleep in Chien's arms. She sat down in the lone rocking chair in the bedroom Lin Lin shared with seven other babies. There were about one-hundred and fifty other babies in this orphanage, and much work to be done. But, it could wait. *It will wait.* She would take this time.

Would I be too old to adopt her if she can't find a family? I can feel it Lord. This one's going to break my heart.

* * *

A day later Aaron was still trying to sort out his feelings while doing bench presses in the Westside Gym on Southwest Boulevard He wanted to have something other than fear and ambivalence to bring home to Katie this evening. He knew she was ready for something more from him – and she deserved it.

His best friend, Mark Cooper helped him rack the bar after doing his tenth rep. Katie and Aaron had met Mark and his wife when they first started attending Crossroads Church. Aaron was still young in his Christian walk and he was instantly drawn to Mark's Christian maturity. The two couples quickly struck up a friendship and Aaron discovered he had found a kindred soul in Mark. He enjoyed their camaraderie, the way they could joke with one another, and strange way they always seemed able to read each other's mind.

Aaron stood up from the bench to help Mark get his weight onto the bar, when he saw an acquaintance, Harold Guthrie walking by on the other side of the room. He waved at Guthrie who saw him, waved back and began coming his way. Guthrie was about ten years older, an inch taller than Aaron, and some fifty pounds heavier – and not all of it muscle. His grey hair was wet with sweat and his matching grey sweatsuit was dark with sweat as well. He wore black socks and white Reeboks.

"How ya doin' Aaron?" Guthrie asked as he stuck out a big, meaty hand.

Aaron shook it and replied "Okay, Harold, and you?"

"Aw, you know, same old, same old. Come down here mostly to get a break from the wife and kids."

Mark looked sideways at Aaron. "C'mon, let's get back to it."

Aaron stepped behind the bench and handed the bar off to Mark who began to steadily pump out the reps. When Cooper reached ten, he stopped and Aaron helped him guide the bar back onto the bench rack.

"What do you mean, Harold? I've only met your family once, but they seemed great," Aaron said.

"Oh, don't get me wrong, I love my wife and kids. Wouldn't trade them for the world. But, you know, sometimes a man needs space and time, and they take that away from you. The only place in the house I can call my own is the garage. Every waking minute is spent doing chores around the house or running the kids someplace, or helping them with their homework."

Mark didn't look pleased. "Isn't that part of the commitment though?" he said as he put weight back on for Aaron. He looked at Aaron. "How much?"

Aaron stretched his arms over his head. "Oh, let's keep it light today. Just bump it up to three-ten."

"Alright, no need to rub it in, wise guy. Remember, you may have the brawn, but I've definitely got you in the brains department."

"Well, it may be commitment," Harold interrupted, pointing a finger at Mark. "But it sure isn't everything they tell you it's gonna be. My oldest son is off in his own world all the time. You say something to him and he just grunts back at you. I spend my life providing for him and that's the respect I get? My girl is thirteen going on twenty-two. She thinks I'm the most stupid thing on earth. Never stops to think how I got where I'm at now. The wife and I rarely have time to ourselves, and when we do, all impulses are gone. I don't know. Sometimes I think guys like you, with a young beautiful wife, ought to think twice about having kids. Maybe live a little while you can."

The words rang in Aaron's ears like a bell. *Live a little while you can. But could Katie?*

"Well," Aaron said, "I'd better get back after it."

"Yeah sure, see you around kid."

"Thank you, merry sunshine! Come back when you can't stay so long," Mark muttered after Guthrie had walked out of earshot. Mark looked down at Aaron who was lying on the bench preparing for his next set of ten. "Don't believe half of what he says."

"I don't know what to believe," Aaron said as he nodded his head and lifted the weight off the bench. His mind wasn't into the lifting and he struggled to complete ten reps. He racked the barbell and stood up, beads of sweat running down his face. Mark looked at him for several seconds then said, "Hey, brother. I know you've been struggling with this. But don't put too much emphasis on what Guthrie was telling you. He doesn't seem like a man who has worked at keeping things in his life fresh and exciting, now does he?"

The two men cleared the weights off of the barbell and walked over to the lat machine to do standing tricep pushdowns.

Aaron spoke without straining as he did his reps. "I guess not, but what exactly do you mean?"

"Well, look at him. Does he look like he works at anything in his life other than his job? You and I know from experience that marriage takes work. My guess is that kids require even more. It's a package deal. You get what you put into it, you know?"

Aaron finished and stepped aside so Mark could do a set. "Yeah, I see what you're saying," Aaron said. "But Guthrie did have a point, that if you're not ready, then you shouldn't do it."

"Absolutely," Mark said "but I don't believe it's work that you're apprehensive about. You've never been the type to shy away from that. Something else is going on."

Aaron was a little annoyed. He wondered how this was Mark's business but didn't say it out loud because deep inside he knew that answer. "What makes you so sure?"

"I know you buddy. You're the type who's always there for your friends, but when it comes to admitting your own struggles or needs, you can't do it. You hide it, or make jokes, but you never confide in anyone about it. I see it in you all the time."

"So then you know I don't want to talk about it. I think talking is overrated as a form of communication anyway."

"I think you just like to play the silent brooding type. You and James Dean."

Aaron looked at Mark without any humor. "Yeah, a rebel without a clue."

*   *   *

Katie uttered what must have been her tenth prayer as she performed the final preparations for dinner. Aaron would be home soon, and she wanted to confront Aaron about his apathetic attitude. What was going on with him? But, she wanted it to be positive, and she hoped the outcome would be that he was as committed to having a child as she was.

Help me Lord. Guide me. Give me the words that can reach out to Aaron. Help me to be patient and understanding. Help Aaron to be sensitive to your lead. Thank you Father, that you're always near.

She raked her hand through her hair and checked her clothes for stains. She'd thought about wearing something he'd like, and making his favorite meal since it was her turn to cook, but she knew he'd think she was just setting him up – which would probably be at least somewhat true.

So, dressed in jeans and a sweatshirt Katie pulled a roast with carrots and potatoes out of the oven as Aaron pulled into the driveway and into his side of their two-car garage. Soon she heard the garage door shutting, and Aaron emerged from the laundry room that was positioned between the kitchen and the garage.

"Mmm, what smells so good?" Aaron asked as he walked to Katie and put his arms around her waist, still in his workout clothes.

Katie leaned away. "Not you!"

He ignored the comment, walked to the stove, and peeked inside the black roasting pan that was sitting on top of it.

"Pot roast, carrots, potatoes. Sounds yummy. But you know I'll have to workout extra to make up for it."

"You mean they don't keep you gophers – I mean junior accountants – hopping enough at work to keep you fit and trim?"

"Hey, that's Senior Gopher to you – and no they don't. It means I get all of the nasty reconciliations, and research stuff that the senior accountants don't want to do."

"Aha. Speaking of nasty, why don't you go get cleaned up?"

"Okay," Aaron said, leaning forward for a kiss.

Katie responded with a tight-lipped kiss.

"Gee, that was something."

"It's all you get until you clean up, buster."

"Okay, then," Aaron said as he turned and walked down the hall leading to their bedroom. "But when I return you'd better be ready."

"And waiting," Katie said after him.

Okay, he's in a pleasant mood. That's a good start.

Katie set the table, fussing over the positioning of the placemats and silverware. She poured iced tea for both of them then sat down in her usual spot at the dinner table, waiting for Aaron to return. *Why am I so nervous?* Aaron wasn't unreasonable – most of the time. Just about this. But even then, he'd never been mean. He just wouldn't talk. *Lord I hope this goes okay.*

A few minutes later Aaron emerged, freshly showered, with his wet hair combed back. He was wearing white tube socks, jeans, and a gray t-shirt that read "Property of University of Oklahoma Athletic Department," with an unbuttoned blue flannel shirt over the tee.

He leaned over Katie, kissed her on the mouth and smiled. He sat down across from her at the dinner table, and the two joined hands and he said a quick blessing on the meal.

"So, how was your day?" Katie asked as she served herself some carrots.

Aaron shrugged. "Lots of grunt work that no one else wants to do. But it was okay. Sometimes I just wish I'd gotten my act together sooner in life. Maybe I'd be a senior accountant by now."

Katie smiled at Aaron and put her hand on his. "You know, everything has a reason. You're still young."

"Thirty-one isn't as young as I once was."

"Well, silly, everyone can say that about their age. It's what you're doing with your life now that counts. At least life is a lot more stable for you these days," Katie said as she paused to think. *No time like the present, while he's contemplative and talking.*

"Babe, that's part of the reason why I feel like we're ready to have kids. Don't you think? I mean the Lord has blessed us with stable jobs, and a very peaceful, contented life. It doesn't seem like the time could be any better." Katie stopped to let that sink in.

Aaron bent forward over his plate. Katie could see his jaw muscles working as he chewed. They seemed to be working harder than normal.

"Aaron, don't you think?"

Aaron laid his fork on his plate and looked up at Katie. She felt his eyes lock in on hers. She loved looking at his brown eyes. She could see everything in them. All of his emotions and thoughts seemed to roll across them like a ticker-tape. Looking in his eyes now, she sensed fear and frustration. She had suspected he'd been hiding something. Now she knew it.

Katie used her napkin to wipe a spot off the gleaming oak table while she waited for Aaron to respond. She knew he would. Over the years he had learned to take his time and form his words wisely, especially when he was speaking about a touchy subject, like now.

Aaron cleared his throat. He did that when he was apprehensive. "Dear . . . I mean . . . I don't know . . ."

Katie nodded her head, encouraging.

Aaron sighed and shook his head. "The thing is . . . I just don't know." His head dropped a little and he stared at his plate.

Katie couldn't believe her ears. Her heart was breaking already. She knew where this was headed. This time, though, she felt anger and resentment boiling up inside her. *Why can't he commit to this, or at least tell me what he's thinking?* She laid her napkin down on the table and took a drink of tea.

"What do you mean you don't know?" Katie asked, the pitch of her voice rising a decibel.

Aaron rolled his eyes. "It means I don't know – plain and simple."

"Well, why don't you? It's not like I haven't given you all the time you should need." *Or should want.*

Aaron sighed. "I know, I know. Yes you've given me ample time, and yes, I probably should have figured things out by now. But it's just not that simple."

Katie stood up and began pacing. She could feel the anger growing hotter by the second. "What! What! What's not that simple, Aaron?" She noticed that her voice was dripping with disdain. She knew she would feel bad about that later, but right now she didn't care how her voice sounded. "We love each other, don't we? What could be so hard? Don't you care about my happiness?"

"Of course I do. What do you want from me, Katie?"

Katie stopped and put her hands on her hips. "I would like to get just one straight answer from you."

"That's just it," Aaron said, holding his hands out in front of him in exasperation. "I don't have a straight answer. I don't know anything I should. I don't know how . . ."

"I don't know, I don't know, I don't know. I'm sick of hearing I don't know!" Katie said, yelling full out now.

Aaron sprung to his feet, causing his chair to tip over behind him. Katie could see his eyes hardening in anger. "Well if you'd just shut up long enough . . ."

"Shut up! Don't you tell me to shut up! I have a right . . . I deserve to know!"

Aaron walked around the table and stood about fifteen feet in front of Katie. "Maybe I can't tell you!"

"You mean you won't tell me! I've had about enough of this!"

Aaron's shoulders slumped and Katie knew immediately that the fight had gone too far. *Oh dear God. I didn't mean for* this.

"Me too," Aaron said in a voice strained with anger and resentment as he started walking down the hall toward their bedroom.

"Now where are you going?" Katie called after him.

"Out!"

"Don't you turn and run away. I'll still be here when you come back. This problem will still be here." Katie stood in the thick silence, tears streaking her cheeks. She knew she was out of control, but she couldn't seem to stop herself. She felt as if she had stepped outside herself and was watching a crazy woman come unglued right before her eyes. Except, much to her horror, that crazy woman was her. Katie's frustration with the whole situation had been pent up for far too long and now it seemed to be boiling out of control onto both of them.

Aaron returned in an instant with his shoes on and his keys in his hand. He stopped at the coat closet to retrieve a coat.

"I know," Aaron said in a voice filled with anger and hurt. "I'm sorry I'm doing this to you," he said as he pulled the coat on.

"Are you really just going to leave like this and run away from our problems?"

"I'm not running away. You're out of control and I'm out of control. We're both angry. I'm going to take a drive and cool off," Aaron said as he walked past Katie and into the kitchen.

"But . . ." Katie called after him.

Aaron stopped and looked at her harder than normal. Katie realized she had pushed too far and couldn't talk him out of it. She looked at him for a moment then turned, walked to her room and shut the door. She was sobbing now. How could this have happened? She sat down on the bed and pulled her knees up to her chin, with her arms wrapped around her shins. She rocked back and forth. *Why God? Why is this happening? Don't you care? The only man I've ever loved and I feel like I'm losing him.*

She heard the garage door opener as it raised, then lowered the garage door, followed by a car pulling away. Katie closed her eyes and rocked some more as she cried. She felt more alone than she'd ever felt before in her life.

What now, Lord?

Chapter 4

Aaron drove east until he reached Highway 97 then turned north. He didn't know where he was going. He just wanted to drive around and cool off. At the intersection of 41st St. he turned back east, toward Tulsa.

How can I tell her what I feel when I don't even understand it myself? She didn't even give me a chance to talk before she blew up at me!

To break the silence, he turned on the radio. Certainly they had had their share of arguments in the past, but he had never left the house like this before. Although he had every intention of going back home, he wasn't ready. He needed to escape the pressure, and the increasingly gnawing sense of failure he felt.

After driving several miles east he crossed a railroad overpass and came to some stoplights at the intersection of 41st Street and Southwest Boulevard. He decided to start back toward home, so he turned west onto Southwest. Up ahead, on the right side of the road he saw the neon sign from a bar: "The Good Times Tavern." He read the sign out loud. Aaron considered how the owners came up with that name. "*They* must not have kids either."

As he neared the parking lot entrance, at the last second he decided to pull in. He whipped the truck hard right and into the parking lot, the driver's side tires hopping the curb in the process. He eased into a space, put the car in park and sat there in the cold with the engine idling.

He felt his body bristle and stiffen as if repulsed by what he was doing. It wasn't that he condemned anyone inside the bar, but he knew that Jesus had rescued him from a life of drunkenness once before and he had decided that it would be best to avoid situations like this one.

You don't belong here. You belong at home with Katie. Katie . . .

He could picture her beautiful face, and those expressive blue eyes. Then he felt the anger boil up inside him again. Why was she pushing so hard when he obviously wasn't ready? Why had she become so angry with him? Couldn't she see how hard he was trying?

"To heck with it," he said to no one as he slung the door open, hopped out of the cab then slammed it shut. He felt the cold night air slap him in the face as he walked stiffly toward the entrance of the small brick building. He almost felt ill, as if every fiber of his being was telling him not to go in. But he was angry and right or wrong, he was going to do this. *If Katie wants to be mad at me then I'll give her a reason to be mad.*

As he reached the door he could hear a muted thumping sound, presumably coming from a jukebox someplace inside. He opened the door and his presumption was confirmed as he was greeted with the blare of an old classic rock tune coming from the jukebox on the wall opposite the entrance.

The bar was dark and smoky. Any ambient lighting seemed to be coming from the various neon signs hung around the bar. The place was moderately full, and the few tables and booths he saw were all occupied so he walked to the bar, which was to his left. He reached the far end and sat down. No one seemed to pay any attention, which was fine by him.

After mixing drinks for a couple sitting very close on the other side of the bar, the bartender came to take his order.

"You're new here," she said, snapping a large wad of gum as she looked him up and down.

Aaron nodded, still looking down at the scarred mahogany veneer on top of the bar.

"I'm Darlene. What'll it be?"

Aaron looked up as if startled by the question. He didn't even know what he was doing in this place, let alone what he might drink. He hadn't been in a bar in ten or more years – since before he met Katie and became a Christian.

Darlene appeared to be in her young to mid-twenties. She had long blond hair pulled back into a thick braid. Despite the dim light he could see that she was wearing very tight blue jeans and a black tank top with a pink button-up shirt over it. The shirt was unbuttoned to her waist, where it was tucked into her pants, revealing the upper part of the tank top and a portion of a small tattoo of some sort on her left shoulder.

"I'll have a beer."

"Which kind?"

"Um, whatever's on tap."

Darlene nodded, drew the beer from a tap and sat it down in front of Aaron on top of a small napkin.

"Three dollars. Want me to run a tab?"

"No, thanks," Aaron said as he dug into his wallet, withdrew the money and tossed it in front of him onto the bar.

Aaron slid out of his coat, letting it drape off the back of the barstool. The cloud of smoke that seemed to permeate the room stung his eyes, so he stared down at the beer in front of him for several minutes. The once thick head of foam had thinned now, and he could see bubbles rising up inside the mug. He finally took a drink. It didn't taste anything like he remembered it. It tasted bitter, but he took another drink anyway.

What in the world am I doing? Why is it that he seemed to have so many questions about life right now and so few answers?

A hockey game was playing on the TV facing him from the other side of the bar. He liked hockey. The excitement and fast pace of the sport appealed to him. It looked as if it was a game based more on reaction than on thinking and that too appealed to him.

Instinctively, he felt like he was being watched. He looked over his shoulder to his left and saw a group of three women and two men sitting in a booth on the same wall as the jukebox. They all appeared to be his age, or near to it. From the bellies that spilled over their belts, the men looked as if they frequented the place often. One of the women was staring at him, so he turned back to the game.

Uh oh, an odd man, er, woman out. Run now!

Aaron wondered how he had sunk to this point. Could it be that Katie was right? Was he really running from his fears, and that's why he couldn't talk about it? *Wonder what Pastor James would say about this?*

Aaron thought back to his high school days. He attended Webster High, just a few miles from the bar he was now in. He had been a jock and a partier, who had graduated with less than two-hundred other kids so he pretty much knew everyone in his graduating class. He remembered the wild weekends spent trying to coax girls into bed, drinking, and fighting. Was that what he was really trying to do – prove his manhood – like Pastor James had suggested? What did it mean to be a good man anyway? Aaron knew the biblical answer to the question, and the more he thought about it he was convinced he wasn't there. *Have I just been living a lie?* Going from one extreme to the other to find out what it was like to be a good man? No, deep inside, he knew that Jesus was the real deal. But why didn't He seem real right now?

Aaron took another drink from his beer. He had never even met his father. Didn't know where he lived. Maybe he was someplace wondering whatever happened to that brat he left back in Tulsa . . . *Or, then again, maybe not.*

Aaron felt a hand on his shoulder and turned to find the woman from the booth.

"Want some company?" Aaron noticed that the "s" was slurred.

He didn't need this kind of attention. "No, but thank you anyway," he said, trying hard to be polite.

"Well, in that cashe, mind if I have a sheat?"

Aaron shook his head quickly. "I'd rather not, I'm marr…"

"Shanks, don't mind if I do," she said, oblivious to his polite protest.

Before he could launch a protest the woman tried to slide onto the chair next to him but in her condition she stumbled and almost fell over backwards. Aaron reached out and caught her by the arm to steady her. She smiled at him and said "Shank you."

Aaron looked at her for the first time. She seemed to be about as tall as Katie, a little bigger, and not nearly as good looking. She had on heavy makeup and perfume.

"My name'sh Amber," she said with a husky voice as her eyes drew to a narrow slit. Aaron didn't know if she was trying to be seductive or if she was getting sleepy. "What's yoursh?"

Aaron paused for a moment, frantic, trying to find a way out of the present predicament and then blurted out, "Uh, Harold." Aaron felt panicky. Even if he had been attracted to Amber, which he wasn't, the last thing he wanted to do was betray Katie or his vows to her and God. Not to mention the fact that he'd just lied about his name. *That's two strikes*

Amber looked at Aaron sideways and giggled. "You don't look like a Harold."

Aaron shrugged his shoulders. "So, my mom guessed wrong." He moved the beer from his right hand to the left, raised it to his mouth and paused, revealing his wedding ring to Amber.

"Married?"

"Yup." Aaron could feel his skin crawling.

"Just here to take a break, maybe get away?" Amber wouldn't be deterred.

"Something like that."

Amber sighed. There was a long uncomfortable pause while Aaron looked at his beer and Amber figured out her next question.

"Today's my birshday. My friends over there . . ."

"I'm very sorry," Aaron waved his hands to interrupt. "I don't want to come off rude, but I'm really not very good company right now and I'd much rather be alone. No offense."

Amber stuck her bottom lip out in a playful pout. "Was it shomething I shaid?"

Aaron groaned as he looked down at his wedding ring. The simple gold band was a powerful symbol of what his commitment to Katie should be. "No, Amber, it's not. It's something *I* said about six years ago."

"Loser!" Amber hissed as she slung her drink into Aaron's face and half stormed, half staggered away.

The bartender rushed over, still popping her gum, with paper towels for Aaron and a damp rag for the bar. She never actually looked at him and Aaron wondered how she did that. As Aaron wiped himself off Darlene wiped off the bar and popped her gum some more. Aaron stood up.

"Guess I deserved that."

"Probably," Darlene said as she walked away.

"Probably," Aaron said to the vacated spot where she had been.

Aaron slid back into his coat and began walking to the door. If ever he needed a sign that he was in the wrong place that was surely it.

As he passed Amber's table one of the two men shouted, "Hey, buddy!"

Aaron stopped, closed his eyes, and looked up toward the ceiling. This was turning from bad to worse. He begrudgingly turned and looked at the group. He felt his trapezoid muscles beginning to knot up in a mix of fatigue, anger, and embarrassment. "Yes?" he said.

"You owe my friend here an apology," said one of the men. He had a goatee, long black hair and dark eyes. The other had cold, pale blue eyes, and very short hair in a sort of crew cut.

"Yes, you're right." Aaron looked at Amber who was still pouting while her girlfriends tried to console her. "I'm really very sorry for the incident. I don't want any trouble, so I'll just move along now."

Aaron turned to leave but the two men stood up. The women with them were all looking at Aaron with something less than pleasure.

Crew Cut smirked at Aaron. "Maybe you bought trouble when you insulted our friend here."

Aaron felt the first twinges of anger gnawing in his stomach followed by a small jolt of adrenaline as he sensed the impending outcome. He forced the most endearing smile he could muster and took a deep breath. "Okay, one more time," he said under his breath.

Aaron turned and looked at Amber again. "Once again, I'm sorry. I apologize. I…I don't know why I'm here. I don't belong here. I belong at home with my wife. But this is what I get for being at the wrong place at the wrong time I guess." Aaron paused to let his apology have its desired affect, but nobody looked like they were buying. "You know, normally, I'm more charming than Jiminy Cricket, but I've had a very bad day and I just want to go home." Crew Cut seemed bewildered by Aaron's passivity, so Aaron turned around to leave again, hoping to make his escape without further incident. But Goatee scrambled up from his seat in the booth and shoved him from behind. Aaron stopped, with his back still turned to them. In the old days, that was all Aaron needed, and it was on. But today he was trying to live like he'd truly been changed, and to minimize any damage caused by his willful indiscretion

"Running away?" Goatee asked, mocking him.

"Yup, that seems to be my forte these days," Aaron said, thinking about Katie as he walked out of the bar and into the parking lot and the frigid night air.

Aaron's frustration had long passed the boiling point and now it was spilling over in a most unsavory way. He didn't know how to deal with the fear that was consuming him right now. He was afraid of being a father, and he was afraid of losing Katie. The fear made him angry and resentful. The unwanted attention from Amber and her friends was only serving to exasperate the situation. He had made nothing but wrong choices since he left the house for his drive, and now he was paying the price.

He was halfway to his truck when he heard the bar door open and someone yell, "Hey, you getting smart with us?"

Aaron stopped dead in his tracks. He was growing weary of the cliché-riddled cat-and-mouse game they were playing. Somewhere deep in the pit of his stomach, he could feel it beginning to burn with anger. *God, please help me to walk the walk.*

Crew Cut approached from Aaron's left flank, Goatee from his right. Cast in the yellow glow from the street lamp behind Aaron, and the red glow from the neon bar sign behind them, their faces looked almost demonic.

"Look, boys, I don't want it to go down like this…"

Goatee grinned at his buddy and sneered at Aaron. They seemed to be taking delight in ganging up on him. "We aint' out here for no apology."

Aaron winced inside. Anticipating what came next, he knew he should walk – or run – away, but he was tired of running away.

Crew Cut snickered as he put his palm flat against Aaron's chest and shoved him. He had no choice now so Aaron let him do it and rolled with it. Taking a step back he pivoted on his right foot and threw a quick left hook that exploded on Goatee's jaw and sent him staggering backward, until he plopped down on his backside.

Aaron shook his hand. The force of the punch in the cold night air made it sting. It had been a long time since Aaron had brawled like this, and he was ashamed to find himself in this situation now. But, ashamed as he was, he was outnumbered and knew he had to strike the first blow or he could get hurt.

After hitting Goatee, Aaron rolled back to his left and barely avoided a wild roundhouse swing from Crew Cut that glanced off the top of his head.

Next he planted on his left foot and dug an uppercut into the burly man's solar plexus. He heard a soft grunt, as he doubled over and gasped for air. He followed the body blow with a sharp left cross that landed on his temple and dropped him to his knees. By this time Goatee had staggered back to his feet and hit Aaron with a solid punch that caught him under his right eye. Aaron stumbled backwards but regained his balance quickly. It didn't hurt yet, but he knew it would probably leave a mouse that he wouldn't be able to hide from Katie.

Just then from somewhere nearby, he heard the distinct, familiar sound of a police siren. All three men froze, staring at each other. After a short moment Aaron dropped his arms and unclenched his fists. Crew Cut staggered to his feet and the other two men turned to run back into the bar.

But it was too late. From the west, just down Southwest Boulevard Aaron saw the lights as the blare of the siren grew louder, so he just stood there. *Busted.* He looked back over his shoulder at Crew Cut and Goatee who were just then entering the bar. Aaron wondered what he should say when the police pulled in. He doubted they would believe him if he told them that it was self-defense. He could always try "male bonding" exercises.

A wave of impending humiliation rushed over him. He would have to call Mark to bail him out of jail. There would be court costs, community service – at the least. And he didn't even want to think about Katie's reaction.

As the police car roared toward the parking lot Aaron's heart pounded. He prepared himself to "assume the position" when he noticed that the car wasn't slowing down. To his amazement and indescribable relief, the car roared right on by and down the road.

Aaron looked to the night sky and let out a big sigh. The steam from his breath was tinted with the color from the neon sign. He thanked God right on the spot for his grace and then walked to his truck.

He started the engine and crept out of the parking lot, heading west, towards home. He was shaking now, from the adrenaline rush. His legs felt too weak to even step on the accelerator.

He turned the dome light on and checked the rearview mirror again, this time looking at his face. There was already a red whelp under his right eye. His breath reeked of beer and his clothes stunk from the combination of the booze that was poured on him, sweat, cigarette smoke, and other smoke that he didn't even want to consider. He was so ashamed. How could he face Katie?

And how can I step foot in church again? Lord, please forgive me.

Chapter 5

Katie Phelps awoke to the sound of a dog barking off in the distance. She looked to her right at the window and could see evidence of bright sunlight through the closed blinds and drawn curtains. Her heart jumped. *Aaron.* Remembering their terrible fight the night before and all she had said, she glanced to her left and saw that his side of the bed was empty, showing no traces of having had an occupant during the night.

Her mind raced through her memory banks. After he had left she cried until her head felt like it was splitting in two. Her eyes, even now, felt swollen and irritated from all of the tears. She tried to stay awake until he got back. She wanted so badly to tell him she was sorry for the fight, but at some point she had fallen asleep.

She threw the covers back and sprung from bed in one motion, hurrying down the hall. Never before had she spent a night feeling so all alone. She ached to talk to him, to tell him she was sorry, to feel his arms around her, and make things right between them again. Reaching the living room she breathed a sigh of relief when she saw Aaron, asleep on the couch. He was still in his clothes and he had no blanket. He was semi-balled up, facing the back of the couch so that his back was to her. She walked over to him, and as she drew within five feet the smell hit her.

Stopping dead in her tracks her mind raced. What had he done last night? *Oh no. Please Lord, help.* He smelled as if he'd been wallowing in a sewer. She sat down on the edge of the couch, the stale smell of cigarette smoke, alcohol and cheap perfume was strong. She shook Aaron by the shoulders until he began to rouse.

She heard the muffled sounds of his voice. "What did you say?" she asked.

Aaron sighed and rolled over to face her. "I'm sorry," he said in a thick, sleepy voice.

When she saw the small black and blue mouse under his right eye she gasped and moved away from him.

"Who . . . What . . . Aaron Phelps, don't tell me . . . What did you do last night? Get drunk and pick a fight?"

Aaron was squinting up at her. "Well, uh, not exactly. I think I was maybe going to get drunk but there was this terrible misunderstanding..."

"Tell me the truth. What happened?"

"I don't suppose you'd accept something like 'I was at the wrong place at the wrong time' would you?"

"No!"

"Okay, okay," Aaron said in exasperation as he propped himself up on his right forearm. "There was this woman..."

"Woman?"

"Who poured scotch and soda on me but it's not what you..."

"What were you doing with another woman?"

"I wasn't *with* another woman. She..."

"I'm not sure I want to hear this," Katie said.

Aaron ducked his head. "All in all, it certainly wasn't my finest evening."

He opened his mouth to speak again but Katie cut him off before he could get started.

"Wait. You go shower and get yourself cleaned up. I'll put some coffee on. I'm sure you need it. When you come back we'll talk." Katie needed time to compose herself, to think.

Aaron struggled to get up from the couch, almost rolling off of it. He started shuffling toward the hall leading to their bedroom but stopped when he reached Katie, but she didn't want to hear anything just yet. Still reeling from all that had transpired in the last twelve hours, she didn't know whether to be mad or just cry.

Aaron opened his mouth to say something but she shook her head. Not looking at him, or anything in particular, she pointed in the direction of the hall. When he lingered a second or two longer Katie stomped her foot and pointed again until he dropped his head and drug himself away. She waited until she could no longer hear his shuffling footsteps then let out a big sigh. She wanted to cry but she didn't have any tears left in her.

Numb, she walked to the kitchen and began to put on a pot of coffee. She didn't know what to think or feel. In the six years they had been married they had been in some pretty heated arguments, but never like this.

How did we get here?

She finished putting the coffee on and turned around to look out the kitchen window. *What woman . . . Did he . . . Was he . . .*

She shook her head. *No, he wouldn't do that. He couldn't.*

She felt as if her world had come to a screeching halt and she was careening out of control. How had he ended up in a bar? She knew he was mad and hurt when he left and she knew it was mostly her fault. With a heavy sigh she sat down at the little round table in the breakfast nook at the far end of the kitchen. She heard the faint sounds of the shower running from the other end of the house. Even though the sun was out a slight chill lingered and she shivered. Sitting in her t-shirt and sweatpants she huddled into herself, resting her heels on the seat of the chair. She felt like she was shrinking from within. *No, you can't do this Katherine Ann. You have to face this head on – all of it.*

If she weren't so upset she would've been puzzled. She knew how Aaron had been before they met. He was always honest with her and had told her about his past. But, since he had come to know Christ, he had never even hinted at wanting to go back to that life. He had always been very humble in acknowledging what God had delivered him from.

Katie bit her lower lip as she looked outside. She could see the bare, leafless branches of some maple trees quivering in the December wind. Knowing Aaron, he hadn't been able to understand where her frustration was coming from so he'd decided to do something to really earn her disapproval. "That would be just like him," she said out loud to no one. She knew her husband well enough to know that when he was angry or hurt he could be a real smart mouth. He probably got into the scrape by popping off to someone.

Over the years she had watched him constantly struggle with low self-esteem. Katie had always assumed it stemmed from his father's abandonment of Aaron and his mother. Surely that would be a heavy burden for a young boy. However, as he continued to mature in the Lord he'd managed to tame his insecurity to some measure, but even now, if he felt threatened, put down or demeaned, he could still lash out like a trapped animal. Katie shook her head, certain her berating had only made things worse.

The coffee had finished so she got up and poured herself a cup then took it back to where she had been sitting. She held the cup in both hands and huddled around it. Hearing the shower shut off she closed her eyes and waited.

She didn't know what to do or say. She never dreamed she would be faced with this problem. *Trust in the Lord with all your heart. Lean not on your own understanding. In all your ways acknowledge Him and He will direct your paths.*

Within a few minutes she heard his footsteps coming down the hall. He was moving like his normal self now. Since it was Saturday he hadn't shaved. Between the stubble of his beard and the small black eye he looked pretty rough. Katie watched as he pulled a coffee cup out of the cupboard, poured a cup, and sat down across from her. As he took his first sip he looked over the rim at her. His eyes looked very clear and focused. *He doesn't look hung over. Maybe he's telling the truth.* Nevertheless, she felt her stomach tighten in a mix of confusion and resentment.

She looked back at her husband. She could feel the tears forming in her eyes. *No! You won't cry.* She sniffled, then wiped her eyes and took a deep breath. "So, let's hear it."

Aaron recounted to her how he had just intended to go for a drive and cool down but ended up in the bar. He recounted the story about the redhead, and how she had thrown her drink on him when he told her he was married and wasn't interested. Then about how the two men with the redhead had picked a fight with him when he tried to leave the bar.

When he was done he stopped talking and looked at Katie as she stared down into her coffee cup. The silence was more frigid than the morning air. She felt terribly conflicted. On one hand she couldn't help but feel angry, betrayed. On the other hand, she found herself tempted to feel sorry for Aaron. It seemed as if his poor decision led him into circumstances that snowballed out of control. Bottom line, she did in fact believe him and she would choose to forgive him – even if her pride said "no." He had always been an honest man and he had looked her straight in the eye the whole time he was talking. Besides, what good would it do not to believe or to forgive him?

"Well," Katie finally said, "if this were someone else's life, that story would almost be comical."

Aaron dropped to his knees in front of Katie and put his head in her lap. She ran her fingers through his damp hair, a force of habit.

"That's me," Aaron said. "Even at my worst I'm always good for a laugh. I'm sorry."

"I know."

"Am I forgiven?"

"Yes." Using her forefinger under Aaron's chin she raised his head up so she could look at him. "I know you felt like I was attacking you. I'm sorry."

Aaron closed his eyes and shook his head his face flushing. Katie had rarely, if ever, known Aaron to cry. She felt her defenses melting away. *We'll work through this.*

"So what now?" Aaron asked.

"I don't know."

"I've been talking to Pastor James some," he said. "Maybe we could go talk to him together?"

Katie smiled, and, unbelievably, tears began forming in her eyes. Aaron's willingness to seek counsel encouraged her. It surprised her to learn that he had already been talking to James, but she would get to that some other time.

She exhaled, trying to keep her composure. "Sounds like a great idea. I'm interested in hearing how you're going to explain that shiner to him."

"I'll say you did it."

"Do you really think he'll believe that?"

Aaron grinned. She recognized the mischief in his grin. "He has a wife," Aaron said, "he'll understand."

She bent forward and he gently kissed her.

Katie felt as if her world were slowly starting to revolve again.

* * *

Wu Chien rocked Lin-Lin in the silence of her room. The baby's seven roommates had been sleeping well for over an hour, but Lin-Lin had had another "episode." Her breathing had become very shallow and soft. This time it was more frightening because her lips had turned a dusky blue. This was the first time Chien had noticed that happen. She was going to have to call the doctor. She feared that this baby might be taken from the orphanage – and her – and put someplace else because of her condition.

She hummed as she looked into the baby's small, almond shaped eyes. Chien could see a fire in those eyes despite her sickness. "Lin Lin," she whispered, "you're going to be a fighter, I can tell. Even now you have a determined look in your eyes. The Bible says we've been made more than conquerors through the blood of Yesu. I hope you learn that and hold onto that as you get older. It will serve you well."

Chien stroked the little patch of thin black hair on top of Lin's head. Once she reached a year old they would shave her head and they would continue shaving it every year or two until she reached about twelve years old. This tradition would help the child's wispy hair grow nice and thick. It would also help prevent the spread of lice and scabies, both of which posed a constant threat in an orphanage full of children.

The baby clung to her finger, and looked up at her with beautiful, sparkling eyes. Since that morning she had found her, Chien had wondered about many things. Where she was born; who her mother was; and what would become of this precious being? But now her wonder was turning into worry. What was wrong with Lin-Lin?

She also wondered why she was thinking so much about this particular baby. The orphanage had been full of children much of the time she had worked there. She had held many babies, but this one was different. This one was special somehow, but she couldn't quite put her finger on it.

She thought of the rich Americans that had come and adopted children from this orphanage. The Americans were never allowed to see the orphanage's facilities because of their sub-par conditions, but on two occasions she had helped to deliver the children to the fancy hotels where they stayed.

Is it possible that Lin-Lin could be so lucky? I'd willingly give her over to a family that could provide for her like we never could here at the orphanage. She's so sick, but maybe...

Chapter 6

Ben Phelps sat alone in the living room of the six hundred square foot, one bedroom, furnished apartment he had rented for the last fifteen years in Van Nuys, California. With the lights off, the room darkness was gathering in the fading twilight.

He'd turned fifty-three today. Another birthday spent alone, almost in anonymity. He didn't want to die alone, but he knew he deserved that – and probably much worse. The passing of another year in his life had given him cause for reflection, and he looked back on it with a mixture of deep regret and disgust.

He reached up and turned the lamp on above him. Then, picking up the Bible he had received while he was in prison, he flipped pages until he reached the one verse that gave him the most comfort at times like this, when he was racked with guilt – Psalms chapter thirty-four, verse eighteen.

"The Lord is close to the brokenhearted and saves those who are crushed in spirit," he read out loud. He knew the promise found in first John, chapter one, verse nine. He even believed it – at least intellectually. But that promise seemed too good for him. More than he deserved. The Lord surely knew how many times he had asked for forgiveness, but this verse, this was the one he had clung to in desperation for so many years now.

He had wanted to return to Tulsa for many years – ever since he had finished his parole. But he couldn't seem to bring himself to do it. Not only would he be facing many unknowns, but he would also be facing the part of his past that haunted him the most. Besides, he didn't even know if she or he was alive, much less living in Tulsa. He didn't even know his kid's name.

He stood and walked into the kitchen and drank from cupped hands under the tap. He dried his hands and mouth on an old ratty dish towel and turned to the small refrigerator.

"Hmm, let's see. Shall I dine on Hungry Man or Swanson's tonight?" he said out loud just to break the smothering silence. He pulled a Salisbury steak dinner from the freezer and put it in the oven. He didn't need to look at the directions. He'd eaten far too many of these dinners and he knew exactly how long it should cook, and at what temperature for the old oven to get it done.

He turned on the radio and sat back down while he waited for his meal to cook. He owned a small television, but watched it very little. College football season was about over now. Bowl season was starting soon, and even though he'd lived in California for nearly thirty-one years, he still followed his beloved Sooners from Oklahoma.

The words to the song from the radio rang in his ears. "His blood is enough…" Although he truly believed and trusted in God's salvation, he couldn't help but fight with the doubts that continually crept in. Is it really? Could God truly overcome all he had done wrong?

After all of this time, could he ever really go back home?

He rested his head on the chair, rubbed his eyes, and reflected on a life that was once so full of potential, but now seemed to be such a waste. Young and stupid. That's what he had been. He didn't care about anything or anyone – including himself. After he abandoned his wife and child out east in Tulsa, he thumbed his way to California. Along the way he committed his first crime when he took money from an unattended cash register at a convenience store somewhere in Arizona.

Phelps stood and walked to the one window in his tiny living room and looked out at the street in front of him. Cars passed by in the business of life. Probably, he thought to himself, with much more purpose and much less guilt. He arched his back, bending as far over as he could without falling over. The day's work in the shipping department at the manufacturing company had been a particularly long, hard one.

Watching the world pass by, he remembered how he seemed fated to fall in with the wrong crowd. He ended up using and dealing drugs.

Marijuana, LSD, uppers and downers – he used and sold them all. He had a regular enterprise going in which he pushed to other users in order to fund his own habit and have enough left over to pay the bills. He soon became strung out, and burnt out. As his life spiraled downward, he began stealing regularly to fund his ever growing habit. He also got sloppy in his "business" dealings, and then one day it happened. He tried to sell to the wrong person and suddenly found himself in handcuffs, in the backseat of a police car, racing to his new life in prison.

Sentenced to twenty years in prison, he was forced to dry out while there, with very little medical assistance. The time in prison was more horrifying than he could imagine. He witnessed more unspeakable things than he had ever cared to. As hard as he tried, he couldn't totally repress the memories, and sometimes during the night they haunted him to this day.

He returned to the kitchen and checked on his dinner. He grabbed the tray gingerly between his thumb and forefinger and spun it on the rack so that it would cook more evenly. He ambled back to his post in front of the window.

As terrifying as prison was, he thanked God everyday that his road had landed him there. In prison he'd met a man who had changed his life forever: Joe. From the moment he first set eyes on Joe, he could tell there was something different about him. He seemed to be less weighed down by the oppression of prison. Although he was completely humble in spirit, it was as if Joe rose above the sewer that was their existence. They first struck up a casual friendship then soon formed a strong bond as they helped watch each other's back from the would-be murderers and rapists. During that time Ben finally asked Joe why he always seemed so happy in such a miserable place. Joe told him about Jesus, and how he had found Him in prison and in the process discovered a peace that couldn't be corrupted – even in that cesspool.

Ben was slow to respond, but Joe seemed very patient, as if time didn't really matter to him. It took almost a year of on-again-off-again religious discussions before he was convinced that what Joe had was the real deal, and he gave his heart to Christ. That day he bowed his head with Joe during lunch. With the catcalls of the other prisoners around them echoing in his ears – he repented right then and there from his sins and committed his life to Christ. Ben still got chill bumps as he remembered the unmistakable feeling of Jesus' grace washing over him, making him clean for the first time, it seemed, in forever.

Ben returned to the kitchen, poured a glass of iced tea and took his dinner from the oven. He stood at the small bar that separated the living area from the kitchen and ate his dinner straight from the tray.

Although he had a new life, he, like Joe, still had to pay the price for his previous sins. He spent over eight more years in prison until he finally received his parole and was released from jail. Several employees of the prison who had seen the transformation in his life testified on his behalf.

During his parole he kicked from one menial job to another until he landed a job as a janitor at Mason Manufacturing – where he still worked today. During that time, after more searching than he could ever imagine necessary, he found a church that he felt comfortable in and began attending regularly.

In the months and years that followed he settled in to a meager, minimal existence. His weekdays were a constant grind of the same routine and schedule – a familiar existence he had learned to appreciate and live with while in prison. Except for his parole officer, he had very little meaningful contact with anyone outside of work or church at first. But over the last several years he had volunteered time on holidays at various shelters around the northern L.A. and Van Nuys areas. After several years he even began volunteering with a prison ministry as a helper and a counselor. He harbored the secret hope that by helping others, he might redeem himself from his guilt.

He finished his dinner and pitched the empty tray into a trash can under the sink. "There, dishes are all done." He grabbed a flannel shirt to use as a jacket from his closet then went outside, closing and locking the door to his apartment behind himself.

He would do it. He had to. He knew there was little if any chance of vindication with the people he'd left behind, but he must try. He had to reach out, and if possible pay some sort of retribution for his wrongs. He knew Jesus had paid the ultimate price to redeem him from the price of justice. But he also knew that while he was free from the Father's condemnation, he wasn't free from the earthly consequences or guilt. But he had to try. He took a deep breath as he walked into the small leasing office to talk with them about giving notice on his lease.

God is close to the brokenhearted and saves those who are crushed in spirit. Jesus, you're all I've got right now. Please save me.

Chapter 7

The following Tuesday afternoon Aaron found himself sitting in one of the matching wingback visitors chairs that fronted the desk where James Patterson was seated. This time Katie was sitting in the matching chair to his right. Aaron had his arm draped over the rest with the pinkie finger of his right hand hooked around the forefinger of her left hand.

They had agreed in advance that their goal was to seek James' guidance in regaining their equilibrium as a couple, and to try to discover why their fight took them where it did. It had seemed so much more intense than normal. They both wanted to avoid that ever happening again. They believed by knowing how it happened they could prevent the scene from occurring again in the future.

Aaron had just told their pastor what had happened to them – everything – including his little "indiscretion." Aaron credited the pastor for his low key reaction. He didn't jump to his feet and condemn him to hell. Instead, he took it all in with very little reaction.

"How did that make you feel?" James asked Aaron.

"Now *that* sounded like something a shrink would say," Aaron said.

James chuckled. "Well, I like to pretend sometimes."

Aaron thought for a moment. "Ashamed, humiliated, bewildered, all alone..."

"Go on, finish the thought."

"I don't really know what else to say. I willfully did wrong. What more can I say than that? I made a very bad choice that landed me in circumstances that I'd never dreamed of, or wanted. When you boil it down, I think it was my insecurity and pride taking over. I feel like I'm letting Katie down. I feel like I'm not living up to my end of our bargain. When I went to the bar I was mad. But I never thought *I* could end up in a situation where another woman would make a pass at me or that I would get into a fight, so I didn't guard against it."

"In Romans chapter seven," James said, "Paul makes this confession, 'For I have the desire to do what is good, but I cannot carry it out. For what I do is not the good I want to do; no, the evil I do not want to do – this I keep on doing.'"

"Sounds like he was prophesying about me."

"The point is that if *Paul* of all people struggles with this, we will too. Not just you, but me too. It's how we handle these struggles that matters. Satan is looking for ways to derail you. You belong to his enemy."

Aaron looked at Katie. She was his silent partner in the conversation – engrossed in it without saying a word.

"I know I need to deal with some of the things in my past," he said, "I understand that now."

James looked at Katie. "What's your perspective on all of this?"

Aaron turned to listen to Katie. They had also agreed there would be no "he said, she said." They were working together, as a team – as a couple that loved each other and wanted to resolve the problem.

"I don't understand how we could come to this point," Katie said. "We've lost the ability to communicate with one another effectively. We have the worst fight we've had in our six years of marriage. Then Aaron slips up like he did." Katie paused and looked at Aaron.

He knew what she was thinking. She didn't want to cause him further hurt or embarrassment. Aaron, smiled at her and said, "It's okay, go ahead."

Katie took a deep breath before continuing. "What's going on? I mean, this has all started from my desire to have a child. What's so wrong about that? Good Lord, people have children every day. Why does it have to cause us so much pain?"

"Of course nothing is wrong with wanting a child, Katie. That's a very normal desire. But are you certain that's God's will for your life?" James said.

Katie looked startled, as if she had never even considered the question. "I don't know, I guess I just assumed." Katie paused as she collected her thoughts. Aaron loved to watch her when she was concentrating. She had a habit of moistening her lips when she was concentrating. She was doing so now.

"When I was a little girl, my first toy was a baby doll," Katie finally said. "I'm sure I played with all the other toys that a baby played with, but my earliest recollection is playing with this doll Daddy bought me for Christmas. Momma had some old cloth diapers she let me use to pin around the baby. I had some old baby bottles that I would pretend to feed her with. I played with that doll for years. As I grew up, the expectations were that I would go to college, get a degree, work, and be independent. But I also expected to someday marry and have kids. That's it. Had I grown up in today's world, I might not have been so preconditioned to this expectation. But this is what I know. This is who I am and the fact is, preconditioned or not, I *want* a child. I *want* to experience giving birth and being a mother."

"Have you ever told Aaron?" James said.

Katie looked at him as if he'd asked her to name all the elements on the periodic table. "Well, I guess I just assumed he knew."

"Look at me, both of you," James said.

Aaron diverted his attention from Katie to the pastor. He could tell she was really struggling and it hurt him to see her like this.

"Here's what I see. Number one. Neither one of you are truly searching for what God has to say about this. You say you are, but what I'm hearing is me, and I, and my. I'm not hearing you tell me that you've really dug down, trying to discover God's will. It's not about us; it's about Him. Katie, you can't fathom a plan for your life other than the great American dream and the nuclear family. There's nothing wrong with that dream –

unless you put it before God, and only you and God know if you're doing that."

Aaron shifted in his chair and glanced sideways at Katie. At least she seemed to take the stern words well. He knew that James would never intentionally hurt her, but he was beginning to see that sometimes taking a good, hard, truthful look at yourself was just flat-out painful.

"Aaron," James continued, "you have baggage from your past that you still need to give to God. You refuse to see how God can use you for His will, regardless of the circumstances. It doesn't have to make sense – He certainly doesn't need to explain himself to you. You just need to believe that He can make it work. In Genesis chapter fifty, verse twenty Joseph is talking to his brothers and says 'You intended to harm me, but God intended it for good to accomplish what is now being done, the saving of many lives'. God doesn't cause the bad things in your life to happen, but he does want to take them, and use them for good. You need to grasp hold of that knowledge, and let it be your guide. Understand?"

Aaron nodded his head. From the corner of his eye he could see Katie looking at him. He took her hand in his and held it.

"Second," James said.

Aaron and Katie both laughed. "My, we're a mess, aren't we?" Katie said.

James smiled and shook his head. "No more than me and my wife, or anyone else for that matter. It's called the human condition and we're all afflicted by it. Actually, you two are about as healthy a couple as I've seen. Anyway, and Katie you've already alluded to this, but the second thing I'm seeing is a fundamental breakdown in communication between you two. Katie, you assume Aaron knows and understands your expectations and desires but you haven't truly voiced them to him like you did just now to me. Aaron, you admitted to me yourself that you haven't confided to your wife your fears and concerns like you've told me. How can Katie understand where you're coming from unless you tell her?"

James stopped and smiled at them, a buoy in the storm. He picked up a pen from his desk and began twirling it in his fingers. Aaron could feel his neck muscles and shoulders bunch in tension as he concentrated on their conversation. "You two are a wonderful young couple and have been a great addition to our church family over the last couple of years. There's nothing here that can't be fixed. Issues concerning family and children are always the most personal, the most intense. The feelings are deeper, and felt more intensely than any others. You're at your most vulnerable."

Aaron nodded his head. What Pastor James was saying made sense to him. He hadn't realized it until now, his father's rejection of him was still haunting him to this day.

"I understand," Aaron said, "how the feelings are more intense. That would explain why our argument was so much worse. But how did I end up where I did?"

James shrugged and held his hands up. "A very, very poor decision. We all have weaknesses and vulnerabilities. Satan looks for ways to take advantage of, and exploit them. But, nothing you did is unforgivable if you'll just ask. You know that."

"Yes, I do," Aaron said. "And I have."

Katie looked at her watch. "I guess our time's up?"

"Only if you want it to be," James said. "I can go longer if you wish."

Aaron and Katie looked at each other. Katie shook her head. Aaron could tell she was tired and needed time to absorb what they had discussed. They all stood and Aaron stuck his hand out to James. "We're kinda new at this 'deep inner reflection stuff' and we don't seem to have much stamina for it. But thank you Pastor James – for everything."

James took Aaron's hand in his right, and reached for Katie's with his left. He stood holding both their hands. "It's truly my pleasure," he said. "Before you go, let's pray."

The three stood holding hands while James prayed, asking God to help Katie and Aaron, to give them strength and guidance, and finally, to reveal to them His plan for their lives.

When the pastor finished, Aaron looked at Katie. Her eyes were wet with tears that hadn't yet fallen. James hugged them both before they left. When they reached Aaron's truck and climbed in Aaron felt emotionally spent and physically exhausted. He looked at Katie.

"I'm not cooking," Katie said, staring straight ahead.

"Me neither."

"What do you mean? You never do the cooking."

"That's just 'cause you won't let me."

"You're too messy."

Aaron smiled and looked at her. "Have been all my life, but you love me anyway."

"Yes, I do," Katie said. "Messy can be fun sometimes."

Chapter 8

The baby was about a month old now. During that time she had
gained hardly any weight. She seemed sickly and was very lethargic much
of the time. Wu Chien knew the baby needed more medical attention than
she had been given, but she hadn't been able to convince the doctors of this.
She felt as if she were dismissed because of her lowly station – a caretaker in
an orphanage. And now, as she fed the baby from a bottle, the kind old
woman looked deep into the child's eyes.

"My Yesu says that we should cast all of our cares on him. So I pray
every day for you mei mei."

Turning away from the bottle, the baby yawned. The bottle was
nearly empty so Chien sat it down then laid the baby on her shoulder, patting
her on the back.

Rocking, Wu Chien closed her eyes, laid her head back and sang
softly to Lin Lin. She yearned for this child to be okay. She wanted to be
able to teach Lin Lin about her Master's love. She did the best she could to
teach all of the children about Jesus – knowing she risked her well-being to
do so if she were ever caught. Her husband was already home with the Lord,
and she understood more than ever what Paul meant when he said "For me to
live is Christ, and to die is gain." Her mission was this orphanage and the
children it housed, but her heart was already at home in heaven.

She was startled back to the present when the baby girl coughed,
then spit up on her back. She jumped up out of her chair and the baby started
crying. Chien cradled the baby in her arms and noticed that she was
wheezing and her lips were once again a dusky blue on the outer edges.
Panic gripped her as she rushed to the office to use the orphanage's only
phone – the baby still in her arms. She didn't bother with the mess on the
back of her shoulder. That could wait. After so many years of working in
the orphanage she no longer owned any clothes that weren't stained anyway.

She punched in the doctor's number. This time she would try her hardest to make them help the poor child – she had to. When she hung up, she scrambled to gather diapers and supplies, and put them into an old torn up diaper bag that the workers shared when they took the babies outside of the orphanage. She dug through her pockets and the desk drawers until she found just enough yuan to pay for a taxi. Before too long she was able to hail a taxi and gave the driver directions to the doctor's office.

In the taxi, the baby was still wheezing and whimpering. She stroked Lin Lin's hair as she prayed. *My Yesu, this baby needs you now. Please be near to her like you are to me. You're her only hope.*

*   *   *

Katie woke up at 12:30 a.m. the following Friday night and immediately noticed that Aaron wasn't in bed beside her. They had gone to bed at the same time and gone straight to sleep. She had noted that this had been the pattern to their nights since they had talked to James Patterson a little more than a week ago. Go to bed, kiss goodnight, and go to sleep – nothing else.

Christmas was less than a week away. Katie had hoped to be able to tell her parents on Christmas day that she was pregnant. Now she just hoped to talk to her husband and move past this horrible episode, but he had been so withdrawn. He hadn't been mean, just quiet and distant. She knew he was struggling with all that had happened and trying to make some sense out of it, and she wasn't about to open her mouth again until she knew for sure it was the right time.

Katie rolled from her side to her back and folded her arms behind her head. She heard the faint sound of music coming from the living room. She lay still for a moment and listened, then she began to whisper a prayer, "Lord, Father. Forgive me where I've been wrong. Let Aaron know he's forgiven too. Lord, you make your mercies new everyday. I ask that you pour them out on us now. Jesus, I love you and I know you love us. Please move in us as you see fit so that we can honor you with our lives. In Jesus' name, amen."

She slid out from under the covers and stood up from the bed. She slipped into her dark blue, terrycloth robe and drifted down the hallway that led from the bedrooms to the living room. No lights were on, but the moon shone brilliantly through the half-drawn curtains, so she could see Aaron sitting among the shadows on the sofa.

As she approached the sofa Aaron looked up at her.

"Did I wake you?" he asked.

"No. May I join you?"

"Sure."

The two sat in silence for what seemed like an eternity to Katie. She could hear two female voices on the stereo singing about the blood of Jesus. She could also hear Aaron's breathing and the old mantel clock ticking the seconds away. It occurred to her that she'd been able to hear a different kind of clock ticking for quite some time now.

"This is that group that goes to our church," Aaron finally said.

"The one that's on tour now?"

"Yeah that's them – *Come To Pass*."

"I like it. They're good," Katie said.

"Yeah," Aaron said, "they are. I always thought it would be fun to play the drums. Maybe it's because drummers are able to take out their aggressions on the drums."

Katie didn't answer. Instead she just waited. She knew her husband, and she could tell he was working up to something.

Aaron leaned forward on the couch, resting his forearms on his thighs. He was wearing a t-shirt and some old navy blue sweat pants.

"You know how I never knew my dad."

Katie's heart jumped with the sudden realization of what her husband had been going through. "Yes," she said with a calmness that betrayed the inner turmoil and empathy she now felt for him.

"Mom tried her best."

"She did well," Katie said. The night had ground to a halt, more silent than ever. Even the sound of the stereo seemed to fade away.

"I always wondered what was wrong with me that my dad would leave like he did. Mom tried to teach me that it takes a bigger man to walk away from trouble and do what's right than it did to follow in trouble's path. I guess somewhere I thought that if I could be the toughest it would prove my worth. Worth for what, I don't know."

Katie's heart was breaking for her husband. She fought away the urge to hold and comfort him. Instead she sat still, listening, hanging on every word, but trying to act calm and relaxed all at the same time.

"Mom never said anything before she died, but I know the way my life was going disappointed her. I guess I've come to realize that at the time, in some way, I was also rebelling against her faith in Jesus. I mean, if he loved the little children, then why did he let my father leave?"

"Because your father chose to," Katie said. "He made the conscious decision to do the wrong thing."

"I know. Free will really stinks sometimes."

Aaron reached over and took her hand in his. Katie desperately wanted to melt into his arms, but squeezed his hand instead.

Aaron looked up at her. She could see the whites of his eyes in the moonlight. They seemed bigger, and sadder, than normal.

"The thing is this – how do I know what to say when my son strikes out with the bases loaded in the last inning? What does a father say to his daughter when she has that first heartbreak? Those are things I keep asking myself over and over. I don't know. I never had that myself. And what about the really important stuff like teaching a son that meekness is not being a wimp, or a pushover, but power that's under the control of God? Or telling my daughter that true love waits? How can I be a Godly example when I do things like I did at the bar?"

Katie let out a loud sigh. "Babe," she said, "I met you my senior year in college. You were just a freshman."

"Yeah, I'd spent the three previous years messing around."

"You were even pretty wild that first year in college."

"Yeah, I suppose so. I only started going to the campus Bible study to be around you."

"Yeah, I know," she said. "You even began following me to church, but I never actually went out with you."

"So what's your point?" Aaron asked.

"The point is, you met the Master while following me to church. You went from this wild rebel looking for his next good time or scrap – whichever came first – to someone madly in love with Jesus and hungry to learn more about Him. It even seemed for a while that you had lost interest in me."

Aaron shook his head. "Oh, I hadn't. Truth be told, I think it was love at first sight."

"But, do you think I would've gone out with you if you hadn't come to know the Lord?"

"I guess I hoped my boyish grin and rugged good looks would win you over."

Katie could see his eyes twinkle in the darkness. "You were, and still are, very cute. But, no, I wouldn't have dated you – no matter how tempting. But God changed you when you gave your life to Him. He made you a new person. I saw it, and witnessed it firsthand. He transformed you into a new young man who was capable of sweeping me off my feet and taking my breath away. He made you what you are today." Katie paused. Through the thick still of the night, Katie could sense a connection between the two of them that was palpable.

"Don't you think He can make you into a wonderful father? I think he can. No, I *know* he can. Plus, he's got all of the materials to work with already."

Aaron ducked his head, but Katie could still feel him smile. She knew it was that wry, sheepish one he used when he didn't know what to say.

"You're right," he said. "I can acknowledge that in my head, but my heart has a tough time believing it."

"That's always the hardest."

"But I've let you down so much," he said.

"Honey, we've let each other down. All I could hear was my biological clock ticking away. Had I listened more closely to you and the Lord, I might have realized sooner what you're struggling with. I never said I'm sorry."

"No need to. You've done nothing wrong. You never do."

Katie put her hand on Aaron's knee. "Yes, there is a need to, and don't put me on a pedestal. You'll only set us up for a fall if you do."

"Okay, you're right."

"I'm sorry, Aaron."

"It's okay. I love you," Aaron said.

"Me too," she said.

Aaron leaned back against the sofa and put his arms around Katie. She felt herself fall into his arms. Laying her head on his chest she closed her eyes, thankful that God was healing them and their relationship.

"I'll always wonder . . ." Aaron said, his voice trailing off.

"Wonder what?"

"Where is my dad now? Does he ever think about us? What would life have been like if he hadn't left?"

Katie rubbed her hand across his chest. She was really beginning to harbor resentment toward this man she never met. How could he knowingly cause so much hurt in Aaron? *I'll have to ask God to help me with that.*

"Who knows," she said. "Maybe your life would've been so different that we would've never met. But, probably, whatever made him leave would have made you and your mother miserable if he had stayed. It could've been worse."

Katie felt Aaron nod. "Yeah," he said. "You're probably right."

They sat in the quiet for several minutes. Nearly an hour had passed. Even though she wasn't quite sure where this would ultimately lead, Katie knew they had made a major breakthrough. Her heart soared with hope. *Thank you Lord, for those wings of eagles.*

"So," Aaron finally said. "Maybe we should think about starting over?"

"Only when you're truly ready to commit one hundred percent to wherever the Lord leads us in this."

"Okay, it's a deal."

"I'm going back to bed now," Katie said, knowing she wouldn't be able to sleep. "Are you coming too?"

"I think I'll stay up a little longer. Maybe listen to that CD some more."

"Okay," Katie said as she stood up and ran her fingers through his hair. She put her fingers under his chin and lifted it so that their eyes met. She could see the depth of emotion and thought boiling in those eyes. Her heart was full of love and compassion for him. Things made so much more sense now.

"Well," she said, unleashing a smile that was ninety-nine percent angelic and one percent naughty, "I'll be waiting."

"In that case," Aaron said, as he turned off the music and threw the remote on the couch. "I think I'll come with you."

When You Come Home

Chapter 9

The next day Aaron and Katie arrived at the Cooper's home precisely at 6:00 p.m. As Katie knocked on the door Aaron turned and looked out over their yard. He had been anticipating spending a nice, relaxing, fun evening with their friends. He felt like he and Katie both needed it. Since neither couple had kids, they spent a good deal of their free time together and the two couples were as close as friends could be.

Sherry answered the door. "Come on in. We've been looking forward to this."

Sherry Cooper was the physical antithesis of Katie in many ways. Her hair was as blond as Katie's was black. While Katie's hair had an abundance of natural curl, her hair hung straight down, almost to her waist. At six feet tall, she was considerably taller than Katie's five feet, seven inches.

"Us too," Katie said as she handed Sherry a homemade blackberry cobbler.

"Oh my, that looks wonderful," Sherry said.

"This is the last of the blackberries we picked when we made that trip over to Porter last summer," Katie said as she and Aaron stepped into the foyer of the house and removed their coats.

Just then Mark showed up and hit Aaron on the arm. "Hi, Champ – uh, I mean brother."

Mark and Aaron were also a study in contrasts. At six foot six, and only one hundred ninety pounds, Mark Cooper was much taller and ganglier than Aaron's six one, two hundred and ten pound frame. In comparison to Aaron's square chin and brown eyes, Mark had pale blue eyes with angular facial features and a pointed nose that held up wire rimmed glasses. Aaron was always amazed that Mark was never in to any sports like basketball or volleyball and he often teased them that they could be ringers for a co-ed team.

"So, Rocky, have you started training for Golden Gloves?"

Aaron recoiled a little at the playful reminder of his own stupidity but decided to blow it off. He knew that Mark would rag on him a bit, if anything just to drive home the lesson. But he also knew that Mark cared for him and would be there, like a friend should. "I'm fine, Bullwinkle. Thanks for asking – I think – and whatever happened to the confidentiality of an accountability partner?"

"I charge extra for confidentiality."

Aaron grinned. "I see. Maybe Sherry and I need to have a little talk, huh?"

Sherry bumped Mark with her hip. "You stop that," she said.

Mark looked at her as if he had no idea why she had done that.

Katie gave Aaron a sideways, empathetic look as if to say "Ouch."

Given their recent troubles, Aaron knew she would be worried about his state of mind after the comment so he winked at her to set her mind at ease.

"Come on in to the kitchen," Sherry said. "I've got dinner ready. I was thinking that since we're all just family here we could serve ourselves."

"Works for me," Aaron said.

Sitting in the dining room at the Cooper's stately mission-style table, the foursome dined on Caesar salad, lasagna, and French bread. The talk was mostly light-hearted and small. However, Aaron noticed that there seemed to be some tension between Mark and Sherry, but he wasn't going to mention anything just yet. He thought it better to wait a while and see if they would bring it up.

They continued talking well after all four of them had finished eating, before clearing the table. Finally Sherry stood up from her place. "I should get these dirty dishes rinsed and into the dishwasher before they dry like this and need a chisel to get clean."

Katie and Aaron both rose to help. With all four of them pitching in, within just a few minutes the dinner mess was cleaned up.

Sherry looked at Aaron. "You'll want coffee with your cobbler, won't you?" she asked.

"Yes, please," Aaron said. "A taste of sweet and a taste of bitter, I call that the principle of counter irritant."

Soon the two couples were sitting in the living room chatting. The conversation ebbed and there was an extended period of silence. Aaron knew for sure, then, that something was up. As long as they had been hanging out together there had rarely, if ever, been an extended period of silence. He could still sense an air of tension in Mark and Sherry. He was just about to ask them what the problem was when Sherry looked at Mark.

"I can't stand this anymore," she said, looking directly at her husband.

Aaron noticed Katie frown, but neither of them said anything.

"Okay," Mark said, taking his wife's hand.

Turning to address Aaron and Katie, Mark had a serious look on his face, which was another unusual sighting when they got together.

"Guys, I know the timing's bad, and we're so, so sorry. But I don't know any other way to say this, so I'm just going to say it. We're pregnant!"

Aaron put his arm around Katie's shoulders, shielding her. He could almost feel her flinching at the announcement.

"Oh guys, don't be sorry, that's wonderful news," Aaron said. "I finally get to be an uncle!"

Katie just sat, staring straight ahead. She appeared dumbfounded to Aaron. He rubbed the back of her shoulders. After a moment Sherry looked directly at Katie. "Kate, sweetie," she said, in a tone that was imploring her to speak, "say something."

Aaron noticed that tears had begun forming in Katie's eyes. His heart ached for his wife. Why did she have to go through this pain? *Jesus, maybe I deserve this, but she doesn't.*

In a voice thick with emotion Katie finally spoke. "I'm truly happy for you," she managed to squeak.

"You're, you're not mad at us?" Sherry asked. "I mean, we know you've been trying to have a baby. Given all that's happened lately we didn't really know what we should do."

"It's kind of like a catch-22," Mark interjected. "On the one hand we knew this news would sting. But on the other hand, if you found out from someone other than us we thought it would be worse, so we decided we should tell you."

Katie rose to her feet and moved across the living room floor toward her friend. Aaron rose with her, as Mark and Sherry did the same. For the next few moments Katie and Sherry hugged and cried on each others shoulders.

Aaron grabbed Mark in a bear hug and squeezed.

"I didn't think you had it in you," Aaron said to conceal the lump in his throat.

Mark smiled. It seemed to Aaron to be a smile made up of equal parts relief as well as joy. "Thanks, brother," Mark said.

Mark and Aaron looked at their wives who were now both scrambling for tissues.

Katie grabbed Mark and Sherry by the hand and looked at them. Still sniffling, she said, "Oh, you guys. I'm so sorry you felt like you had to protect us. I guess I never realized how much it showed."

"Maybe only to us," Sherry offered with a weak smile.

"Anyway," Katie continued, "you shouldn't feel sorry or worry. Your life, your happiness, they don't hinge on what's going on in our lives. We love you guys and we want God to bless you with all the kids you want."

Mark laughed. "For starters we'll take just one, please."

"Okay," Aaron said, "enough of this group hug junk. Let's have some cobbler."

So, the friends moved into the kitchen for cobbler, much to Aaron's delight, and ended up playing cards and talking. The conversation often turned back to the expecting parents, what would be bought, and all the plans that needed to be made in preparation for the arrival. It didn't take long before Katie and Sherry had planned a Saturday shopping trip.

Aaron admired Katie for her dedication to their friends, and the way she tried to hide the longing in her heart that was so painfully obvious to him.

*   *   *

The ten minute drive back home passed with a strained silence. Katie felt as if she were in shock from the news. She felt guilty, selfish, envious and angry, and despite her best efforts she couldn't seem to fight off the emotions. As they drew near to their home she couldn't see the distant hills for the nighttime darkness, but she knew they were out there and she felt as dark, barren and as lifeless as those hills.

Aaron eased the car into their garage and turned off the motor. He hit the button on the garage door opener to make it go down, then turned and faced Katie.

"Hey, you okay?"

"I don't know," Katie said as she unbuckled her safety belt and opened the car door.

Katie went into the house with Aaron just behind her. She sat her purse down on the washer in the laundry room that connected the garage to the kitchen.

Stepping into the kitchen, she plopped down at the table. Aaron sat down across from her. "Why is this so difficult? Why does everything have to be so – so emotionally volatile?"

"I'm not sure," Aaron said as he reached across the table and took her hand. "I guess perhaps it's like Pastor James said. Maybe these intense emotions are just inherent to the desire to have children."

"Well, I don't like it," Katie said. Her head was pounding and she just wanted to crawl into bed and go to sleep.

She noticed Aaron studying her, his brow creased. "What?"

"Oh, nothing," he replied.

Katie felt impatient. "I know that look, buster. Your wheels are turning. I see the smoke coming out your ears."

Aaron grinned at her. "My lovely wife, always gracing me with your favor."

Katie started to tell him she didn't feel like joking but he put his finger up to her lips, so she stopped short. Her curiosity was piqued now.

"We've had a lot to think about lately," he said.

"Yeah, you could say that." King of the understatement – that was her husband.

"So, maybe we should go visit a doctor?"

She felt her heart leap for joy but it was quickly replaced by suspicion. "Just like that? I . . . No, wait a minute. You're just saying that to make me feel better. Do you have any idea what we would be getting into?"

"Well, yeah, I think I have a basic understanding of the concept," he said.

"Oh, don't be a wise guy. We cannot even think about getting into this unless we're both fully committed. I love you, and please forgive me, but I have doubts about your commitment level right now." Katie cringed at her own words. She didn't want it to seem like she was going to hold things against him forever.

"Look, just listen to me for a minute," he said. "Yes, I understand you have doubts about me. I don't blame you. I have doubts about me all the time. But, I've spent a lot of time thinking about this. It all boils down to one thing – faith. I've got to believe that if God wants me to be a father he'll make me the best one I can be – if I'll let him."

Katie longed to believe him. He was saying all the right things, but she couldn't stand the thought of going through these last few weeks again. She started to speak but he interrupted her before she could get started.

"No, let me finish. Hear me out. So much of life is about faith. Faith that God exists, faith that Jesus is God's son, born of a virgin, crucified, buried and rose from the grave for our sins. I believe that – every bit of it. You said it yourself, babe. God has changed me. He has taken me from someone whose life was going nowhere but down the tubes to a man that gets to be married to you."

Katie smiled and ran her hand across his cheek. "You can be so sweet, but I'm just so afraid."

Aaron raised his hand, "Uh, been there. But you were right. If God can change my life, he can help me overcome my fears and make me into a good father as well. Who knows, maybe I can somehow give a kid something I never knew."

Katie didn't think it was possible just now, but she felt the heat traveling up her neck again, and her eyes beginning to well up. She was so tired of tearing up, but on this subject she seemed entirely incapable of stopping it. Rubbing her eyes, she stood up and met Aaron halfway in front of the table. He put his arms around her waist and pulled her close. Katie felt overwhelmed with emotion.

"Gosh, I can't go through the rest of my life constantly welling up like this. Are you positive?" she asked.

"Yes, I am."

"Completely?"

"Yes."

"But not just for me."

"How about for us?"

"I like the sound of that," Katie said.

"Me too. But, I was thinking, we might try to beat the doctors to the punch."

Katie closed her eyes and smiled as she leaned up to her husband's ear. "I was wondering when you were going to get around to that," she whispered.

Chapter 10

It was a cold, cloudy day in January when Ben Phelps pulled up against the curb opposite Aaron and Katie Phelps' house. He put his 1993 Ford Taurus into park, leaving the engine and the heater running, and turned to his right for a better look at the house. Two weeks ago, he sold or gave away most of his belongings, packed the rest up into his car and made the trip from Van Nuys, California to Tulsa, Oklahoma. He took his time on the trip. To his surprise he had been able to find the little gas station on the outskirts of Yuma, Arizona he'd robbed when he fled Oklahoma thirty-one years ago. It didn't look anything like he remembered. It was modern and bright, but he entered anyway. He had no way of knowing how many times it had changed hands since his last visit, but he bought a bottle of Dr. Pepper, paid for it with a one hundred dollar bill and told the clerk to keep the change. He had arrived in Tulsa a week ago, located a hotel that let him pay by the week, and found a job working nights at a manufacturing plant in West Tulsa.

Before he left California a friend had helped him do some internet research and he was heartbroken to learn that Suzie Ann Phelps had died from a car wreck some thirteen years ago. The two years he was married to her seemed like three lives ago. But he could still remember her striking, jet black hair and those eyes that seemed like they could see through anything. How had he managed to blind her and convince her to marry him? It disappointed him to know that she never remarried. A woman like her deserved to have someone by her side – someone she could grow old with. The guilt seared through his stomach like a hot poker. *I wish I could tell you how sorry I am.*

He had also learned that her son – his son – Aaron had married a Katherine Reynolds seven years ago. Getting their address was easy. And now, here he sat. He could tell the house was empty. He figured both of them worked. Before approaching them he wanted to just swing by and see

Aaron's home. He wasn't sure why – if anything maybe to get a sense for how he lived. The house sat on a small acreage. Ben admired the house and the land. Going from prison to his apartment in California he hadn't seen this much wide open space in many years.

But he wondered if he had made a mistake. *Maybe he doesn't care, or need to meet me.* He felt his heart beat harder at the thought of coming face to face with his son. What would he say? "Hi, I'm the man who abandoned you and your momma," he mumbled out loud in the empty car. He knew "I was just in the neighborhood..." wouldn't work either. What does one say when confronting such a terrible past? *Lord, I can't do this!*

Ben was just about to put the car into drive and pull away when a large ray of sun erupted through the clouds. He almost felt like it was spotlighting him. As the sun helped to warm the inside of his car, he was reminded once again of the verse – his verse: "The Lord is close to the brokenhearted..."

He pulled away from the curb and drove off, sure that somehow, some way, the Lord would give him the strength to face his son.

*   *   *

Two weeks later, Aaron and Katie found themselves sitting in the office of Dr. Richard Pugh, one of the leading fertility doctors in the state of Oklahoma. He was dressed in khaki pants and a light blue silk shirt with large, bright yellow floral patterns on it. Aaron thought he looked a bit too festive for his tastes, but he appreciated the effort. It seemed to fly in the face of such a dark problem like infertility.

His office was on the third floor of the Crest Building at the corner of 13th Street and Utica Avenue. The wall just to Aaron's left was covered with framed diplomas and certificates. The opposite wall faced the west and had two big picture windows that overlooked Utica. Even though it was cold outside, Aaron found himself wishing he were out there rather than inside the clinic.

They were conducting their initial consultation with the doctor and, as such, it was basically a fact finding interview in which Dr. Pugh was asking them questions. By the highly personal nature of the questions, it was apparent to Aaron that working with a fertility doctor wasn't a "take two aspirin, and call me in the morning" proposition.

Pugh interviewed Katie first. "Have you ever had a sexually transmitted disease?"

"No," Katie answered. She was sitting upright and appeared to be considerably more at ease than Aaron felt.

Aaron twiddled his thumbs.

"Have you ever had an abortion or miscarriage?"

"No."

"Have you ever been pregnant before?"

"No."

Aaron drummed his fingers on his knees.

"Do you have any family history of infertility problems, like, say, endometriosis?

"No, not that I know of. My mother never spoke of any problems like that, and my little sister, Jane, isn't married or trying to have kids."

Aaron noticed the resolve with which Katie was forging ahead. He realized that he had better suck it up when it came his time.

"How's your monthly cycle? Same number of days every month?"

"Used to be fairly consistent, but it seems as I've gotten older I've noticed more and more variances. Often times, now, I'm as much as a week or more late."

The doctor nodded his head to himself. Aaron only noticed because it was the first reaction of any sort he had seen. Pugh and Katie volleyed back and forth with similar questions and answers before the doctor turned on Aaron.

He asked several of the same questions, but some were, of course, very different.

Aaron understood the questioning. He knew the doctor was looking for red flags – areas he could start investigating immediately. Still, opening up like this to a close friend was troublesome for Aaron, much less a complete stranger. Katie listened in silence, absorbing it all. She looked at Aaron in an encouraging way, as if to say she was proud of him for being brave with the doctor.

"Have you ever had any trauma to your testicular area in the past?"

Aaron almost laughed. He knew it was a serious question, but it sounded so ridiculous. "Forgive me if this is crude, but do you mean racked?"

"Yes."

"Well, um, yeah. I mean, I've played sports all my life, so of course I have."

"Ever require medical attention?"

"No, just the usual stuff you learn to fight through – the pain, dizziness, and nausea. You know."

The doctor smiled, empathetic. "Unfortunately I do."

"Any history of testicular cancer within the males of your family, like your father, brothers, uncles or grandfathers for instance?"

Aaron felt Katie tense up. He looked at her and gave her a small smile. She nodded at him.

Aaron sighed, yet another area he had been deprived of – family history. "I don't know. I've never met my father, both of my grandfathers are dead and I don't have any brothers. My uncles on my mother's side are all still alive, and all have more than one child."

"That's fine," the doctor said. "No problem."

After what seemed an eternity the doctor quit asking questions, and put his pen down on his desk. He leaned back in his big leather chair and looked at Katie. Aaron found himself hoping that the doctor would tell them he couldn't help them. But, he was determined to see this through in a positive manner. He had yet to overcome all his fears, but he felt God's presence with him like he hadn't in quite some time. His resolve was strengthened daily with the knowledge that God was there as Lord, guide and friend.

"So, let me tell you about myself," the doctor said. "I'm an aggressive doctor. I have no problems going straight to the high-tech, high dollar treatments. I'm pedal to the metal and it will be up to you to put the brakes on with anything you're not comfortable with, or don't want to pursue."

"What forms of treatment do you use?" Katie asked.

"Well, of course, a lot of the treatment strategy depends on the individual cases themselves. We'll go as low key as fertility drugs, all the way up through artificial insemination to IVF."

"IVF?" Aaron asked.

"Invitro fertilization."

Aaron shifted in his chair and leaned toward Pugh. He liked the feeling of taking the offensive in the questions department. "How long have you been doing this?" he quizzed.

"I'm in my fifteenth year."

"You've seen it all then," Katie said.

The doctor shrugged modestly. "Well, I don't know about 'all', but I've seen a lot."

Aaron took his turn. "What about money? How much? When do you expect payment?"

"The amount depends on the treatment. Between drugs and my fees, IVF is usually about fifteen thousand dollars a cycle. We usually expect full payment by the end of the cycle, but we try to work with you as much as possible."

Aaron and Katie looked at each other in disbelief. Aaron was stunned. Fifteen thousand dollars was a significant percentage of their combined annual income. "Wow," Aaron finally mumbled.

The doctor was unflinching, but empathetic. "I know – there is certainly an element of sticker shock with the treatment choices."

Aaron noticed that Katie was shaking her head, almost imperceptible. "How many 'cycles' does it usually take?" she asked.

"Well, of course, we shoot for just one. We have had some couples do as many as three – with and without success. It all depends on how far you're willing, and capable of going with it."

"Do you know if insurance will pay for any of it?" Aaron asked.

Pugh shook his head. "You know, that's the irony. IVF has proven to be much more successful, percentage wise, than artificial insemination, yet AI is the only thing the insurance companies will cover. Go figure."

Aaron struggled to swallow. "So," he said, "what's the first step?"

"The first place to start is with you, Aaron. We need to do a complete workup on you and see where you're at."

"You mean a physical?"

"Yes, we'll do a physical, but we'll also need to start with a semen analysis."

"Oh," Aaron said. This conversation was growing worse by the second.

"I understand, it's not pleasant. But I'm sure you understand that the most logical place to start is with the male. It's much less invasive than any exams we would do on your wife, and it can be more conclusive. If we find that you're sterile, then that pretty much settles it. Understand?"

Aaron rubbed his eyes with the thumb and forefinger on his left hand. He hadn't anticipated this. He looked at Katie to see if he could tell what she was thinking and feeling.

She looked back at him. Her beautiful blue eyes were wider than normal.

"You don't need to decide now, of course," Pugh offered.

Aaron closed his eyes for a moment. *Lord, be the lamp for our feet, and the light on our path.*

"We might as well do all of the tests to see what we're dealing with then go from there," Aaron finally said.

"Okay, we'll schedule your tests, go over the results, and then we can decide," Dr. Pugh said as he stood up from his chair.

Katie rose from hers and Aaron gladly followed them to his feet. The doctor walked around his large desk and shook both of their hands. He seemed genuine in his concern.

"I'm not going to tell you this is easy. It's not. It's one of the hardest things you'll do. But, we've had good success and we'll do everything we can to help you."

"Thank you, doctor," Katie said.

"Yeah, thanks," Aaron followed.

Pugh opened his office door and guided them out. "Let's take you to Maggie's office and she'll get you scheduled, Aaron."

As they walked down the hall and through the waiting area the doctor said, "We'll want to get the semen analysis first thing in the morning. We've found that to be the optimal time."

"Okay," Aaron mumbled. He glanced around the waiting room. There were two other couples waiting. The men had their heads buried in a sports magazine and appeared oblivious to their presence. The women seemed lost in their own worlds. There was a tangible sense of desperation –

as if the walls were saturated with it. Aaron was beginning to understand why.

Aaron was scheduled to return in a week, at 8 A.M. As they left the building and walked to the car Katie grabbed his hand.

"You going to be able to do this?"

Aaron swallowed hard. "Yeah, I am."

"What about the money?"

"Honestly, I don't know how we could afford it," he said.

Katie seemed dejected. "I know. I never dreamed it would be that much."

"But," he said, "we'll take it one day at a time and see what happens."

"One day at a time."

"Yup."

Katie kissed Aaron, her lips soft on his cheek. "Sounds like a plan."

"It's all we've got right now, babe."

"We've got the Lord."

"True."

"He could make the way for us. We just need to trust His plan."

Aaron pointed his finger toward the sky. "Ah, there's that word again. Easy to spell, but hard to put into practice."

"What word?" Katie asked.

Aaron stopped as they reached the car, ran a hand through Katie's hair and smiled. "Faith."

Chapter 11

Two weeks later, Katie was back in the doctor's office with Aaron, going over his test results on a cold Monday morning in mid January. Katie had marked the passing of another month without a pregnancy mourning another chance gone, lost time. So coming to the doctor this day gave her some hope, even if just a little.

"Well, Aaron," the doctor said while reading Aaron's chart, "your results turned out fine. Your blood work looks good. Sperm count and motility are all in the normal ranges. There doesn't appear to be any problem with you."

"You mean other than my propensity for being a knucklehead," Aaron said, forcing a small laugh. Katie saw his shoulders relax some, and she could sense that he was relieved – and she was relieved for him. She suspected that his recently battered self-esteem and confidence would take a huge blow if he believed he was letting her down once again.

Katie turned her attention back to the doctor. "So, I guess that means . . ." She let her voice trail off, knowing what it meant.

Pugh nodded his head. "It means we need to start running some tests on you, Katie. We'll start with an overall exam. We'll take blood, check hormone levels and the like. When did you have your last pap?"

Changing positions in her seat, Katie cringed at that thought. "About six months ago." Katie knew this meant that whatever the problem was, it was likely with her. She had been reading up on infertility issues on the internet and had seen a lot of evidence that indicated female problems were much more complicated than male.

The doctor interrupted her thoughts. "Everything okay, I presume."

"Um, yes. This means that the problem is with me, right?"

"It means that if," Pugh paused for effect, holding both hands up, palms facing Katie, "*if* there is a problem, it's likely with you."

Katie looked at Aaron who nodded at her with empathy. She couldn't believe what she was hearing. Her lifelong dream of raising her own children had apparently been a farce.

"This means it's going to be a whole lot more complicated, doesn't it?" Katie said.

Aaron laid his hand on hers. Her eyes settled on him, but she didn't see him. It occurred to her how confused he must be. He was finally ready to do this, and now she was the one with problems.

"Listen, Katie," Aaron said. "The doctor's trying to tell us that it doesn't mean a thing yet."

The doctor observed the couple with his hands folded in his lap. Katie figured he must've dealt with freaked-out women many times in his career. "Aaron's right," he said, "we don't know a thing until we do some tests on you."

Katie shook her head. "But I've read the statistics. It's rare that a couple tries for two years or more without a pregnancy if nothing is wrong."

"Katie," Pugh said, "assuming doesn't get us anywhere. Let's take it a step at a time. Let's find out if there's a problem someplace, then we'll determine if and how we're going to treat it. Okay?"

"Okay," Katie said as she bit her lip. But she knew deep inside that something was wrong. She could feel it. She'd had the sense for some time but had never told anyone, not even Aaron.

"Let's go ahead and do the examination and blood work now. I want to schedule you for an HSG in three days."

"HSG?" Aaron said.

"Hysterosal pinogram," the doctor said. "Basically, it's a test we'll do to make sure Katie's tubes are clear."

Aaron nodded his head.

"Katie," the doctor said, "do you feel up to doing the exam today?"

Katie could feel herself shrinking inside. "Sure." She noticed that her voice sounded like it was coming from someplace outside of her body. Had she really prepared herself for all of this? What if she didn't want to go through with it? Aaron was looking at her and the doctor was alternating between watching Katie and Aaron. *No, I'm not backing down now. The Lord is my rock.*

Katie reached for her husband's hand. "Yeah, I am, but you and I will need to talk some more about how far we want to go."

"Okay," Aaron said, squeezing her hand.

The doctor nodded and stood from his chair. "Okay, then. Let's walk across the hall to an examination room."

Katie heaved herself up from her chair and took a tentative step on shaky legs. Aaron reached for her coat and purse and carried them for her. "Let me hold these," he said.

She flashed a weak smile at him. "Thanks." Katie followed the doctor across the hall and into an exam room. *Oh great!* The exam table was covered in the sterile paper that would always wrinkle and bunch up, sticking to her whenever she would try to sit or lie down on the table. At the foot of the table were stirrups covered with pieces of brightly colored cloth that looked like socks. Aaron looked at them and his eyes grew big. Despite her dejection, Katie laughed out loud.

An exam tray was on a cart beside the table. Aaron nodded towards the speculum that lay on the tray among the other instruments. "Are you using that thing today?" he asked as Pugh shut the exam door.

"Yes."

"Uh, Katie, are you all right if I just go wait in the lobby?"

Katie chuckled to herself. So big, so tough and scared of a little piece of metal. "Yeah, sure, babe. I'll be okay."

The doctor smiled discreetly. "It's okay, Aaron. We'll send a nurse for you when we're done. Katie, I'll step out for a sec, while you put that gown on," he said, pointing to one of the exam gowns lying on the table. "You know the drill. I'll get a nurse, and we'll be back in just a few minutes."

"Okay," she said as he walked out and closed the door.

After the door shut, Katie felt Aaron's arms go around her waist. "Uh, what are you doing, mister?"

"I figure at least I can stay and help you get undressed," he said.

"Oh no, chicken boy! You don't stay in here with me, you don't get to help."

"Aw," he said as he walked in front of her. "I know this is bugging you, babe. I'll stay in here if you want me to."

"It's okay," she said. "I'm sorry, I guess the realization that something's wrong with me has just thrown me for a loop."

"Well, first off, we don't know anything's wrong yet," he said, "and secondly, what did you expect? Isn't that why we're here?"

"Yeah, crazy, isn't it? Come to find answers then get upset once you get some."

Aaron shrugged his shoulders. "I quit trying to figure out women a long time ago," he said as he leaned over and kissed her.

She kissed him back. "See you in a few minutes," she said.

"Sure." Aaron left the room, closing the door behind himself.

Katie slipped out of her clothes and into the hospital gown that had been provided for her. She folded her clothes with care and laid them on a side chair, then sat down on the table. It was silent in the room and all of a sudden her breathing seemed loud.

She thought back to long before she knew Aaron – when all she knew of marriage was just the promise of someone like him – and all the times she compiled a secret list of baby names she might one day use. She had just assumed this was the plan. Now she wasn't so sure. Did God really want them to have a baby? Maybe Aaron was right all along.

Her thoughts were interrupted by a knock on the door. "Come in," she said.

The doctor entered, followed by a nurse. "Katie, this is Angela, she'll be with us throughout the examination," he said.

Katie nodded.

"Okay, if you're ready, lie back on the table and put your feet in the stirrups."

Katie took a deep breath and clenched her teeth tight. *Ready or not . . .*

*   *   *

"Mr. Phelps."

Sitting in Dr. Pugh's waiting room, Aaron looked up from his golf magazine and saw a nurse looking at him.

"You can come back now," she said as she stepped away.

Anxious, Aaron nearly jumped out of his chair to follow the nurse down the hall into Dr. Pugh's office. Katie was dressed and sitting in the same chair she had sat in each time they had been in his office. Relieved to know that he was in working order and the spotlight would be off of him, Aaron still found himself wishing that it *was* his problem, so that Katie wouldn't have to endure any more trauma. Aaron sat down in his designated chair, gave Katie a smile of encouragement, then turned to the doctor.

This time Dr. Pugh was dressed in a pink oxford shirt, Levis and ostrich skin cowboy boots. Aaron thought he looked like a bad version of *Urban Cowboy.*

"Katie didn't ovulate this month," he said.

Aaron raised his eyebrows at the doctor. For the first time in a long time he was speechless. "You can tell just by looking?"

The doctor nodded his head and waved his hand back and forth. "There are certain tell-tale signs."

Aaron looked at Katie who appeared to be in shock. "I knew it," she uttered. He put his arm around her and rubbed her shoulders.

"So, what's next?" Aaron asked.

"We'll determine why she didn't ovulate and then we'll determine the best course of action."

"How will we determine that?" Katie asked.

Her voice sounded pinched off, small and distant. Aaron's heart went out to her. Although he wished he could shield her from this disappointment and pain, he knew he couldn't. He could tell by looking at her that somewhere deep within her, in a place he'd never fully comprehend, she was now under an emotional assault.

"The HSG might provide some answers. Also, we'll do an ultrasound and look for signs of cysts or endometriosis. Each of those problems would or could prevent or hinder ovulation. We'll be systematic and thorough. We'll find the answer. Any questions?"

Katie ducked her head. Aaron sensed she was fighting to keep her composure. "No."

"Okay. Maggie will get the HSG scheduled and we'll go from there."

Aaron stood, then Katie. Aaron noticed that her motions seemed stiff and forced. "Thanks, doc," he said as they walked out.

They made their next appointment with Maggie then left the doctor's office. The elevator ride passed in a blanket of silence. Aaron could hear Katie's breathing – which seemed to be more shallow than normal. They exited the elevator then the building. Walking out, Aaron grabbed Katie's hand. As they crossed the parking lot and arrived at his truck he opened the passenger side door for her.

"You okay?"

"No."

"I'm sorry," he said.

Katie just nodded.

"I'm here for you, you know. Just like you've been there for me."

Aaron couldn't tell if Katie was going to cry, or punch something. A single tear slid down her cheek. With deliberate care Aaron wiped it off with the back of his hand then engulfed her in his arms. Huddled together in the winter cold and gloom, Aaron whispered, "Seems to be the season for this."

Katie nodded again.

Aaron thought of the verse in Ecclesiastes. *There is a time for everything, and a season for every activity under heaven. Lord, may the next season come soon.*

*   *   *

It was 9:00 a.m. Lin-Lin and all of her roommates were asleep when Wu Chien stepped into their room to check on her. Ever since the last scare Chien had been fearful of staying away from her too long. That night had been such a long horrible night. After waiting for medical attention for five hours, the doctors simply dismissed the baby, saying she had a touch of the flu. Chien had tried in vain to convince them otherwise, but the doctors wouldn't listen to her. But she knew there was something more than just the flu going on. She had been around many babies who had the flu over the years, and none of them had turned blue.

There were now twelve children sharing the room Lin-Lin was in. The room could hold a total of fourteen children. Lin-Lin's bed was the last one on the right row of seven by the window opposite the door. Chien walked the length of the room between the two rows of beds to the baby's crib. She leaned over the metal side and held her hand in front of the baby's mouth to make sure she was breathing – and she was. Chien sighed as her shoulders sagged in relief. The baby's breaths were often so shallow that she couldn't tell by simply looking so she had taken to checking in this manner when the child was asleep.

Chien stroked the baby's head.

"Lin-Lin, I heard today that some of Yesu's missionaries from America will be visiting us soon. My boss, Chang Li calls them 'foreign representatives', but you and I know the truth, don't we? There will be an American doctor with them. Maybe he will listen and help us. I praise you Yesu for your provision! I know you hold the entire world in your hand, yet you're so caring and loving, even to the least of these like Lin-Lin. Please hear my prayer Yesu and bring her help."

She turned and walked the length of the room back to the door. Chien paused at the door and turned to listen to the nighttime sounds. Tears filled her eyes. She was tired from another long day. She wondered if these children would ever know how truly special they are. Each one, hand knitted in the womb by the Father himself, now just thrown away by her own country.

Please heal us, Yesu.

Chapter 12

The next day Aaron awoke at 6:30 in the morning and slipped out of bed without disturbing Katie. She seemed to have done a lot of tossing and turning that night, but she was asleep now and he wanted her to get as much rest as possible.

It was a Saturday, and Aaron was thankful for a two-day vacation from the invasive world of fertility in which he and Katie found themselves captive. He looked forward to allowing his mind to ponder the more pleasant things in life – which so far, he had decided, could include bamboo slivers stuck up his fingernails. He also hoped to divert their attention, at least for a day, away from the entire topic of pregnancy and babies.

He washed his face, brushed his teeth, slipped into his sweat pants, then moved down the hall to the kitchen where he put coffee on.

Opening the cabinets, he rummaged around until he found all the ingredients to make corn muffins. He turned the oven on to preheat, mixed the batter, sprayed a muffin pan with oil then poured the batter into the pan and put it in the oven to cook. By this time the coffee had finished brewing so he poured himself a cup. He leaned on the kitchen bar and sipped his coffee. *Ah, nothing like that first cup.*

Their house was an open floor plan. There were no walls to divide the family room from the dining area, and only the bar on which Aaron was resting separated the dining from the kitchen. Consequently, he could see out the big bay window in the front of his living room while standing in the kitchen.

He stared out at the hills for some time. He was struck by how lifeless they seemed in contrast to the way they burst with energy during the rest of the year – rich green in summer, or brilliant orange, red or yellow in fall.

He turned and walked two short steps to the oven and peeked in. The muffins weren't ready yet.

"Desolate," he thought as he turned back to the windows. He spent more time looking out windows and thinking during the winter. It was too cold to play golf or enjoy any other outdoor activities.

Lately, though, he'd been thinking that life seemed to be a mirror of nature in some ways – alive and active or dormant and dead. At times it seemed to be full of rich vibrant color, and other times of black and white, or varying shades of gray. Occasionally he wondered what purpose the bad times served. He had heard in Sunday school and in Pastor James's sermons that God allowed them for each person's benefit. They were supposed to help people grow by challenging a person's faith, or resolve, or both. "God cares more about your character than your comfort," the good pastor would say. Aaron always found that a bit amusing. "But what if you're already a character," he would think to himself.

He heard a door shut at the other end of the house so he turned back to the oven and checked on his corn bread. "Perfect," he mumbled out loud as he took the now golden-brown muffins from the oven and sat them on the counter to cool. He set the table for two – a small plate and butter knife for each. He placed some butter and a jar of strawberry rhubarb preserves they had bought at a restaurant on the east side of Tulsa on the table between the two place settings.

Aaron slipped into a pair of old loafers and stepped outside in his t-shirt and sweat pants to retrieve the paper. A shiver ran up his spine as he was slapped in the face with a strong gust of cold wind. Looking up at the gray sky, he couldn't help but think about how unfair this all seemed for Katie. Anything bad that came his way, he believed, at least partially, that he deserved. But she sure didn't. She'd always been so faithful. Not perfect, but as close as he had ever seen. Now to have this challenge set before her, the one thing that could most shake her world just didn't seem fair. He picked up the paper and spun to go back inside.

What are you doing? This is your day off. You're supposed to enjoy the day.

Aaron stepped back into the warmth of their house and the rich smell of the breakfast that awaited them. "Now that's what I'm talking about," he said to himself.

He found the basket he'd seen Katie use to put hot bread in, and lined it with a clean towel. He then filled the basket with the muffins, wrapped the towel over the top and put it on the table. When that was done he poured himself coffee and sat down. He didn't bother to pour any for Katie because she would add creamer and sugar to hers. She used so much creamer that he often referred to her coffee as blonde coffee.

In the hall Aaron heard footsteps shuffling down the hardwood flooring. He spotted Katie, still in her pajamas and wearing a pair of his tube socks. Her hair had been only partially combed back, just enough to get it out of her face, and she was wearing her glasses instead of her contacts. Even now, Aaron was stunned by her beauty. Her presence always seemed to bring an abundance of life and energy – as if nature itself were coming to attention. He stood up as she reached the table and put his arms around her. She didn't melt, but more like melded into his arms as she lay her head on his upper chest and shoulders.

"Good morning," Aaron kissed the top of her head.

"Mornin'."

"You didn't sleep well, did you?"

"I've slept better," Katie said, still locked in Aaron's arms.

"Well," Aaron said as he turned Katie where he could look into her lovely eyes, "I've made my world famous corn muffins for breakfast."

"Yum," Katie said.

Aaron knew she wasn't overly big on breakfast.

"Is that all, after the way I slaved over this wondrous treat?"

Katie smiled up at Aaron and batted her eyes. "Why, I'm sure they're quite lovely, Mr. Phelps."

"Don't mention it, Miss Dee." Aaron grabbed his cup and walked to the coffee pot. Can I pour you one?"

"Yes."

"Sugar?"

"Of course"

"Creamer?"

"Um, *yes*."

"One cup or two?" Aaron asked as he grabbed a teaspoon from the silverware drawer.

Katie stepped up next to him and yanked the spoon from his hand. "Gimme that," she snapped, only half joking.

"Why, is that the way a young, well bred, sophisticated socialite speaks to her adoring husband?"

"It is when he's being a butt."

"Oh."

Aaron and Katie sat down at their table. They held hands as each said their own silent prayer.

After the prayer Aaron grabbed a corn muffin, split it into halves and spread what he was certain was the perfect amount of butter on one half of the muffin then ate nearly the entire half in one large bite.

"Hungry?" Katie asked.

"Not really," Aaron answered with his mouth too full. He knew it annoyed Katie. "Why do you ask?" he said as he cocked his head sideways.

Katie grabbed part of the paper and held it high, in front of her face. "Well, thanks for letting me sleep in some, and thanks for breakfast."

"You're welcome. What kept you awake?" Aaron asked as a formality. He was pretty sure he knew the answer.

Katie let the paper drop to where she could look over it at Aaron. The look on her face said "need you ask"?

"That's what I thought," Aaron said, his voice now soft and gentle, the playfulness instantly replaced with concern.

He looked at Katie. There was a different look in her eyes. They seemed far away, as if she were withdrawing.

"I can't help but worry about it, Aaron," she said. "I know you're supposed to leave things in God's hands – to have faith – but it's just so hard. This is the most difficult thing I've ever faced. It seems like so many people who have no business being parents can have babies at will, but we can't."

"We haven't yet, you mean."

"Yeah, sure, whatever," Katie said, as she wadded up the paper and threw it down on the table. "You know, save the positive thinking schtick for someone who wants to hear it, okay?"

Aaron was surprised by his wife's reaction. Katie had been a fireball for as long as he had known her. It was one of the things he had always loved most about her. But instead of positive energy and passion, she'd been growing more and more on edge, and had become prone to caustic outbursts like that. He reached across the table and took Katie's hand in his own.

Aaron looked into her eyes and held his gaze. He had run once, he wouldn't do it again. "I love you," he said.

"Yeah."

"I mean it."

"I know."

"Hey, what's your favorite verse? Isn't it Jeremiah chapter twenty-nine, verse eleven?" Aaron said as more of a statement than a question. "I know the plans I have for you, declares the Lord. The Lord wants to give us good things."

"Oh, does he?" Katie said, her voice drenched in bitterness. "You know, I'm really starting to wonder about that."

Aaron stood up from the table and walked into the kitchen for another round of coffee. "Why's that, Katie?" he asked. "Wasn't it just a couple of weeks ago you were preaching at me about having faith? Believing that God can make me a good father if that's his will for us. What happened to that?"

Katie's head dropped into her hands, the hard edge giving way slightly. "I know, I know," she sighed. "I'm just having such a hard time hanging on to that right now. I guess maybe I've never been tested like this."

Aaron returned to the table, sat down and grabbed another muffin. He took a bite without adding butter and waited for her to continue.

"I guess you think you've got a plan, and you know what you want in life, but in the end, that doesn't seem to matter. I just want us to have children so badly and I'm not sure if it's going to happen."

Katie stood up and began clearing the table. Aaron grabbed another muffin out of the basket before Katie could remove it.

"Isn't that your fourth?"

"Naw, fifth. I snuck one."

"Piggie."

"I thought maybe we could go for a walk later, if I can get through the door."

"We'll see," Katie said, looking sideways at Aaron. "I can always use your two-wheeler and haul you up and down the street."

Aaron stood up and followed his wife into the kitchen. "Hey we're not going to get anywhere like this. Let's make this a good day," he said as he stepped behind her and wrapped his arms around her waist.

"What do you have in mind, mister?"

"Well…"

"Besides that?"

"What else is there?" Aaron asked.

"Shopping."

"Ugh," Aaron groaned. His wife's idea of shopping involved spending hours wandering through countless stores until she bought a top, or that one special pair of pants that looked just like dozens of others she'd passed up a half dozen stores ago.

"Now, come on. It'll be a chance for us to talk, and people watch. Plus, you'll be able to walk off your breakfast."

Aaron shrugged his shoulders, but Katie continued. "If you're a good boy we'll eat lunch at Dairy Queen and I'll let you get a Dilly Bar for dessert."

"That sounds more like it."

"And if you're extra-special good, there may just be a very special prize tonight."

Aaron felt his pulse began to race, but he tried playing it cool. "Hey, that's cheating. Isn't that just a thinly veiled form of bribery?"

Katie turned and kissed Aaron on the mouth and held it. Then she pulled away only enough to look up at him. Her eyes shimmered with life. She smiled in a way that suggested she had a secret, but she wasn't going to tell. "Uh huh," she said, her eyes big.

"Okay. Just making that clear."

* * *

Katie and Aaron returned from their shopping excursion late that afternoon. Aaron limped into their living room and collapsed onto the couch.

"Wimp," Katie said as she walked down the hall toward their room, shopping bags, like trophies in her hand.

"Hey," Aaron yelled after her, "even the toughest man can be worn down by hours of looking at clothes."

Katie smiled to herself as she inventoried her purchases. She found it humorous that men could run for miles in the name of "pushing yourself" or "competition" but a few hours of strolling through stores dropped them like flies – at least hers anyway. Their day-long outing had been fun and it helped take her mind off her worries. Even if momentarily, it was a much needed break. But now, once again, her thoughts turned towards he present troubles. The desire for a baby seemed to be consuming her, and that worried her even more. Yet, she couldn't stop thinking about it. What if they could never have a child? How would she cope? She knew the Sunday school answer was that God would help her. But she wanted more than that. Besides, she was beginning to doubt His love for her.

She stacked the items into a neat pile to be dealt with later then walked back down the hall and into their living room.

She leaned over Aaron and kissed him on the cheek. "Well, you were a very good boy – I didn't hear any heavy sighing or see any eye rolls. So you'd better rest up."

"There's only one thing that could inspire me to such pristine behavior."

"I know, and I am quite flattered."

"Boy that ice cream was good!"

Katie glanced sideways at Aaron. He had his eyes closed, but there seemed to be a smug grin of self-satisfaction peeking at the corners of his mouth.

She looked out the bay windows and down the road. She thought she had noticed a moving van sitting in front of that new house to the south of theirs. One of the things she loved about the sub-division they were in was the size of the lots – which ranged from one to three acres – yet they did have neighbors around so they weren't in complete isolation.

Katie sighted the moving truck again. "Hey, did you notice that moving truck in front of the new house down the road?"

"Yeah," Aaron mumbled.

"Want to go meet our new neighbors?"

"Not right now, I'm still recuperating."

"Oh, give me a break. Well, I'm going to walk down and introduce myself," Katie said.

Aaron sighed. "Hold on, I'll go with you."

They put their coats back on and walked out their front door to the street and turned to their right. The house was about a hundred yards down and across the street from theirs. It was a two-story traditional with a series of three dormers that spanned the front.

They walked in silence, with their hands buried deep into their coat pockets to keep them warm. As they approached the house, Katie noticed two children running up and down the ramp that led into the back of the moving truck. One child was a girl who appeared to be seven or eight. She had long blonde hair. The other was much smaller, no bigger than a two or three year old, but she seemed to move much better than most children that age. She had black hair that was pulled into pig-tails on each side of her head.

As they approached the rear of the truck they heard a male voice from inside. "Hey you monkeys, be careful now."

"Okay dada," the littlest one said. Just then, both girls noticed Aaron and Katie. "Dad, someone's coming," said the oldest.

Katie smiled as she approached the girls, and they smiled back. Aaron waved at them, but they looked away from him.

"Hi," Katie said to them.

Then the person from inside the truck came out and greeted them. Katie guessed him to be in his early to mid forties and he appeared to be relatively fit. He had dark hair that had grayed into a nice salt-and-pepper mix.

"Hi," Aaron said. "I'm Aaron Phelps and this is my wife, Katie. We noticed you moving in and thought we should come down and introduce ourselves."

The gentleman smiled at them and stuck out his hand. "Hello, it's nice to meet you. I'm Tony Humphrey. My wife Gayle is in the house trying to get a few necessities unpacked. You know how that is."

Katie elbowed Aaron in the ribs as she stuck her hand out in front of his to shake Mr. Humphrey's hand. "It's a pleasure to meet you, Mr. Humphrey," she said.

"Aw, just call me Tony," he said as he walked down the ramp to the kids.

"These are our girls. This is Clair," he said as he put his hand flat on top of the oldest one's head.

She smiled politely and said "Hi," her voice so soft Katie could barely hear her.

He scooped the little one up in his arms. "And this one is our Kellie."

Katie thought both girls were beautiful, but she was immediately drawn to the youngest, noticing that the little one was definitely of Asian descent. Her skin was brown, and her eyes were almond shaped. Like the oldest she was very beautiful, but there seemed to be a slight trace of something that Katie couldn't quite make out in those eyes.

"Clair, run in and get your mother so she can meet our new neighbors."

"Oh no, we don't want to keep you," Aaron said. "I'm sure you're exhausted from the move. We'll check back in on you in a day or two. Just wanted to say hi."

"Well, okay," Tony said. "I'll tell Gayle you stopped by. I'm sure she'll want to meet you."

They all said good-bye, then Katie and Aaron made their way back up the street to their house.

"He seemed nice enough," Aaron said.

"Yes, and those girls were beautiful."

"Sure were. I wonder if that Kellie is a foster child or something."

"I don't know," Katie said. But she hoped to find out more about this unique family that had moved into their neighborhood.

Chapter 13

Wu Chien held the orphaned baby and watched the doctor from America as he examined an x-ray of Lin Lin's heart. The small fish symbol on the pocket of his white coat pleased her. She guessed that the doctor was in his early forties, but it was difficult to tell with foreigners. He was slender and medium height. He had blond hair and bright blue, kind eyes and a large, meaty nose. The large noses on the visiting Americans had always been a source of private humor and fascination for her. *Da bizi*, they called them – big noses. She rarely, if ever, saw a fellow countryman from the Republic of China with such a large nose.

Filled with anticipation Chien was happy to see this day arrive. Her worries had grown as the baby's "blue" spells continued to occur. She hoped and prayed that the doctors could determine what was wrong with Lin Lin and help her. The doctor frowned at the picture and Chien's concern grew. He motioned for his colleague, a female doctor with long brown hair pulled back in a ponytail to come over. Looking at the x-ray from several different angles, the two talked in whispers. After a few more minutes the female doctor nodded her head and walked away.

Wu Chien came to attention as the male doctor neared. He said something she didn't understand to the interpreter, a young girl who appeared to be college age, or near to it. The girl nodded her head and the doctor began speaking.

The doctor said something and stopped to wait for the interpreter. "The baby has a congenital heart defect known as tetralogy of Fallot."

Chien frowned. The interpreter spoke proficiently in her own Mandarin dialect, but except for the words "heart defect," she didn't understand anything else the doctor said. But she understood enough. Her hands trembled as fear began seeping into the corner of her heart.

The doctor must have sensed her fear, because he put his hand on hers and looked into her eyes. He said something else, then the interpreter spoke some more. "That means it's a problem with her heart. Basically, there's a hole between two openings at the bottom of her heart. This causes very low blood pressure. As a result, not enough oxygen can get into the bloodstream to carry to the rest of her body. When she turns blue, and her breathing is very shallow, that's called a 'tet spell'. This also explains why she hasn't gained any weight."

"What can be done to treat it? What are her chances?" she asked, stopping to wait for the translation and response.

The doctor sighed and looked away from Chien for a moment. She could see the worry etched in his furrowed brow when he looked back at her. "This requires surgery," he said "and unfortunately, since we're not in America we don't have the resources available to perform it. One out of every four babies with this condition die before they reach age one. I fear that given her living conditions and the medical attention that is available, her chances are less than that."

Chien maintained a calm façade, but inside a storm of fear swelled within her. What would become of this baby? How could she help Yesu's child? Then she remembered Jesus' promise that he would never leave us nor forsake us. *Please be near this little one, Yesu.*

"Is there anything at all that we can do to help her?" Chien asked.

"Not really, not without surgery anyway. From your account, and another doctor's previous exam, it appears that her tet spells are particularly acute, so I'm going to prescribe two different pills for her when she has the spells. Give her one of each. But understand, they won't fix the problem, they'll just help her through the episodes."

When the interpreter finished Wu Chien said, "*Xie xie.*"

The doctor smiled, his face kind and open, leaned forward and tapped at the small fish emblem embossed on his lab coat and then to his heart.

She looked back at him, her eyes moist with tears and nodded her head once, just a slight gesture.

"You're welcome," he said. "Wait here while I get the pills."

A few minutes later, Chien was in the back of a taxi, returning to the orphanage. She looked down at the baby cradled, safe and sound in her arms. Her head swam with a million thoughts and worries. She knew that normally babies weren't allowed to be put up for adoption until they were six months old. Would that be too late? Would Lin Lin die before then? Chien could hardly bring herself to think it. Maybe they could make an exception for Lin Lin. Adoption appeared to be her only shot at the life-saving surgery she needed, but Chien knew that the chances of a "special needs" child being adopted were even less than a healthy child. Her only hope was in Jesus.

Thank you, Yesu, for the hope we find in you.

*   *   *

Katie sat alone, in their dark living room, devastated by the news she'd received earlier that day. She had gone to her appointment with Dr. Pugh, their fertility doctor, with renewed hope and within an hour her hopes had been crushed. She scrambled to her feet, retrieved a dust rag from their utility room and began dusting. She had to do something – she couldn't just sit while she waited for Aaron to get home from work. He hadn't been able to make the appointment with her this time due to obligations at the office.

"One ovary..." she muttered through clenched teeth as she rubbed vigorously on the coffee table. Dr. Pugh had done an ultrasound that day and determined that she only had one ovary – apparently a genetic disorder more common than widely known. To add insult to injury, apparently the one ovary she had wasn't in very good shape either. The ultrasound revealed that she also had multiple cysts and endometriosis.

Tears rolled off her cheeks and dropped onto the coffee table. She rubbed the oak tabletop even harder. Alone in the dark, she dropped to her knees and pounded her fists on the coffee table. *Why, God? Why?* She was angry – and not just in general either. She was mad at God. How could a

God that claimed to love his people allow them to suffer such disappointment? She thought back over her childhood – how she'd given her life to the Lord at ten. She'd spent her years living for the God she loved. She'd never rebelled against her parents or their faith. She'd loved the Lord and dedicated her life to Him – even in high school and college, when the pull against a life lived for Christ was at its peak. And now, this was how He rewarded her? *Forget it. I don't need it.*

Just then she heard Aaron pulling his car into the garage, so she got up, turned a light on in the living room and sat back down on their couch. What a strange, unfair twist of fate. Aaron had been working to overcome his fears of parenthood and now, come to find out, it was all for nothing because his wife was infertile. Aaron didn't know yet. How would she tell him? "Hi, honey, guess what? You're off the hook!"

Aaron entered the house through the utility room that adjoined the garage. As he entered the living room he took one look at Katie and stopped. He stared intently at her for a moment then asked, "Hon, what's wrong?"

Katie's chin quivered and she just shook her head.

Aaron hurried over to her and sat down on the couch beside her. "Babe," he said softly, "what's the matter?"

Katie lurched forward, gasping through the tears she could no longer fight back. She felt Aaron's hands, gentle yet firm, take her by the shoulders and pull her close to him. She crumpled into his arms, sobbing uncontrollably.

"C'mon Katie, tell me what it is," Aaron implored.

But Katie couldn't. She felt as if she had been sucked underneath a flood of grief. She heard Aaron whispering, and though she couldn't make out his words, she knew he was praying. Anger erupted in her like a volcano and she yanked herself free from his grasp.

"If you're praying, you might as well forget it!" she said, her voice dripping with sarcasm. "It's all just a sham. *He* doesn't really care anyway."

Aaron looked at her in pure shock and bewilderment. "Okay…how about just telling me what's going on?"

"I had my appointment with Dr. Pugh today."

"Yeah?"

"Well, let's just say you don't have to worry about being a father anymore, because it isn't going to happen. My lifelong dream turns out to be some kind of cruel joke."

Aaron shook his head. "What exactly did he say?"

Katie moaned. She could tell he was trying so hard to be patient with her. "He did an ultrasound today. I only have one ovary and it isn't any good."

"One ovary? What do you mean by 'it isn't any good'?"

Katie stood, walked to the fireplace and faced it, looking at the picture of her parents on the left side of the mantle. Somehow just staring at the picture made her ashamed of her reaction – ashamed for being so angry at God. As far as she knew, her parents had never doubted the Lord. They had, and still were serving Him faithfully, every day of their lives. Then again, they'd obviously never faced what she was facing.

"Apparently, I was born without one of my ovaries," she said, still staring at the picture without really seeing it.

"But you've got the other one, right?"

"Yes, but I also have PCO syndrome accompanied with endometriosis on the one I do have. The doctor says I may never have been ovulating, and if I ever was, it was just every other month."

"PCO?"

"Poly-cystic ovaries – or in my case 'ovary'."

"I don't understand – you still have your monthly cycles."

Katie turned and faced Aaron now. Her legs felt weak so she sat down on the fireplace hearth. She felt like she was letting him down.

"I said the same thing. The doctor said that was because the walls of my uterus were still building up as if I were going to ovulate so that they eventually became so heavy that they sloughed off anyway. That explains why my periods have been so inconsistent."

Aaron walked on his knees from the couch over to where Katie was seated. He grabbed her hands in his, squeezing them tight – tight enough Katie figured so that she couldn't yank them away again. She looked into his eyes, rich with love and compassion for her.

"What's this talk about God?"

"I don't know," she said. "I'm angry. I feel like He's betrayed me."

"I'm sure he understands what it's like to be betrayed."

Katie looked down and nodded.

"Hey," he said, leaning low enough that he could still look at her. "Don't be ashamed. *I* am certainly not one who could or should judge you for how you feel. I was merely pointing out that I think it's okay to be mad at God. He's big enough. He can take it. But more importantly, He understands. He knows how you feel."

"Yes, but this is so devastating. I feel like I'm the butt of a terrible joke. I feel like He doesn't care, or love me."

"Yes, but how you feel doesn't change the fact that He *does* love you."

Katie forced herself to look at him. "What do we do now?"

"I don't know. We'll find a way to deal with this, like we've been dealing with everything else – one step at a time, with the Lord's help."

Katie felt empty. Without this dream she didn't know what life meant anymore. "I'll try."

Aaron pulled her close and held her tight. "That's my gal. I love you."

"I love you too."

"I remember something very wise someone told me not too long ago."

"What?"

"That if the Lord wants me to be a dad – if he wants us to be parents – he'll make it happen despite the odds or circumstances."

"I hate it when you do that," Katie said with a slight smile.

"What?"

"Use my own words against me."

Aaron kissed her on the cheek. "In that case, babe," he said in a terrible Bogart impression, "you shouldn't be so right all of the time."

Chapter 14

On Sunday morning Aaron walked into the Crossroads Community Church alone. It was bitterly cold, with a strong north wind that seemed to cut to the bone. It seemed even worse without Katie. Except for the occasional illness, it was the first time Aaron could remember attending church without her at this side.

She had told him that she didn't want to go and she was giving up on God. Never before had he seen his wife in such an emotional state and he was worried. It scared him because he didn't know how to deal with it.

As Aaron entered the building the church pastor, James Patterson, was at the entrance. He greeted Aaron with a friendly smile and a handshake.

"Where's Katie?" James asked.

Aaron scratched behind his ear. He didn't know how to respond. He didn't want to out-and-out lie. "Uh, she couldn't make it."

"I'm sorry to hear that. I hope she's not sick," the pastor said with a look of concern.

Aaron shook out of his coat, trying to seem casual. "Oh, nothing like that," he said. Then he stopped and looked around. People were coming and going through the halls of the church. Still worried about his wife, but not certain what to do, he saw the compassion in Patterson's eyes and came to a decision. "Can we go someplace and talk?"

"Sure, let's go to my office," James said as he turned and began walking.

Aaron stayed close behind and they wound through the church's halls back to the pastor's office. Several people stopped to say hello to James and Aaron as they passed, so the trip to the office seemed to take forever.

They reached the church offices and strolled through the reception and secretarial area straight into the pastor's office. James stepped to the side and let Aaron enter first. Then he pulled the door shut as he entered.

"So what's up?" James asked as he leaned against his desk.

Aaron told James everything. How they'd been visiting the doctor and what Katie had found out the previous week.

"So now," Aaron said in summary, "she has decided that God must not care about us if he would let his people go through something like this."

"I see," the pastor said.

"So what should I do? I feel like we've been nothing but a very bad melodrama for the last few months. It seems like we've just crumbled at the first sign of adversity."

The pastor was tapping on his chin. Aaron could see that he was giving their situation careful consideration. "I think it's up to you now to take the lead. *You* need to be patient and supportive."

Surprised at the pastor's response, Aaron's eyes narrowed and he clenched his teeth, causing his jaw muscles to flex. "Believe me, I am. I understand what it's like to be confused, even angry at God. It's not good, but I can relate to how Katie's feeling."

"Don't take me the wrong way, Aaron, I'm not trying to criticize or condemn anyone. This is confusing for me as well. On one hand, Katie's so well grounded that I'm tempted to advise that you give her some time and let her figure things out for herself. However, it worries me to see a member of my congregation pulling away. That's the last thing she needs. What she really needs is to be surrounded by the support and love of her church family as well as you. That's what I meant about you taking the lead and being patient. Let her lean on you just like you leaned on her a while back. Have you been out with the Coopers lately?"

"No," Aaron said, "not in a couple of weeks. Sherry's been having a lot of morning, day and night sickness and hasn't felt much like company.

And also, when we are together she goes on and on about the baby and I think Katie resents it."

The pastor lifted his brows in surprise. "Hmm, that doesn't seem like Katie."

"It's not like Katie resents the fact that they're having a baby," Aaron said. "It's more like she resents how they go on and on without concern for how it makes Katie feel – or at least it seems that way. I know we're oversensitive, but it's just so hard…"

"I guess people who've never been in your situation can't ever fully understand."

"Well, pray for us, will you pastor?"

"Yes, of course I will. And remember, God *does* have a plan. I know it sounds trite, and I know it may be hard to see right now. But everything happens for a reason. Hang on to that. Help Katie hang on to that. Would you like for me to pray now?"

"Sure."

The two men grasped each other's hands and James began to pray. "Lord, we come before you as humble servants. You have told us to cast our cares on you, for you care about us. Father, I pray now for Katie and Aaron. Heal their hurt. We know that although we cannot understand your ways, your ways are higher, your ways are better, and your plan is perfect. Carry them through this painful time so that they can come through it giving glory to You, Father. For all this we ask in Jesus' name, amen."

Aaron thanked the pastor and exited the office. Although more resolved, he was still confused. He couldn't see how all of this pain could bring glory to God. *But I place my trust in you.*

* * *

Later on that Sunday afternoon, Aaron was half watching the football game on TV and half sleeping when the doorbell rang. He heaved himself up from the couch and went to answer the door.

As he opened it he saw an older gentleman standing four feet from the door. He was wearing an old pair of black dress shoes, tan corduroy pants and an old brown coat. His hands were buried deep in his pockets and his breath was creating large billows of steam. He looked to be in his early to mid fifties with graying hair, about Aaron's height and at least forty pounds lighter, which would put him at about one-seventy. Aaron studied him for a moment, thinking that he looked familiar. Aaron noticed that the man seemed to be looking at him just as intently. His face was lined. And there was a mixture of joy, surprise and profound sadness in his brown eyes that seemed to convey a story.

"Can I help you?" Aaron said after a brief pause.

"Is this the Phelps residence?"

"Yes it is."

"Are you the son of Suzie Ann Phelps?"

"Yes…what's this about?"

The man looked down at his shoes and scratched behind his ear.

About that time Katie came up behind Aaron to his right and said, "What's up?"

Aaron shook his head and stared at the man.

After an awkward pause, the man looked up at Aaron and met his gaze. "I'm Ben Phelps," he said.

Somewhere in the periphery of his consciousness Aaron heard Katie gasp.

There was another long silence, accented by the stillness of the cold winter afternoon. Aaron's mind raced as curiosity and anger battled for control of his emotions. He didn't know whether to invite him in, slam the door in his face, or flatten him then slam the door in his face.

"The same Ben Phelps that abandoned his wife and newborn son some thirty-one years ago?" Aaron blurted in a voice as hard as stone.

Aaron heard Katie whisper "*Aaron…*" behind him. He glanced at her with a harder look than normal.

"Yes, that's me," Ben said. Aaron noticed a slight waver in his voice.

"So, what do you want?"

"I…I don't really know. I've moved back here now. I know this is very awkward…very difficult, but I wanted to meet the child I fathered. Maybe get to know you, find out what your life has been like…"

Aaron noticed the man shivering in the cold. Somewhere in his conscience a still small voice was telling him he shouldn't be so hard hearted and unforgiving, but still, he wasn't about to invite him in.

"You want to know what my life's been like?" Aaron said in disgust. "Let me summarize. I learned to play catch by throwing a tennis ball against the wall of our apartment building. I spent my childhood walking to ball practice and games by myself because my mom was working her evening job and there was no one else to take me. When I hit my first homerun my coach was the one who bought me an ice cream cone. My best friend's dad bailed me out of jail when I was sixteen. There was no one to stand by my side at Mom's grave. Wait, you *did* know she's dead, right? Get the picture?"

Ben looked down and nodded his head with one short motion. "Yeah," he said, still looking down. "I know this won't make any difference, but I'm sorry. I'm sorry for leaving you and your mother. She was the finest woman I've ever known. I'm so sorry for not being there for you like I should have been. Yeah, I'm sorry for a lot of things that I can't do anything about. I get the picture."

"Save the apologies," said Aaron, balling up his fists. "They're about thirty years too late."

Ben looked up at Aaron, but didn't meet his eyes. He pulled a piece of paper from his pocket and held it toward Aaron. "Here, this is my phone number and address if you would like to contact me sometime."

Aaron looked at the paper and stuck his hands in his pockets. Katie reached around him and took it from Ben's hand. She smiled at Ben then walked away. As Ben turned back toward his car Aaron shut the door and stood in the entryway, his hand still on the polished brass doorknob. He watched Ben Phelps, his father, drive off. His head was spinning and his stomach felt queasy. He had dreamed many times of meeting his father, but he was unprepared for the blunt reality, and the rawness of his own emotions. Aaron placed his hands flat against the cold window pain and wondered if Ben felt the same emptiness and desperation that he felt.

After several minutes Aaron's shoulders slumped and he walked back to his spot on the couch and eased down as if he were unsure of his balance. He turned off the television. Suddenly, football seemed very insignificant.

Leaning forward he held his head in his hands as pangs of guilt skewered through his conscience. He had been rude, and worst of all, unforgiving. He knew the Lord is a God of forgiveness. *I can't, I don't have it in me.*

Katie walked back in and sat down by him. The warmth of her hand felt good as she grasped his hand in hers.

"Guess that wasn't exactly my most gracious moment," Aaron said, still looking down.

"No. But just about anyone would understand. I do. That was quite a bombshell."

"Yeah. I still don't know what to think. Why now? Why at all? It's not as if we don't have enough chaos going on in our lives right now."

Katie laid her head on his shoulder. "I know," she said. "It kinda makes me wonder."

"Kinda reminds *me* of a soap opera."

"Maybe," Katie said, laying her hand on top of his, "but you'll always be my hunky leading man. I'm so confused myself, I don't really know what to say to you, babe. I know a few weeks ago I would've talked about this grand plan that God has for us, but now I'm not so sure. It all sounds like nice platitudes, but nothing that carries any real meaning anymore."

Aaron struggled to contain the anger that burned in his stomach. "That makes two of us. Our lives are overwhelming us. And yet, I know this sounds so overused, but all I know is to turn to God."

Katie ran her finger up and down Aaron's arm and sighed. "Maybe you can cover for the both of us."

"Hey now," Aaron said, trying to shake off the shock. "You know I can just barely cover for myself most of the time."

"I'm sure you'll fight your way through it."

"Oh," Aaron said, "very funny!"

"No pun intended."

"Sure… I'll do my best…"

I hope.

*   *   *

What a fool!

Ben Phelps sat alone in his rented motel room. *Lord, did you do this to set me up? Is there a reason for this, or does this go back to me reaping what I sowed? Father, I love you. I can't turn my back on the One who saved me from the darkness of my life, but I don't understand this. I knew it would turn out like it did. And I deserve it, Lord. My past is despicable. Even today it still haunts me. What should I do now?*

Ben could hear the muffled roar of the eighteen wheelers as they rolled by on I-44, about one hundred yards from his room. The trucks were either entering or leaving Tulsa on the Turner Turnpike. Like a coward he had fled Tulsa on that same toll road so many years ago. He hooked up with I-40 in Oklahoma City heading west, and never looked back.

Maybe that's what I should do now.

He pulled back the thick drapes covering the lone window and the room was flooded with red light from the neon sign for the Rio Motel.

I don't know, Father, that I can stand this much longer. No family, no friends. Is this any way to live my life?

He blinked away tears as the flashing neon sign advertising a pool rhythmically pierced the red glow with blinding white light.

But my life is no longer my own, is it? You bought it with your blood on Calvary. You redeemed it for eternity – even if I can't find redemption here on earth.

Ben collapsed onto the bed, and lay flat on his back with his right forearm over his eyes, shielding it from the irritating lights. Death right now seemed like an answer to prayer. He longed for family. He ached to feel the soothing touch of Jesus. He longed to be free at last from his chains of guilt and shame and embraced by his Lord.

He had accumulated a small savings over the years. Maybe he could leave it to some homeless shelter or children's home where at least someone here on earth might have a fond memory of him after he had passed.

Time was his enemy, and yet that's what he seemed to have the most of. Time. Time to think, time to regret, and time to hurt. He longed to go to that place where time was no more.

Chapter 15

The next Tuesday evening at dinner, Katie was restless and irritable. Aaron had prepared a big pot of stew and a pan of cornbread for dinner, but Katie was just picking at her food. She knew she had to do something to get out of her funk. She couldn't continue to be so bitter.

Dinner was passing in unpleasant silence like it had since she'd first received the bad news from Dr. Pugh. Katie wanted to talk to Aaron, to tell him how she felt, but instead she was sullen and distant. She couldn't seem to find the words to say. She felt empty and drained.

Worse, Katie felt badly for Aaron. He was trying so hard. He often encouraged her to open up and talk, but to her shame she often rebutted him with harsh words or a dirty look. Aaron would reply with a grin and one of his patented wisecracks – often drawing more of her ire. But in his eyes, she could see that she was hurting him with her distance. Those eyes used to be full of joy and mischief but now appeared tired and worried.

A loud clank from Aaron's direction jolted Katie out of her thoughts. She looked up at him and his eyes met hers.

"Katie, I can't stand this anymore."

"I know."

"This…This isn't *us*. This is *you* over there and *me* over here.

"What if this is all I have?" Katie said.

Aaron pushed his food away from him. "Well, I'm sorry," he replied, "but I don't buy it. You have so much more…"

Katie cocked her head to one side. It irritated her that Aaron acted like he was able to get inside her head and feel her hurt. There was no way he could understand. "How do you know?"

"I just know! I've been your husband long enough to have picked up on some things. I admit, I can't fully comprehend the hurt you're going through right now. I understand there's this mother thing – this instinct and drive to bear children. I'm not trying to come down on you. I love you. I'm trying to help you…maybe help you deal with it. You deserve happiness and I'd do anything…give anything to make that happen."

Katie sighed. "I know… There are things… things that drive people, things that make people what they are. And since we found out that I most likely will never have a baby, I feel like I've lost it – whatever 'it' is."

"Well maybe you need to find it. Or find a new 'thing'."

"But I don't want a new thing…" Tears began to form in Katie's eyes. She wiped them away with the back of her hand and wiped her nose with her napkin. *How could Aaron possibly love a wreck like me?* "I want you, and me, and baby makes three – that's all."

Aaron stood up from the table and walked around to where Katie was sitting. He kneeled in front of her and wrapped his arms around her.

"I'm sorry," Katie said.

"Don't be," Aaron said. "You aren't wrong to feel how you feel. Things are what they are."

"Yes, but here I am wrapped up in my anger and pity while you deal with your own bombshell. Your long lost father comes to meet you – I know that rocked your world too."

"Yeah, but worrying about you has kept me from thinking about it too much," Aaron said.

"Glad I could be of service."

"Jesus told us that he came to give us not just life, but life more abundant." Aaron held up his hands. "Before I say it, I know this isn't going to sound right, but you've got to believe that He has something planned for you that's greater than you ever dreamed of. I mean, who can dream bigger than God?"

Katie sighed and ran her fingers through Aaron's hair. "Come on. Let's go to the living room."

They made the short walk to the living room and sat down. Aaron put his arm around Katie and she laid her head back against him and closed her eyes. She felt tired. "I know," she said. "I think part of my emptiness comes from my pulling away from Him. Honestly, I'm tired of being angry at Him. I feel like I've been flailing against the wind."

Katie opened her eyes to look at Aaron and caught him grinning. She immediately recognized it. "What?" she said.

"Oh, nothing."

Katie frowned. "Don't give me that, I know better."

"Okay, okay. I was thinking maybe that's God's version of the 'rope-a-dope'."

"Rope a what?"

"Muhammad Ali used to do this thing where he'd cover up as well as he could and just let the other guy wail away at him. In theory, the other guy would punch himself out, and then Ali would turn on him. He called it the 'rope-a-dope'."

"I'm not quite sure I approve of that analogy," Katie said. "Who's the dope?"

"Usually, it's me. But in this case… I've been thinking."

"Oh gosh, that's all I need!"

"Well, as best I can anyway." Aaron sat up and turned to better face Katie. In doing so he forced Katie to sit up as well.

"Hey, I was quite comfy, thank you very much."

"I'm sorry. We'll resume the cuddle position shortly. I think you need to take a few days off work."

"And do what?"

"Get away," Aaron said. "Go back home, see your folks."

"Just like that, go back to Okemah without you?" Katie said.

Aaron shrugged. "Well, just for a few days, I mean, I wouldn't want it to be for too long."

"I suppose I could. I've got plenty of vacation time saved up. But, you don't want to come?"

"I'd love to, but I can't. I'm swamped at work. There's an auditor from the IRS coming in this week and I get the privilege of being his lackey for the next week or two."

"Ick, sounds like having a root canal would be more pleasant."

"And less painful, too. Actually, I've worked with Terry before. He's a pretty cool guy. Anyway, I think going back home would do you some good. Get some perspective. Relax. Let Mom fuss over you and let Dad pick on you."

"Well, it *has* been a while. Are you sure?"

"Positive."

"What will you do?" Katie closed her eyes and smiled. As soon as the words left her mouth she knew she would regret it.

"Oh, I don't know," Aaron said. "Run around in my boxers. Eat Cheetos in bed. Maybe turn on Bob Seger real loud and dance around the house. Maybe throw a stag party, or dress up in your underwear."

"Okay!" Katie said, laughing now. "Enough! That's a mental image I could've done without." Katie slapped Aaron playfully on the arm. "Besides, you big oaf, you couldn't fit in my underwear."

"So, it's settled?"

"Yes, I guess so. I'll call the office, and Mom and Dad in the morning."

"Great."

Katie grabbed Aaron's hands in hers and looked at him. "Thank you," she said.

"Don't mention it." Aaron leaned back against the couch and patted for Katie to join him. Katie leaned back in his arms, and for the first time in a while, she felt as if God were smiling down on her – if only just a little. "What would I do without you?"

"Have underwear that isn't stretched out or torn up."

Katie laughed out loud. "Oh my…"

*   *   *

Wu Chien knocked on the orphanage director's door. Casting aside her fears of being chastised for being too forward, she'd decided that she must at least try to get Lin Lin into the adoption program. *Please Yesu, be with me.*

The office walls had once been a bright white, full of hope. But over the years they had yellowed with age, grime and pollution. The director, Fu Si Chuan, was slouched over his old, weathered desk. She could see that his black and grey hair had thinned enough so that he had a bald spot on the crown of his head.

He looked up from his work and peered over his glasses at Chien. "Yes?"

"*Ni hao*," Chien said, her smile wavering with nerves. Chuan, she thought, was a good man. But thirty years as the director of an orphanage had made him cold and calloused. She prayed for him every day. Without the Lord, Chien had determined, it must be hard not to become that way in these circumstances.

Fu Si Chuan nodded once, quick and succinct.

"You know that Lin Lin is not well?"

Chuan sighed and straightened up. "Yes."

"We don't have the money to get her the surgery she needs."

"No."

Chien continued, but with care. She knew that his short answers meant he wasn't in the mood to be bothered by this. "Shouldn't you consider submitting her paperwork to be adopted?"

"No."

"But…"

"No," Fu said, cutting her off. "We only have the funds available to apply for one child. We need to use them wisely and pick the child that has the greatest chance of being adopted."

"I understand," Chien said. That was what she feared. She had worked at the orphanage long enough that she too understood the system. It was unfortunate that they were one of the poorer orphanages in Chongqing. Some of the newer, nicer, richer ones had the resources to submit several babies.

But something in her pressed her forward. She had to keep trying. If she didn't, she felt as though she were letting down the child and betraying Yesu's calling on her. "But what about placing her as a special needs child? Is that a possibility?"

"No!" Chuan said again, his voice hardening.

Chien looked down at her feet, trying to make amends at being too forward. She could see that the linoleum flooring in the office had aged as poorly as the walls. "Please forgive me," she said, still looking down. "I did not mean to offend you."

"I know," he said, his voice softening. "It's very difficult to make these decisions. But the Party only grants us so much money. We still have to feed the children that are here, pay the bills and pay our workers. None of which we are able to do very well."

The Party. She had never spoken outwardly against it because to do so would put her in danger. But inwardly she despised the Party. The communists had persecuted the church and perverted that part of the message they did allow public. Now, thanks to Party policies, her country was forced to abandon many of their children, and in doing so, abandon their future.

At last she looked up again, but didn't make eye contact with Chuan. "Thank you, for your time," she said as she turned to leave.

"Wait," he said.

She stopped and turned back to look at Chuan. He was standing now, looking out the only window in the room. His hands were clasped behind his back.

"We've lost other children over the years due to sickness and poor conditions. The Party doesn't like that. It appears as if we can't take care of our own." He paused and snorted as if he hadn't missed the irony.

Chien was also struck by the irony, but didn't say anything. Instead she prayed in her heart, asking God to touch Chuan and use him for His purpose.

"Maybe," he said after a lengthy pause. "Maybe we can find some special funding because of her heart condition. I will check into it, but don't get your hopes up or say anything to anyone else."

"*Xie xie,*" she said, thanking God also, in her heart.

"You have been my most trusted, loyal worker for many years," he said.

Chien looked down again, accepting his kind words with humility.

"I know this one is special to you, but be careful that you don't push too far on this. There are many other children that need you also."

Chien looked up at him, surprised by his strong words. What did he mean by that? She really didn't care. Her life had been lived. She loved China, but it was no longer her home. Home was with her Lord, and with her husband. If it meant losing her job, or even her life, she would fight for these children. Especially Lin Lin.

"I will be as careful as I can," she said.

"Good," he said, smiling at last.

Chien left the office and went straight to Lin Lin's room. Picking her up, she held the baby close and whispered in her ear. "Good news, Lin Lin, there's a chance. Praise You, Yesu. There's always hope for those who trust in Yesu."

*   *   *

It was cold and windy, but the sun was shining brightly in a brilliant blue sky as Katie drove through the streets of Okemah, Oklahoma. Looking around, it was as though she were transported back in time. Nothing seemed to have changed. Despite the downtown's small size, it still boasted all of the same charming early twentieth century architecture in its buildings and store fronts, and Katie reveled in the old town feel created by the cobblestone streets and old ornate buildings. The little town seemed to move at the same slow pace it always did – as if in defiance of the frenetic pace of life in big cities.

Aaron might just be right, Katie thought. Maybe she did need some extra time to get away, refocus, refresh. She did, however, dread one thing. Her mother could always tell when something was wrong – no matter how hard Katie tried to hide it. Her parents had always been the picture of faith. Abraham himself would've been envious of their steadfast trust in the Lord. Katie tightened her grip on the steering wheel. She knew that it wouldn't do any good to tell them about hers and Aaron's struggles. There was no way they could understand.

Just outside the southwest end of town Katie turned her maroon Honda Civic down a gravel drive that led to her parents' farm, and her childhood home – the only home she had ever known until she left for college. Okemah's sole claim to fame was as the birthplace of Woody Guthrie, and Katie was thrilled when she left to attend college at the University of Oklahoma in Norman, Oklahoma, just outside of Oklahoma City. But lately, she found herself pining for the simple days she remembered growing up in Okemah. Now, as she approached her parents' home she couldn't help but smile.

As Katie pulled up to the brick, ranch style house, her parents stepped out onto the front porch. Her mother, Margaret Reynolds, was dressed in jeans, a button-up blouse and a cardigan sweater. She had clasped her hands in front of her and was already saying something Katie couldn't make out. Except for twinkling eyes and a broad smile, Frank Reynolds was his usual stoic self. He was wearing his normal, everyday attire – a pullover knit shirt under overalls, with a dark blue flannel shirt on top as a jacket. The ensemble was topped off with a green John Deere ball cap tilted back on his head.

Shedding any pretense of being a sophisticated, well-educated city woman, Katie climbed quickly out of the Honda and yelled, "Momma! Daddy!" She bounded up the front porch steps and hugged her mother.

Margaret held Katie out at arms length. "It's so good to see my baby. How are you? You look tired. Are you hungry?"

"I'm fine, Mom."

"Are you sure? I could whip something up in a jiff."

Katie smiled at her mother. She had always said that you could show up at her mother's house at three in the morning and she could produce a seven course meal in a matter of minutes. "No, I'm fine, really. But thank you."

Katie turned to her dad. "Hi, Daddy," she said as he bent over and picked her up in a giant bear hug.

"Hi, Peanut. It's wonderful to see you again."

Frank set Katie down and went to Katie's car to grab her bag.

Margaret put her arm around Katie as they turned to walk into the house and asked her, "So how long are you staying?"

"Just a couple of days."

"Is everything alright?" Margaret whispered.

Katie shrugged. "Things are okay," she said, trying to act nonchalant.

Margaret looked suspiciously at Katie. "Well, we'll talk later."

Frank came in with Katie's bag. "I'll drop this off on your bed," he said as he started up the stairs to Katie's old room.

Katie looked all around, taking in the familiar sights of her parents' home. The memories wafted back into her consciousness, like the scent from the hickory wood burning in the fireplace. The old, antique clock was still sitting in the middle of the fireplace mantle. Many of the same pictures still hung on the walls. Katie looked at the furniture. "Hey, you got some new furniture," she said as she rubbed her hand across the top of the couch.

"Oh yes, we got that about six months ago. Your father's spot on the couch finally gave way. Has it been that long since you've been back?"

"Yeah, I think so. The year before last we spent the holidays at our place. Then of course in December you went to see Aunt June up in Ohio, so we didn't spend Christmas together this year."

"Oh, that's right. Between working the farm in the summer and all of our travels in the RV, I can't keep up with things anymore."

Frank returned from upstairs and nudged Katie as he walked by. "Is she already giving you the tenth degree?" he said with a mischievous glint in his eye.

"Not too bad."

"Give her time."

"Oh," Margaret said, "you just hush. I want to catch up on everything that's going on in Katherine's life. Who knows, maybe there might be some big news coming soon." Turning to Katie she said, "You know, we're ready for more kids anytime you and Aaron are."

Katie felt as if she'd been punched in the stomach. Turning away, she didn't want her parents to see her reaction so she began walking through the rest of the house. Her mother meant well, Katie knew. But now she also felt as if she were letting her parents down in more ways than one.

"Wow, I like what you did in the dining room," Katie said, trying to hide her shaky voice.

"Go on, look around some more and make yourself at home," she heard her father's voice calling from the living room. "We'll resume the interrogation later."

"Frank!"

"Thanks, Daddy," Katie called back.

Oh boy, what could be more fun?

Chapter 16

"And then he just left," Aaron said as he finished telling Mark about his encounter with Ben Phelps, his father. They were running side-by-side along the Arkansas River, on the Riverparks trail in Tulsa. He felt like he needed to talk to someone about it, and since Katie had been going through her own problems, he didn't feel like he could add much more to her load. Aaron was sure Mark would understand where he was coming from.

"So, what do you think?" Aaron asked. They had only been running for two or three miles, so he wasn't too winded yet.

"I don't know," Mark said after a pause.

"What do you mean you don't know?"

"It just seems like you were kinda harsh, that's all."

The two friends each swerved to opposite sides of the trail as they passed an old man walking a small terrier.

As they passed the old man and his dog the dog barked at Mark and Aaron.

"Wolfie!" Aaron heard the old man say. "You stop that!"

As they came back together on the trail Aaron said, "Don't you think I had the right to? I mean after what he did, I would think I'm entitled."

"Yeah, I suppose."

"But?"

Mark was wearing New Balance running shoes and a grey wind suit with white piping down the arms and legs. Aaron could see the collar of a thermal shirt under the jacket where it was unzipped an inch or two at the top. Mark's only other visible concessions to the cold were his gloves and black stocking hat.

"It just seems like there's a lot of things we have the right to do, but that doesn't necessarily mean we should do them. Ya know? Now I know, I'm not in your shoes. I would probably feel just the same way you do. But, you know how Pastor James is always talking about how you shouldn't totally trust your feelings because feelings can be misleading?"

"Yeah, so?" Aaron said.

"This seems like one of those times."

Aaron noticed that Mark wasn't huffing and puffing yet from talking while they ran, so he was careful to make sure that he didn't either. He breathed in deeply through his nose and let it ease out through his mouth.

"You're right," Aaron said. "It *is* easier to be objective when you're not in the other guy's shoes."

"Sure it is. Don't you remember a couple of years ago when I had all that trouble at work?"

"Uh huh."

"Well," Mark continued, "weren't you the one who said that doing the right thing was usually the hardest to follow through on?"

"I don't think I've ever said anything that wise."

"Oh yes, brother. You even looked proud, like you'd had an epiphany."

"Naw, I think it was just some bad Mexican food or something."

Taking normal breaths while running and talking was starting to become a challenge for Aaron. He was trying to decide if he could trip Mark and make it look like an accident when Mark started slowing down.

"Let's...walk...while we talk," Mark said between gasps as he stopped running.

"Wimp," Aaron said as he gratefully slowed to a walk.

Mark took his stocking cap off his head, brushed his hair off his forehead with his fingers and repositioned the thick hat on his head.

"Anyway," he said, "I think yes, you had the right to be mad. And yes, maybe he doesn't deserve forgiveness. But do any of us, really?"

Remembering back to his actions at the bar Aaron nodded his head. "Okay, I'll give you that. I guess I was totally unprepared for all of the raw emotion that seemed to boil up from nowhere."

"I can't even begin to imagine," Mark said as he laced his hands together behind his head to help catch his breath.

"I remember one time," Aaron said, "when I was a young kid and Mom took me to Sears to see Santa Clause. I had looked forward to it all week. We got there and stood in line for what seemed like days. Then when it got to be my turn, I froze. All of a sudden I didn't want to be there. I wasn't ready for the moment."

"Mom says I did that too, when I was about five. I don't remember it though."

"It was the same thing the other day. The exact same. I had spent so long dreaming about that moment, but when the time came…"

Mark stopped and looked at Aaron. "You were scared."

Aaron nodded his head and kicked a rock off into the bushes on the west side of the path. He didn't like talking about his feelings with anyone other than Katie.

"You're like me," Mark continued. "And when you get scared, it makes you mad."

"Yeah."

On the trail ahead, Aaron saw a woman with long blonde hair running their way. She was pushing a stroller that appeared to be designed for off road activities – the kind with two large back wheels and one large front wheel both with knobby tires and she looked like she had just stepped out of a Nike ad.

Aaron looked at his Converse tennis shoes held together with duct tape, his old, tattered sweat pants and the tail of a green t-shirt hanging out from under a faded red OU sweatshirt and decided he must look like an ad from "We-B-Slobs."

When Aaron and Mark stepped aside to let them pass, Aaron noticed that the baby she was pushing appeared to be Asian.

Aaron elbowed Mark. "You know, that's twice recently that I've seen an American with an Asian child. I wonder if she's babysitting for someone?"

"I dunno," Mark said. "Maybe the baby's adopted."

Aaron shrugged. "Could be."

Mark looked back at Aaron and resumed their conversation. "Anyway, you know what you've got to do."

Aaron sighed as they started walking again. "I know what you're going to say, but I don't know if I have the strength."

Aaron turned back for one last glance at the woman and her baby as they disappeared down the trail.

Mark put his hand on Aaron's shoulder. "You'll never be able to offer more forgiveness than you've been given by Jesus."

"I know, I know. I need to do it for me, for Katie, to honor God. My head knows all of that but my heart says 'no way'."

"Those twenty-four inches between your head and heart can be the slowest traveling in the world."

"In my case, it's probably the rockiest too."

"You said it – I didn't."

"I know," Aaron said as they started running again. "I just wish it wasn't true."

The two ran on in silence. Aaron's mind wandered back to the woman and baby they had seen. *Adoption? I wonder what Katie would say...*

*   *   *

It was eleven at night and Wu Chien was on her knees at the side of her bed praying. She poured her heart out to Yesu every night, but this night's prayers had been exceptionally long. This evening she had felt more need than ever before to lift up the children in her orphanage, and even the children of the Republic of China to God.

She clasped her hands in front of her, knuckles nearly white, as she rested with her forearms on the bed. She was especially troubled for Lin Lin. The other babies her age were developing rapidly but her development was almost nonexistent – or at least it appeared that way. It seemed as though Lin Lin didn't have the strength to do the things normal babies her age do. She was still very lethargic much of the time.

But, in her eyes, Chien could see the spirit of a fighter. She didn't know how many more babies she would be allowed to take care of before the Lord took her home, but Chien knew that this one was special. There was a definite plan at work, and she could feel it. She didn't know "how" or "who," but she didn't need to. She only hoped that the "when" would happen soon enough.

Closing her prayers, she stood up to get into bed. As she did, her head began to spin and she felt nauseated. She staggered backwards a step then tried to reach for her bed. She fell sideways, collapsing to her knees and knocking the small brown ceramic lamp off of her old bedside table.

Her breathing was coming in gasps and she was shaking with uncontrollable jerks. She tried to call out for help, but couldn't. For an instant everything went black. She reached out and pulled herself up enough to rest her head on the side of the bed. She closed her eyes and waited. *Please, Yesu. Please let me help this one last child.*

She'd been having these episodes for several years now, but in the last six months they had increased in frequency and intensity. She was afraid to tell anyone, for fear she might be taken away from her only purpose for still being on God's earth. Fortunately none of the episodes had ever occurred in front of someone else.

Slowly but surely the spinning subsided. Like always, her head was pounding. With wobbly legs and shaky arms she lifted herself up and collapsed onto her bed. She strained to pull the covers up over her and closed her eyes once more.

Thank you, Yesu for Your grace to give me one more day with these kids. Especially Lin Lin.

*   *   *

Katie got up early the next day to help with the morning chores. Dressed in an old pair of sneakers, jeans, a black hooded sweatshirt, a medium weight coat, and a red ball cap she collected new eggs from the chicken coop and milked her parents' only cow. Much to her displeasure her father, Frank, took great delight in watching her try to knock the rust off of her milking skills. It took more time than it used to, but at last she completed those chores.

Katie played it off, claiming she was just rusty, but secretly she was nervous. She was trying to psych herself up to tell her parents everything that had been going on. Katie knew they – or at least her mother – would be very suspicious after her reaction to her mother's comment the previous afternoon.

As Frank, Margaret and Katie sat down for breakfast Frank said the blessing over the food and they began filling their plates.

"So, what's the point of having only one cow?" Katie asked as she spooned some strawberries, cantaloupe, and pineapple onto her plate.

Frank shrugged his shoulders as he sipped on his coffee cup.

"Go ahead, dear," Margaret said, smiling at Frank. "Explain to us why we still have a cow left in the barn. Explain why we spend more money feeding and taking care of that one cow than we would to just buy our milk from the store."

"It's the principle," Frank said. "We're farmers. Farmers have cows. I've always had cows. It's what I do."

"So, in other words," Katie said, "you can't let go of your roots so you're just treating it like a hobby?"

"More or less. Besides," Frank continued with a sly sideways glance at Margaret, "I can talk to her. It's about the only conversation I can have around here where I can get a word in edgewise."

"Oh, fiddle. So dear," Margaret said looking at Katie, "you told us why Aaron couldn't come with you, but how is he doing?"

"He's okay. His father showed up at our door last Sunday," Katie said before taking a bite of scrambled eggs.

Frank stopped in mid chew and looked at Katie.

"Oh my dear Lord," Margaret said. "How'd Aaron take it?"

Katie swallowed the eggs and took a drink of orange juice. "About like you'd expect, I suppose. At first he was very surprised, and then he was angry. I think when it was all over he was pretty bummed out – to say the least. He hasn't really told me a lot yet." Katie paused and took a deep breath before continuing. "I think he's been trying to protect me because I've had so much on my mind as well."

Margaret looked at Katie. "Like what, dear?"

Katie knew she was committed now. *Here we go.* "Mom, you know yesterday when you said something about having grandkids?"

Margaret's eyes lit up. "Yes."

Katie could feel her face begin to flush. She took a minute to maintain her composure. "Well, we've been trying," she said with a shaky voice full of frustration. "For more than two years now. And it hasn't happened. Probably won't…"

Margaret began to tear up as Katie did. Frank maintained a steady gaze on Katie, but she could see the concern in his eyes.

Margaret put her hand on Katie's. "My sweet baby," she said. "I would've never said anything had I known. I'm so sorry. Won't you forgive me?"

"Of course, Mom. I know you didn't mean anything."

"Why didn't you say anything before?" Margaret asked.

"I was ashamed to. We haven't handled things so well. Aaron has struggled with even committing to being a dad – with good reason. And I've become like some deranged basket case. You two have always been so rock-solid, I'm sure you've never been mad at God or struggled with your faith..." Katie's voice cracked. She stood up from her chair. "Would you excuse me, please?"

"Honey, where are you going?" Margaret called after her as she walked out the front door.

Katie wrapped her arms around herself against the cold and hurried to the barn. She felt so foolish. Why couldn't she handle this more maturely – more dignified? She wanted her parents to be proud of her and yet here she was running away like a school girl. She went inside and climbed up onto her dad's tractor, sat down, and began to cry.

Within a few minutes Frank appeared at the door. He walked in and climbed up onto the tractor beside Katie.

Katie looked at her father and took a deep breath. "I don't want to hear anything about 'God's plan', okay Dad?"

Frank took his coat off and wrapped it around Katie. "Sometimes," he said, "His ways just don't make any sense – how the world can be so unjust. Unborn babies are killed every day and yet a bright, beautiful, faithful girl like you doesn't get to experience the miracle." He shook his head and ran his big hand across the back of her head. Even now, in his upper fifties, she could still feel the strength in his hands.

"I don't know that I've been all that faithful," she said looking down.

"You ever wonder why we were a little older when you were born?" Frank said.

"I don't know that I ever gave it much thought."

Frank smoothed the cuff of his jeans down over his boot and cleared his throat. "You almost had an older brother."

Katie looked up at her father, startled by this revelation. "You and Mom never said anything."

"No," he said, shaking his head slowly. "We didn't. We kept it mostly to ourselves and a few other people."

"What happened?"

"Nothing really," he said. "It was about four years before you were born." Katie noticed a faraway look in her father's eyes. She wasn't sure she'd ever seen it before.

"The baby just died. In the seventh month."

Katie gasped.

"Your mother had to carry the baby to term and deliver it."

Through her own tears Katie noticed a tear in her father's eye. "How horrible."

"Yeah, and the labor and delivery was very hard. The doctor didn't even let us see the boy – just took him away." Frank spit on the floor of the barn in disgust. "Sometime later they told us he was a boy. We buried him two days later, here in town."

"So why," Katie asked, "are you telling me this now?"

Frank looked at Katie for a moment. Katie could see the love and compassion in his eyes.

"Your mother just holed up in the house. Wouldn't leave it – not even for church."

I can relate…

"I guess the shrinks these days would call it depression. But she was mad at God – mad as Hell, to put it bluntly. She wouldn't eat, wouldn't sleep, wouldn't talk to me any. Just sat in a rocking chair on the front porch. I didn't handle things any better either. I'd just lost a son, my wife was falling apart. I was pretty mad too. I decided that if God was going to turn on me that I'd at least do something to earn it. So I went out and got drunk."

Katie looked at her dad in disbelief.

Frank nodded his head. "Hard to believe, huh. The first and only time I ever touched anything stronger than soda pop. I landed myself in jail. Spent the night in a cell with three other drunks."

Katie shook her head. "I had no idea."

"One of 'em puked on me, so I got him back."

"What did you do?"

"Turned around and puked on him. Once I sobered up they allowed me to make my one phone call. Old man Storms – used to be the town sheriff – came to the jail house and bailed me out."

Frank jumped off the tractor and helped Katie down. He grabbed some chicken feed and walked outside to the coop and began throwing feed through the fence.

"Anyway," he started again, "Sheriff Storms was as fine a man I ever knew. He didn't talk much about his faith, but he knew the Lord. I talked to him a lot over the next several weeks. I told him that after this, God would have to prove to me that he loved us before I'd go back to Him. You know what he said?"

Katie looped her fingers through the holes in the fence and stared down at the chickens. "I'm thinking this sounds very familiar. What?"

"He said that He already has, and He didn't have to again. That was all he said, but I knew what he meant. On the cross, when Jesus took the nails. He was stretching out his arms and saying 'This is how much I love you'. He proved it once and for all. I repented and began going back to church. I prayed for your mother and she eventually came around. I guess we should've told you and Janie, but it got so easy to just not talk about so that's what we did."

Katie bit her lower lip. "I've been so confused and angry. How easily we forget…"

"Peanut," Frank said as he put his arm around her shoulders. "It's okay to be mad at God. He can handle it. It's okay to have questions. But He won't tolerate you questioning how He runs His universe. Just read Job. Your mother and I are human. Yes, our faith is stronger now than it was. But it's the trials in life – just like the one you're going through now – that grew us up in our faith. It's the only way. Where's the faith in 'easy street'?"

Katie nodded. "James calls it trial by fire."

"Exactly. But don't give up hope. He does *love* you. I can't tell you much more, but I know that one fact for certain."

Katie kissed her father on the cheek. "Thanks, Daddy. But I still can't believe you never told us."

Frank shrugged. "I guess we never felt the need to – until now."

"So," Katie said, managing a grin, "is this the part where you give me a Lifesaver?"

"Nope," Frank said as he swatted her on the backside. "This is the part where I kick you in the fanny and tell you to straighten up and fly right."

Katie laughed and swatted her dad on his upper arm.

"Let's go in, our breakfast will be cold and I know your mother's worried sick." Frank stopped and looked Katie in the eyes. "I love you."

"I love you too, Daddy."

And thank you too, Father.

Chapter 17

Katie left her parents home mid afternoon on Friday. She'd missed Aaron, but he was right – a point she wasn't about to admit to him – the trip did her good. In the short stay at her parents' home she had grown to love and appreciate them in a totally different way. She had always had a view of them as these "Super Christians" who never failed God. But she learned that they were in fact, human, and that fact only made her respect them all the more. She knew now that it wasn't always easy and things were plenty tough for them as well, yet ultimately they remained faithful to the Father.

On her way home she stopped at the market and picked up two good sized filet mignon steaks, mushrooms, fresh squash and zucchini, red, green, and yellow bell peppers, a sack of potatoes and a loaf of French bread.

Once home, she found the house in spotless condition – a pleasant surprise from what she'd expected. She also found a large bouquet of red roses in a brand new crystal vase sitting in the middle of the dining room table. There was a note from Aaron welcoming her home – worded like only Aaron could, suggestive without being offensive.

I can't wait until he gets home from work.

She mixed up a marinade for the steaks and put them in a bag to sit. She then preheated the oven to four hundred and fifty degrees and began cutting up the vegetables. Once they were cut up she tossed them in olive oil, spread them out on a baking sheet covered in parchment paper, sprinkled salt, pepper, dried rosemary and garlic on them and put them in the oven to roast. She then washed and shred several potatoes and a block of asiago cheese to make potatoes Julianne.

Once she had dinner on its way she set the table, complete with candles. She wanted Aaron to come home to a good meal, but more importantly, to come home and find that he had his wife back. She was no longer so confident about what their future might hold, but after much praying last night she had determined that they would face it together and trust in God – no matter what.

She heard Aaron pulling into the garage so she put the steaks on to broil. Grilling would have been better but it wasn't an option in the cold. She lit the candles on the table and turned around as Aaron walked into the house. He stopped in the entryway into the kitchen. His eyes showed signs of stress and worry, but his smile told Katie that he was relieved to see her. He walked around the bar to where Katie was standing and stopped in front of her. She put her arms around his neck as he wrapped his arms around her waist. They kissed, long and tender.

With their lips still touching Aaron said "Hi."

"Hi yourself, big fella."

Aaron rested his forehead on Katie's. "Something sure smells good."

"Well, I do have a nice dinner going."

"Oh yeah," he said. "That too."

Katie smiled. She knew she was home now. Aaron changed out of his suit and tie, and helped Katie finish making the dinner preparations.

They worked around each other in a strained silence. Katie could tell that Aaron was trying to hide something that was bothering him.

Once dinner was ready and they had taken their places at the table, they joined hands and Katie prayed. "Thank you, Father, for Your unfailing love. Thank you for Your redemptive power. Bless this food to our bodies, and our bodies to Your service. In Jesus name, amen."

Aaron looked at Katie. "So, how was your visit?"

"Very good. I enjoyed seeing Mom and Dad again."

"So then, I was right, wasn't I?"

"Well, I wouldn't go that far," Katie said as she popped a bite of roasted red pepper into her mouth.

Aaron smiled at her. "Of course not. Why ruin your record now?"

"I was thinking that it's really not that far from here to Okemah," Katie said, ignoring Aaron's last playful jab. "We should go see them more often."

"Okay by me," Aaron said as he took a bite of steak. "Your folks are the sweetest people in the world. They've meant a lot to me since my parents have been gone…you know."

"Yes, I do know." Katie reached across the table and took Aaron's hand. "Can I ask you though, what's troubling you?"

"Yes, you can," Aaron said between sips of tea. "But that doesn't mean I'll answer. I don't want to mess up a perfectly fine evening talking about me."

Katie leaned toward Aaron. "What if I flutter my eyelashes at you and nibble on your ear."

"I could try to contain myself, but I make no guarantees."

"So," Katie said, "tell me. What's up?"

Aaron sighed. "I've decided that I need to offer forgiveness to Ben."

Katie was very relieved to hear this. She knew that Aaron needed to do this, as much for himself as for Ben. She smiled at him, encouraging him to continue.

Aaron got up and took his plate into the kitchen to get another helping of vegetables. "I talked to Mark the other day. He said I was way too harsh on Ben."

"I'm sure that was hard to swallow."

"Do you need anything while I'm up?"

"No, I'm fine."

Aaron returned to his seat. "Of course, at first. But I came home and read through the gospels and some of Paul's letters. Over and over again God offers us forgiveness. Who am I to withhold the same?"

Katie brushed her hair back behind her ears. "I can see how that would be a tough thing to do, but something tells me there's more."

"Boy," Aaron said, "you must be able to read me like a book."

"Pretty much. I think *I* have a better poker face than you."

Aaron cut his steak and took another bite. Katie waited while he chewed. The conversation wasn't going quite as well as she'd hoped for, but she was still optimistic.

Aaron put his fork and knife down, took a drink from his tea and looked at Katie. "I found out today that I'm not getting a raise this year. I was really hoping to surprise you with some good news."

"How disappointing for you," she said. "Did they tell you why?"

"Yeah, said it was the economic conditions. They aren't giving any raises at all."

"So they're okay with *you* though."

"Oh yeah. Say I'm doing great. We're just not going to be able to get ahead as much this year as I'd hoped."

"There are worse things."

"Yes. Things have been," Aaron said.

Katie nodded her head and reached again for Aaron's hand. She could see the depth of his love for her in his eyes. "But, we're still us."

"That we are."

"And we still belong to the Father."

"Greater is He that is in us."

After a moment Aaron got up and began to clear the table.

"Don't mess with that now," Katie said. "Let's retire to the sofa and talk some more."

Aaron took Katie by the hand and they sat down next to each other on the sofa. They sat in pleasant silence for quite some time. Katie was soaking up the renewed feeling of wholeness.

"You know what I've been thinking about?" Aaron asked.

"Well, I know what you're usually thinking about," Katie said as she ran her hand across Aaron's chest.

"Okay," he said. "Besides that."

"Then I haven't the foggiest."

Aaron looked at Katie. "What if – I can't believe this is me suggesting this – we look at…maybe consider…adoption?"

Katie couldn't contain her surprise. She had already given it some private thought, but she had never dared to believe Aaron would be willing.

"Well," she said, laughing in delight, "I think the prospect sounds very intriguing."

"Should we start researching it then?"

Katie kissed Aaron and hugged him tightly. "Yes! I would've never dreamed…I've got to ask you, what made you consider adoption?"

"The other day, when Mark and I were running, we saw a woman who looked American – well at least Anglo any way – pushing an Asian baby in a stroller. Mark thought maybe the baby was adopted. Then I was reading in the Bible where it says that we've been *adopted* into God's family. And besides, if there's one thing I should understand, it's that kids need parents."

Katie smiled and closed her eyes. *God, you are so cool!*

*   *   *

Aaron stopped and watched as Ben Phelps stood by his mother's grave in the Memorial Park Cemetery at 51st Street and Memorial Avenue in mid-town Tulsa. It was an overcast, sunless Sunday afternoon and the cold north wind chilled to the bone. Aaron had called Ben to meet so they could talk but this setting seemed so bizarre.

There was a small bouquet of flowers resting on his mother's headstone. Ben was wearing the same coat he wore during his visit to Aaron's house, but today he was also wearing a stocking hat and gloves. Aaron could see a flannel shirt under the coat.

As Aaron approached Ben from the other side of his mother's grave Ben looked up at Aaron. His eyes still looked sad, just like the first time they'd met.

"This is a really weird place for us to meet, isn't it?" Aaron said.

"Yes, I suppose so," Ben said as his eyes shot back and forth, looking around the cemetery. "I had been considering leaving this weekend before you called. I wanted to visit your mother's grave before I left. I guess I panicked a little and this was the only place I could think of."

"I don't know," Aaron said. "Maybe it's appropriate."

"I reckon so."

There was a long, miserable silence. Aaron stooped down and wiped some dirt off his mother's headstone. "It looked like you were talking when I got here." Aaron's statement was in the form of a question.

"I guess I was talking to your mother, and talking to God. Seeking forgiveness, release…something."

"Why?" Aaron said. Ben looked at him, puzzled. "Why did you leave? What was going through your head?"

"I wish," Ben said, "that I had a good answer but I don't. All I can say is that I was very screwed up."

"I'd sure like more."

"Why, what would it change to know exactly why I left?" Ben asked.

"Probably nothing," Aaron said. He felt as if there were two forces at war within him. He wanted so badly to tell Ben he had chosen to forgive him, but a part of him wanted to scream at the injustice. He stood upright and looked at Ben. "Shakespeare said that 'readiness is all.' I guess I wasn't ready for the moment when it came."

Ben looked at Aaron and his face was full of compassion. He breathed out hard and his breath formed a great puff of steam in the cold. "I don't see how you could be."

Aaron said, "Come on, let's walk. Try to stay warm." The cemetery was empty of people except for Aaron and Ben. They were in the middle of Tulsa and it seemed as though they were isolated, in their own country. Aaron felt as if God had cleared the stage just for them.

"I had fallen in with the wrong crowd at work," Ben said. "Remember, this was the mid-seventies and there were still a bunch of hippies hanging on, hoping for Utopia to suddenly erupt here on earth. We'd leave the shop then do drugs on our lunch hour and talk about freeing our minds and spirits – crap like that. I made bad choices. Very bad. But the worst was when I chose to leave your mother and you."

They were walking on a road that wound east towards the Chapel, between the various sections of the cemetery. The wind whistled through the bare tree branches. Aaron stopped and bent over at the same time Ben did to straighten some flowers that had fallen over on one of the grave markers. They looked surprised at each other then laughed uneasily.

"I always thought that there must've been something terribly wrong with me for you to up and leave like that," Aaron said.

"No, there wasn't. But there *was* something terribly wrong with me."

"So what happened after you left?"

"It just gets worse. Are you sure you want to know?"

Aaron shrugged. "Why not?"

"I ran out of money in Arizona and robbed a convenience store. Ended up in the LA area dealing drugs and consuming just as much as I sold. One day I tried to sell to the wrong person and ended up in prison."

"Hmm," Aaron said as he took care in stepping around a headstone, "some legacy."

Ben laughed without humor. "But, as odd as it may sound, I'm thankful for my time in prison."

"Wow," Aaron said, looking directly at Ben for the first time since they had started walking. "That's not something I'd imagine hearing very many cons say."

Ben picked up a piece of stray trash and threw it into a nearby trash can. "In prison I became friends with a man named Joe who led me to the Lord." Aaron noticed a tiny spark smoldering in Ben's eyes. "No, I don't have a very good legacy to speak of. But in that hell hole I became part of a heritage of grace that shines brighter than any other legacy you could name. I cling to God's grace. It's all I've got."

"Well, we do at least have some common ground," Aaron said.

"Oh yeah? Tell me about it."

"I started following Katie to church while I was in college. I really didn't want any part of that scene in those days. I'd seen how my mom had lived her life dedicated to God, and then died in a horrendous car crash after spending nearly all of it raising a child on her own..." Aaron stopped and looked at Ben. "No offense," he said.

Ben made a gesture as if to wave it off. "The facts are what they are. No sense trying to deny them."

"So, I was pretty down on religion back then. But I wanted to impress Katie so I started memorizing enough scripture that I could at least sound like I was spiritual."

"Uh oh," Ben said grinning. "Give Him an inch and He'll take your life."

Aaron nodded his head then ducked a big gust of wind that kicked up.

"That's what happened," Aaron continued after the wind gust subsided. "It was as if the love of Christ dripped off the pages and somehow made its way into my hardened heart. I started believing that maybe He could truly love someone like me. Before long, I was ready, no, *had* to give my life to Jesus."

The two reached the Chapel and looped back toward their cars. Even though there was a part of Aaron that wanted to remain cold and distant, he felt compelled to learn more about his father.

"Your turn," Aaron said.

"I did my time while Joe and I became brothers in Christ. He mentored me, made sure I was consistently in the Word. Taught me to put on the armor every day." Ben shook his head. "In that place I needed all God's armor. Anyway, I got paroled. Found a small apartment within a bus ride of work and my parole officer. Started working on becoming a member of society."

Aaron stopped at a grave that had a small American flag at its head. The marker indicated that the man was a beloved father who had proudly served in WW II.

Beloved father…

"What happened to Joe?" Aaron said as he looked away from the marker.

"About a week after I left, my parole officer told me that Joe had been stabbed and killed trying to save a man who'd been attacked by a gang of prisoners."

"Must've been hard."

"I don't know…sort of… maybe? You talk about going to a *much* better place."

"Good point."

Ben stopped and looked off to the northwest and skyline of downtown Tulsa. "When I think of Joe," he said, "I'm reminded of the scripture that says that David served the Lord in his time and then he died."

"Now that you mention it, not a bad way to be remembered."

The two men stopped walking when they reached their cars and turned to face each other.

"If only I could be remembered that well," Ben said.

"I forgive you," Aaron said. The empty cemetery seemed to become even quieter, as if the hush had been silenced. "I can't say in complete honesty that I'm sure I want to, but I know I must."

Aaron could see a flood of emotion running through Ben's face. "Well," he said, "that's a start."

"I'm called to it...Mom would want me to. But, I...I don't know how much more I have to offer right now," Aaron said.

"I understand."

"I want to try, though."

"Me too."

Ben stuck his hand out to Aaron. This time, instead of shoving his fist into his pocket Aaron pulled his hand out of his coat pocket and shook his hand. He was thirty-one years old and it was the first time he'd ever felt the touch of his father's hand.

But Aaron knew that there was a loving, mighty hand guiding his steps. And he wasn't sure, but he almost felt his mother's arms around him at that moment as well.

Chapter 18

Katie and Aaron were on the floor of their living room playing with Clair and Kellie. They had invited the Humphreys, their new neighbors from down the street over for dinner. Katie was intrigued by little Kellie and hoping to learn more about her.

During the course of dinner they learned that Tony was a telecommunications analyst for a local consulting firm, Gayle had been a successful sales rep for a pharmaceutical company before quitting to stay at home with their children, and that Kellie really only liked rice – a fact they discovered after she gagged several times on the peas and carrots Katie served her.

Clair and Kellie were rolling a ball back and forth while the four adults were watching them. Clair, who looked very much like her mother, was wearing jeans and a sweatshirt and had her long blonde hair pulled back into a ponytail. Kellie, very obviously of Asian descent, was wearing a long sleeved shirt with little red ladybugs all over it under some Oshkosh overalls. Her hair was up in pigtails on either side of her head.

"So how old is your daughter?" Aaron asked, while looking at Clair.

"Which one?" Gayle asked.

"Both of them," Katie jumped in, sensing that the question had somehow annoyed Gayle.

Aaron looked at Katie and shrugged. She could tell he had no idea why Gayle had taken offense to his question.

Gayle looked at Aaron and pursed her lips, then at Katie. "Clair is seven and Kellie is four."

"Kellie is adopted then, I presume?" Katie said.

"Yes," Tony jumped in with a cautionary glance at Gayle before she could answer. "We adopted her when she was nine months old."

"Well, she's adorable."

"Both of them," Aaron said, hoping to smooth things over with Gayle.

"Thank you," Gayle said. "I apologize if I was a little touchy just then. We have a tendency to be defensive because of some of the totally off the wall, stupid questions we've gotten before."

"Oh, really," Katie said. "Like what?"

"Well," Gayle said, biting her lip. "There's 'are they real sisters'? Then my personal favorite: 'Who are her real parents'?"

Aaron shook his head and laughed in disbelief. "You've got to be kidding me!"

"No," Tony said, "I wish we were. Then there's the classic 'how much did she cost?'"

"No! How horrible!" Katie said. "What were these people thinking?"

"Most of them probably weren't," Tony said, "but I guess you hear those kinds of questions often enough and you become a little guarded."

"So how did you set up the adoption?" Katie said. "Did you go through an agency?"

"Yes, for international adoption that's about the only way you can go. Some of the richer people can afford private adoptions, but most can't. We went through Dickinson in Tulsa."

Just then the girls came running through the living room screaming as Clair chased Kellie. Their shrieks were loud and piercing, but Katie noticed how natural it felt – as if their home was meant to be filled with the sound of children laughing and playing.

"Clair! Kellie!" Tony snapped, to get their attention.

The girls stopped and stared at him with a look that said "Uh oh, busted!"

"Calm down just a little. We're in someone else's house."

"Okay, Daddy," they said in unison as they tore out again.

Gayle started to call after them but Aaron waved her off. "Don't worry about it," he said, "they're not bothering us."

"I know, but I would just hate for them to break something," Gayle said.

Katie shook her head. "There's nothing down where they can reach that can't be replaced."

"Well then, where were we?" Gayle said.

"We were talking about Dickinson," Katie said. "I've heard of them. I hadn't really paid much attention, I guess. Do they do domestic and international?"

"No," Gayle said, "Dickinson does international only."

"What's the adoption process like?" Katie asked.

"Long and arduous," Tony said.

"Yes," Gayle nodded her head in agreement. "Are you interested in adoption?"

Katie looked at Aaron and he nodded his head. "Yes, we think so. We've just recently started considering it. I don't know which would be better, domestic or international?"

Tony shrugged. "Although we've never gone through a domestic adoption, I think both have their up sides and down sides. But if you're really interested in international, Dickinson has introductory workshops you can go to."

Aaron puffed out his lower lip. "Okay," he said, "sounds like something worth considering."

"We can tell you," Gayle said, "it's very rewarding. Honestly, nothing short of a miracle."

"But," added Tony, "the scuttle-butt is that the Chinese are intentionally slowing down the adoption process and are getting more and more stringent with their requirements. So if you are going to adopt from China the sooner you get in, the better because it looks like they might be closing their doors soon."

The kids came back into the room. "Mommy, we're thirsty," Kellie said.

Aaron hopped up off the floor. "I'll take care of them. You all keep talking." He turned to Tony and Gayle. "More lemonade?"

"That's fine," Gayle said, then added "but not very much. And keep it in the kitchen, girls. I don't want you to spill any on Katie's and Aaron's carpet."

Aaron looked at Katie and winked. "We can handle it," he said.

Katie followed Aaron and the girls into the kitchen with her eyes. She was amazed at the gradual transformation that was coming about in Aaron.

"Back to China," she said. "I thought they had so many orphaned girls that they welcomed foreign adoption."

"They did for a while," Tony said. "They've created their own dragon, so to speak. Their population exploded under Mao, but it created too much of an economic strain, and they couldn't feed all of their people so they instituted the one child law."

"I heard about that," Katie said.

Gayle jumped back into the discussion. "But since they're still very much a patriarchal society, if they were going to be limited to one child, most families wanted a boy."

"So that's why so many girls were orphaned," Aaron said as he walked back into the living room.

Gayle shook her head in dismay. "Those were the lucky ones. So now, they're faced with an entirely different problem. With so many little girls adopted out of the country or worse, they're looking at a bad gender imbalance in their society.

"Katie nodded her head. "So that's why they're moving towards shutting down foreign adoptions. It seems so sad."

"Yes, it does," Gayle said.

The evening ended with more discussion of kids, work, golf, and many other things as the two families got to know each other.

But Katie's mind was flooded with seemingly hundreds of questions about the adoption. She had never known a family that had adopted children until now. She knew of one family from church, but they moved away shortly after Aaron and Katie joined Crossroads and they never had an opportunity to get to know them. What if they wanted to adopt from China, would they have time? What about domestic, or other countries?

But seeing the love between little Kellie and her family had convinced Katie that adopting a child could be as much, if not more, awesome than she'd dared to imagine.

*   *   *

It was an unseasonably warm Saturday in February as Aaron and Mark teed off on the third hole at the public golf course in Sapulpa. The temperature was in the upper fifties and there wasn't a cloud in the bright blue sky.

Mark had gone first and hit a nice tee shot straight down the middle. Aaron was feeling on top of his game today and striped a tee shot that flew past Mark's. On such a beautiful day, the course was full of other golfers like Mark and Aaron who were desperate to get reacquainted with their clubs after the long, dreary winter. With the course so crowded play was going to be slow, but Aaron didn't mind. He was thrilled to be on the course on such a beautiful day.

Mark was dressed in khaki pants and a navy blue, long sleeved mock turtle-neck. He whistled. "Well done. You sure hammered that one."

"Aw, I don't think I caught it all," Aaron said with a wry grin as he put the head cover back on his driver. Aaron was wearing khakis as well, but he had on a white knit pullover shirt with a maroon wind jacket over that.

"Mmm hmm," Mark said, slinging his bag over his shoulder and starting down the fairway to his ball.

Aaron kept pace beside him. "How's Sherry?"

"Doing well," Mark said. "She's been complaining about how fat she's getting, but I love it. You know, I've always heard people talk about this 'glow' that pregnant women have and I'm starting to see what they mean. The bigger she gets the more beautiful she becomes."

They reached Mark's ball and Aaron stood off to the side as Mark sat his bag down and selected a club.

"I know one thing for sure," Aaron said, "you're going to be a great dad, brother."

Mark grinned at Aaron. "You may have the power, but I've got the touch. Watch me knock this stiff."

As Mark began his backswing, Aaron's cell phone rang. Mark stopped, let the club head drop to the ground and looked at Aaron.

"I'm sorry," Aaron said as he scrambled to dig the phone out of his golf bag.

Aaron saw on the Caller ID that it was Katie. "Yes, dear," he said as he answered the phone.

"Aaron," Katie said, and he recognized a sense of urgency in her voice.

"What's up, babe?"

"You and Mark need to come quick. I'm taking Sherry to the emergency room."

"Oh, no. What's wrong?" He looked at Mark who had a concerned look on his face.

"I don't know, but she's sick to her stomach and spotting some."

"Okay, we'll meet you there. Which one?"

"Saint John's."

"Okay," Aaron said and broke the connection. He looked at Mark. "Katie's taking Sherry to the emergency room."

"M-my Sherry?" Mark asked.

Aaron nodded his head and both men picked up their bags and began running back towards the parking lot.

They reached Aaron's truck, threw their bags in the bed and hopped in. Aaron slammed it into gear and squealed his tires pulling out of the parking lot onto Highway-33, heading east.

"Did Katie say what's going on?" Mark said.

"I don't know," Aaron said. "She just said that Sherry was sick to her stomach and was spotting."

"That can't be good."

Aaron shrugged his shoulders, but he could see the fear in Mark's eyes. He was scared as well, but wasn't about to entertain the thought of Mark and Sherry losing their baby.

They ran the red light at the intersection of Highways 33 and 97 and turned left onto 97, heading north. Within a few miles they caught Interstate-44 going east, then after a few more miles they transferred onto Highway-75 going back north. Fifteen minutes later they pulled up to the emergency room entrance to the hospital. Mark jumped out of the truck and hurried in, then Aaron drove through the parking garage until he found an open parking space.

As Aaron walked in he saw Katie coming out of a large set of electronic doors just beyond the reception desk.

Katie reached him and they hugged.

"Mark went inside with Sherry," she said.

"We got here as fast as we could."

"I know. They've got her on a fetal monitor and they're concerned because the baby's heart rate is a little too slow. I feel so guilty," Katie said as her eyes began to well up.

Aaron looked around the waiting room and spotted a corner that appeared semi-secluded, so he led Katie over there and they sat down.

"Why? You didn't cause this."

"I don't know. I was so jealous of them..."

Aaron ran his hand through Katie's thick brown hair and pulled her towards him until her forehead rested on his shoulder.

"I'm sure things will be fine. Jealous or not, you didn't cause this. And besides, you're here now, aren't you?"

"I guess," Katie said as she wiped her nose. "I see now how wrong I've been. How my obsessing has caused me to have these terrible thoughts and jealousy. I don't want anything to happen to Sherry or their baby. I love them. How could I ever take joy in having a child of our own someday if I've got this guilt to live with?"

Aaron kissed her on the head. He knew guilt and pain firsthand. He whispered a prayer that only Katie could hear. "Lord, please be especially with Mark and Sherry right now. Comfort them. Strengthen and encourage them. Guide the doctors and make everything all right. Wash us of our sins, and free us of our guilt as we move forward, searching for Your will in our lives. Amen."

Katie looked up at Aaron. "Thank you," she said.

Aaron wrapped her in his arms and looked at the doors leading to the emergency treatment areas. He wouldn't doubt, not this time. *I know the plans I have for you, declares the Lord...*

Chapter 19

Wu Chien sat up in bed on her own for the first time in nearly three weeks. She had been struck down with pneumonia and hadn't been able to tend to any of her duties, nor see Lin Lin during that entire time.

She sat on the edge of the bed, waiting to verify that she wasn't going to pass out or get sick. The fever had finally broken several days ago but the illness had ravaged her to the point that she hadn't had the strength to get out of bed.

She worried about Lin Lin. Chien knew that the baby would be taken care of in the same manner all of the other children were attended to, but she also knew that no one else had taken the interest in her like she had. She thought she had heard her weak cries several times, but she wasn't sure. Maybe she had been hallucinating.

Chien took a whiff of the air in her room and wrinkled her nose. The orphanage never smelled exactly pleasant, but right now her clothes and even her bedroom had the stale, pungent odor of sickness. She looked around her room. An outside window would certainly be nice to help ventilate the room, but all she had were four dingy walls and one creaky old door.

Cautious, she rose to her feet and took a small, tentative step on wobbly legs. Anxious to see how Lin Lin was faring, she decided to clean herself, change her clothes, and go see about the baby. Frail or not, she needed to check on her. Chien had received very little medical treatment during her illness and at one point she was convinced she would die. But tottering on weakened legs, she knew in her heart the reason she was still alive. God had kept her alive so she could be with Lin Lin, and help her find a home.

She showered and dressed as quick as she could and made her way to the kitchen to find a bowl of congee. One of the other workers at the orphanage, Qian Juan stopped Chien as she entered the kitchen. Juan was twenty-one years old. She had a small mouth and nose and warm, dark brown eyes. Her black hair was pulled back into a ponytail that hung several inches below her shoulders. Wearing a pink wind suit with a white, long sleeved turtleneck shirt underneath it, she exuded the same youthful energy that Chien once had.

"You must be feeling better," Juan said, smiling at Chien.

"Yes, much better."

"Good, we were all worried for you. We were ordered to keep the door to your room closed and to stay away. Bao was the only one allowed to be near you, but she wasn't allowed to be with the children while your fever was up."

"How's Lin Lin?"

Juan shrugged her shoulders. "I've been watching out for her as much as I could, but it's been difficult with you and Bao both out. Na and I had to pull double duty."

"But she's okay, though?"

"Yes, I think so. She had another episode two days ago. We gave her the pills, but I didn't think they were going to work this time."

Chien's heart sank, and she trembled from weakness. She needed to sit down.

The kitchen was the one place in the orphanage that seemed cleaner than any other. On the wall furthest from the kitchen door was a large, black stove and oven, and a mismatched refrigerator-freezer, with cabinets in between and around them. On the wall to the left was a large stainless steel sink with more cabinets. Just to the left of the door was a small metal table and two chairs.

Chien reached for a chair and sat down. Juan had confirmed her fears. She knew now that it was Lin Lin she had heard crying from down the hall.

She looked at the large stock pot sitting on top of the stove. She knew she could find some porridge in it. With limited resources, congee was a staple in the orphanage. Most of its residents and workers had it every day, and during especially lean times they ate it for every meal. Consequently, there was always a large pot on the stove.

"Would you like a bowl?" Juan asked, looking in the direction of the stove.

"Yes, that would be good," Chien said.

Juan retrieved a bowl from a cabinet and dipped a small amount of the watery, rice porridge into a bowl. She brought the congee, a spoon, and a glass of water to Chien then excused herself. Chien was hungry and eager to see Lin Lin so she ate in a hurry. The congee was warm and satisfying.

Once she had finished off the bowl she inched her way down the main hall, past the hall where her room was located and to Lin Lin's room. As she stepped through the door she could see Lin Lin in her crib. It saddened Chien that she was the only baby in the room at the moment. She made her way down the aisle between the two rows of cribs to Lin Lin's bed. Chien grasped the side rail and leaned over. The baby was awake and looking around. She was still very small and underdeveloped, but Chien noticed that her eyes came to life when she saw her. The child's lips curled into a small but brilliant grin.

Chien retrieved her from the crib and sat down in the lone rocking chair with her. Lin Lin raised her tiny hand toward Chien, whereupon she ducked her head so that the baby could touch her cheek. The old woman slipped back into the familiar pattern of rocking and humming to the baby.

"Yesu is so good," she whispered. "He promises to supply all of our needs, and I know that includes you too, little one."

Just then she heard a male voice coming from the door. "When I couldn't find you in your room I knew I would find you here," Fu Si Chuan said.

Chien looked down in respect and nodded her head.

"I have good news for you," he said.

Chien's head bobbed back up and she looked directly at the orphanage director.

"We have obtained the funding and special permission to apply for the baby to be put into the system for adoption. She will, of course, be listed as a special needs child."

Chien nodded and smiled. She knew that the "special needs" tag would lessen her chances, but it was still something, a hope to cling to. "Yes," she said, "that is very good news."

"But," Chuan cautioned, "the application will only be good for six months. If the baby isn't adopted in that time then her paperwork will be pulled. And I won't try again."

Chien nodded her head. "I understand."

"Also," he continued, "your health is failing. I'm afraid that we will have to let you go soon."

Panic gripped her heart. She couldn't leave the baby. She must be allowed to finish Yesu's work. "But…" she started to object when Chuan interrupted.

"I will, however, allow you to stay until the six months has passed. You have been a faithful, loyal worker. You deserve as much."

Humbled by his praise, Chien bowed her head. *"Xie xie,"* she said.

The director nodded and left.

"It's not much," she said to Lin Lin, "but it's something. It may take a miracle, but I happen to know someone who works in that department."

*　　*　　*

"Sherry, hi, it's Katie." It was late morning on Monday and Katie had called Sherry from work to check on her. Katie worked as a computer programmer for the city of Tulsa. The pay wasn't all that great but the security and benefits helped make up for what the salary lacked.

"It's good to hear your voice," Sherry said. "Listen, I'm so sorry I scared everyone like that. I know you all were worried sick and I ruined the boy's golf outing."

"Don't worry about it. They're grown-up boys – I think. They'll get over it. I'm just glad you're okay and it wasn't anything serious. I was relieved when Mark came out to the waiting room and told us what was going on."

"Well, you shouldn't have stayed in that waiting room so long. We could have called you at home."

"If I had known it wasn't anything more serious," Katie said, "then we wouldn't have stayed. But until I knew for sure, we weren't about to leave."

"I've never had a urinary track infection before so I didn't know what to think of the spotting. I only know that it scared me to death."

Katie absent-mindedly twisted the phone chord. Pangs of guilt resurfaced as she thought of her past jealousy. How could she call herself Sherry's friend and still harbor the resentment she had felt? It made her feel like a hypocrite.

"Kate," Sherry's voice broke through her thoughts "are you there?"

"Oh yes, I'm sorry. I was just lost in thought."

"Is something wrong?"

Katie hesitated. She didn't want to lie, but she didn't know if she was ready to get into a serious conversation just yet – especially at work. "No, I'm okay," she finally said.

"Are you sure? You don't sound okay."

Katie sighed, then rolled her office chair to the far corner of her cube and the farthest point away from the other cubes around her, stretching the phone cord as taut as possible. "I guess I've just been dealing with some guilt issues."

"Guilt? What about?"

"You," Katie said.

"Me? You didn't do anything to me. You've been a very good friend. I've always been able to count on you, just like I did the other day."

Katie rubbed her forehead. She didn't want to admit her jealousy for fear that it would damage their friendship. Her cube was against an outside wall on the third floor of the courthouse building in downtown Tulsa. One window looked south, out onto Sixth Street. It was another mild day in February. The inviting sunshine made her wish she was anywhere but at work.

"I guess," she said. "But ever since we found out you're pregnant I've been dealing with this overwhelming jealousy."

"Oh," Sherry said. "You've sure hidden it well."

"Yeah, I've gotten pretty good at putting my mask on over the years. Maybe too good – I don't know. It's not that I don't want you to be happy, you know that don't you?"

"Of course."

Katie grabbed a small stack of folders from various projects that were on her desk and began filing them away in the lateral drawer under the window.

"I guess it seemed so easy for you. Everything always seems to come easy for you. Not that I want your life to be hard..."

"Well what *do* you want?"

"I don't know… This isn't coming out right."

"I guess not. Katie, I love you, but I'm not going to apologize for being pregnant, or for having things – for having a life. I realize I'm very lucky and blessed. I understand that."

"I'm not asking for an apology, Sher. And I'm not trying to make you feel bad either. It's impossible for someone who's had – or is having –

her own child to understand what I go through everyday. I see a commercial for baby food on the television and I feel like I've been kicked in the gut. When we go shopping, as I'm walking through the baby beds and strollers, I get this profound feeling of loss – of incompleteness."

"I guess I never gave it much thought because you've seemed to be dealing with it okay."

"Well, my visit with Mom and Dad helped a lot. Before that I was becoming quite bitter," Katie said.

"You've always been so sweet. I bet Aaron didn't know how to handle that."

"Actually, he was very supportive. He's the one who made me go see my folks."

"Well, good for him," Sherry said. "I can see how it's the little things that would get you. I mean, so much of life is about the little things – the little memories, or those unexpected moments of laughter or joy. I apologize for not being more aware."

"Really, there's no need..."

Katie's boss, Pete Marshall, stuck his head into her cube. "Hey, team meeting in five minutes to go over the accounts payable system rewrite status. Middle conference room."

"Hold on," Katie said into the phone. "I don't show this on my calendar, did I miss it?"

"No, upper management's getting testy. They don't seem to understand that it takes more than a couple of days to get an a/p system rewritten."

"Okay," Katie said, "be right there."

Katie watched Marshall walk away then spoke into the phone. "Sher, I've got to go."

"I heard."

Katie bit her lip. "So, are we okay?"

"We're better than okay," Sherry said. "Just remember though, that there is One who understands your heart. You need to give it to Him."

"I'm trying… Seems that leaving it with Him is the hard part, but I'm trying. The scare we had with you kicked me in the rear, though. Gotta go."

"Okay. Love you. Bye."

"Thanks, Sherry, you too."

Katie hung up the phone, grabbed her project notes and a pad and pen then stood up. She glanced out the window and saw for the first time a bluebird making a nest on the outer ledge, just to the right of the window, behind some ornamental fluting.

She smiled. "You, too?"

Katie Phelps, friend to those in waiting.

*   *   *

Aaron pulled into a parking spot at the Metro Diner on Eleventh Street, right next to the campus of the University of Tulsa. It was fifteen minutes till noon, and the lot was already three-quarters full with the lunch hour crowd.

Aaron always liked this place, with its neon signs, and memorabilia of days gone by. But those days were before his time, so he never experienced them firsthand, just like the many things he never experienced growing up without a father. Riding horseback on daddy around the living room. Playing catch in the back yard. Going to church with mom and dad as a family. Little things that many kids might take for granted, he'd missed them all. "Hmm, now there's some positive vibes to dwell on," he murmured as he turned the engine off.

Aaron got out of his truck and looked at the art deco design of the building, with the neon piping up the sides and across the top. He took a deep breath, and let it seep out, not sure if he was ready to do this. *Help me remember, Lord, that I'll never forgive more than I've been forgiven.*

He entered the restaurant and was greeted by Fats Domino's "Walkin' To New Orleans" on the old Wurlitzer juke box. It seemed to transport him back in time to the fifties. No doubt, that's what the owners were going for. But knowing that it had been there since the fifties gave the restaurant an air of authenticity and reminded him once again of his father.

"Can I help you?" the hostess asked from behind a small reception area made from the rear end of a fifty-seven Chevy.

"I was supposed to meet another gentleman," Aaron glancing anxiously around.

"I think he's already here." She led Aaron around a wall made out of clear, glass blocks. Aaron noted a Dutch apple pie sitting in the pie case on a counter next to the fountain machine and his stomach churned. He wasn't sure if it was from hunger or nervousness.

As they rounded the wall into the main dining area, Aaron spotted Ben Phelps sitting in a booth and nodded his head. "That's him," he said. "Thank you."

The hostess smiled. "Sure. Enjoy your lunch."

Aaron had struggled with the decision to call Ben again. But he had thought a long time about their meeting in the cemetery and subsequent discussions with Mark and Katie. He had noted how Ben seemed eager to make up for lost time – although he was skeptical that he could ever call him "Dad." Aaron could think of a million hateful reasons why he didn't want to talk with Ben again, and very few reasons for wanting to see him. But it all boiled down to one thing – he *wanted* to know his father.

Aaron slid into the booth across from Ben. "You cramped for time?" he asked his father, hoping they'd have the opportunity to get to know each other better.

"Naw. I told them at the shop I'd be a little late. I'll just work past quitting time to make it up."

"They okay with that?"

"Yeah, sure. Small shops are usually pretty easy with that kind of stuff. Wouldn't matter anyway. When I've got a chance to see my thirty-one-year-old son for the third time in my life, I'm going to take it. What about you?"

Aaron fumbled with his menu and dropped it on the floor. When he reached down to pick it up he knocked the rolled up silverware onto the floor as well. *Sheesh!* He retrieved the dropped items then took a deep breath in an effort to regain his composure. Sitting down to eat lunch with his father seemed too surreal to Aaron. For most other fathers and sons it was probably a common occurrence. But this was his first meal with Ben – with his father.

"Oh, uh, I work through lunch most days. So when I do take off it's no biggie if I'm late – within reason, of course." He hated small talk, but that was all he seemed capable of at the moment.

Ben looked around the dining area of the restaurant. "I bet it's been thirty-five years since I've been here."

"Changed much?"

Changed much! A million things to ask and say and that's all I can come up with?

"Yes. I guess it celebrates what was ordinary back then. Still a neat place, though."

The waitress spared Aaron more embarrassment when she came and took their drink orders then left to fill them. The two men took a couple of minutes to look over the menu. Aaron was thankful for the opportunity to regroup.

"So boys, are you ready to order?" the waitress said as she returned with Aaron's Dr Pepper and Ben's iced tea.

Aaron looked at Ben and nodded.

"Yes," Ben said. "I'll have the chef's salad, with low-fat ranch dressing."

Aaron grinned wryly at Ben. "I'll have a patty-melt, fries, and a piece of that apple pie."

The waitress repeated their orders. "All together, or separate checks?"

Aaron looked at Ben. He didn't necessarily mind paying for Ben's, but he didn't want Ben paying for his meal. He wasn't ready for that yet.

As if sensing Aaron's apprehension, Ben looked up at the waitress. "Separate, please."

"Okay," she said, then turned and walked off.

"Just wait," Ben said, patting his stomach. "Someday you'll be my age and won't be able to eat like that."

"I'll run extra to make up for it."

There was an awkward silence. Aaron, hated the awkward silence. It seemed to only underline the point that father and son had very little in common. They shared no life experiences.

"It took you a while to call again," Ben said. "I was beginning to wonder."

Aaron looked him in the eyes. There didn't seem to be any signs of judgment so he shrugged his shoulders as he rubbed a water spot off of his fork. "I guess it just takes me a little longer to assimilate things sometimes."

"Lot to uh, assimilate."

"Impressed with my college education?"

For a rare moment Ben looked directly at Aaron. Aaron could see a flicker of pride flash through Ben's eyes. "Not as much as I am with you and the life you've built for yourself," he said.

Aaron didn't know what to say. Could he trust this man, and believe that his words were genuine? "I can't really take much credit. God's given me so much more than I deserve. You should've seen me when I was eighteen, nineteen, twenty years old."

Ben looked out the plate glass window. "Yeah, I should have."

"I didn't mean it like that."

"I know. I guess the Lord saves us from the penalty of our mistakes, but not the memory and the regret."

"I've got some of that too," Aaron said. "Maybe that's part of the consequences."

"Suppose so."

Aaron spotted a black Jaguar pulling into a parking place in front of the restaurant. He recognized the woman who got out as Heather Carter, a local celebrity who had made a recent splash in the national country music scene. She paused dramatically as she exited the car, making sure everyone in the restaurant had time to notice her.

She was pretty in a glamorous way. Her long black hair was stylish and her makeup appeared expertly done. She was wearing wrap-around, dark tinted sunglasses and a black leather biker's coat unzipped over a white blouse with wide collars. Her designer jeans were creased over her heeled leather boots. As she strode to the front door, chin up, Aaron thought she looked how a celebrity should – and completely contrived.

Aaron noticed Ben watching her also. His gaze seemed to be less that of adoration, and more curiosity, maybe even pity.

"I'd take Katie over someone like her in a heartbeat," Aaron said.

"That would be the wise choice," Ben said.

"She told me the other night that we needed to have you over for dinner."

"I'd like that, but I don't want to if you don't."

"Who knows, maybe before too long..." Aaron said. "How would Mom have stacked up to her in your eyes?" Aaron asked as he nodded towards the black Jag.

"Now? Your mother. No contest. Back then, to be honest, I probably would have chosen the glamour girl. I would've thought she had it all together."

"Mom never talked much about you two. I think she was hurt when you left. Most men back then weren't interested in a single woman with a punk kid."

Ben took a sip of tea and set his glass down. He looked down at his salad without eating it. "The way you're circling around..." He looked up at Aaron. "This is hard, I know... I don't have any rights or special standing – I understand that, so I'm trying to let you set your own pace. There must still be a lot of gaps for you, huh?"

"Yeah, I suppose so. Maybe I'll just ask questions until it starts to make sense."

"My past never will. I told you a couple of weeks ago at the cemetery that I was screwed up back then."

The waitress showed up with their food and laid it down in front of them. She asked if they needed anything else and when the two answered no she moved to the next table.

The place was packed now with the lunchtime crowd. The low hum of conversation had escalated to a loud roar as people spoke over each other. All of a sudden Aaron felt like he didn't want to be there. He started looking around when he noticed that Miss Carter had been seated in a secluded part of the restaurant with another woman and two GQ looking men dressed in business suits.

"I don't think Mom ever had anyone take her to lunch or dinner while I was a kid. When I got older and could earn a little money, I'd save it up and take her out for Mother's Day each year."

"At least she had you. She must have been proud."

"I don't know," Aaron said. He cleared his throat, and the lump that had formed there. "The older I got, the more I disappointed her. She never gave up on me, though."

"Me either."

Aaron's eyebrows rose. "Really? How so?"

"We wrote a couple of letters back and forth before I got so strung out that I quit writing to her. She told me she still loved me. That you needed a father."

"Wow," Aaron said.

"Yeah. She was a Christian when we married and I wasn't. She made the classic mistake of believing she could change me. I know it's hard to believe, but I loved her. Once I got out to California, I went downhill so fast that before long I knew I didn't deserve her – as if I ever did. The first couple of years, before she became pregnant with you, we were pretty happy. I even went to church with her on Christmas and Easter. Thought that was my penance. When we found out you were coming along, I guess I just panicked."

Aaron nodded his head and looked down at his half-eaten sandwich. "I can relate to that. Katie wants kids."

"You're not okay with that?" Ben said.

"I think I am now. But I wasn't. Kinda went off the deep end – but maybe not as much as you."

Ben laughed without humor. "I'm not sure anyone has gone off as bad as me. Tell me about it."

Aaron recounted the whole story, including the bar fight and up to their adoption considerations, as the two men ate their lunch. Aaron noticed that Ben seemed entirely immersed in Aaron's story – as if every scrap of information was new insight into his son.

When Aaron finished telling his story he looked at his watch. It was a little after one now and the lunch crowd had dwindled to just a few.

"I better get back to the office," Aaron said.

"Me too, I suppose. So are you two going to adopt then?"

Aaron shrugged. "I think so. Seems pretty hard though."

Ben looked at Aaron. "Take it from me, if it was easy, everybody would do it. Don't be like me. Face it head on. If it's the Lord's will, then you should embrace it. Ultimately, you'll never go wrong doing His will – even when it seems too tough."

Aaron looked out the window. It seemed odd to him for Ben to try and give him advice like this. A small part of Aaron wanted to ask him who he thought he was. But the larger part of him welcomed it. Aaron realized now that there was more to his father than he'd ever imagined. Maybe he was the same man only in name. Their conversation had revealed that they did in fact have something in common, albeit most of it seemed to be centered on regret and sadness because of their pasts. Yet oddly enough, it seemed an appropriate place to start. Aaron was reminded of Psalms 139, which talked about God's all-seeing eyes and inescapable presence. He was convinced that God was at work in his heart. At long last he was willing to surrender to God's call.

Aaron laid enough money to cover the bill and tip on top of his check and stood up. Ben did the same and slid out of the booth.

They walked out the front door and faced each other. Ben had parked at one end and Aaron at the other.

Aaron extended his hand. "Thanks," he said.

Ben shook his hand. "No, thank you. Will I get to see you and maybe Katie again?"

"Soon. There's so much more I need to ask. I promised God and myself that I'd react with grace this time, unlike the first time I saw you. But this still isn't easy. I guess it's going to have to come in bits and pieces."

Ben smiled and turned to walk to his car. He called over his shoulder, "I'll be waiting then."

Aaron smiled at the irony, then turned in the opposite direction to his own car.

Me too.

Chapter 20

Nearly two weeks later, Katie bit her lip as stepped into the offices of the Dickinson International Adoption Agency at 8:45 a.m. on a Saturday with Aaron at her side. The offices were on the second floor of a two-story office building at 71st and Lewis in Tulsa. Although the décor was tasteful and understated, Katie couldn't help but feel a nervous energy that made her jittery. She didn't know what to expect. Could she really trust someone else to help her fulfill her dream?

A receptionist greeted them. She had long, straight brown hair and was dressed in a white pant suit. "Hi, I'm Danielle," she said with a warm smile. "Look around, and make yourselves at home. The workshop will start at nine, in the large conference room." She pointed at a pair of double doors stained in the same cherry wood color as the reception desk, just past her, on Katie's right.

Katie was grateful to be at the workshop. She had checked Dickinson's web site and found that they would be having this introductory workshop on international adoption. She called to see about a reservation, and she and Aaron had finagled the last two spots. The next workshop wouldn't have been for another three months.

Katie heard Aaron say "Hey, look over here," as he took off down the hall to their left, but she ignored him, stepping instead into the large conference room. She shook her head, bothered that he could be distracted so easy, but she was too anxious to object. Rows of chairs were lined up, enough for at least fifty people facing the north end of the room where a projection screen was set up. A table with coffee, juices, and pastries stood to one side of the room.

On the other side was a series of tables with pictures and informational brochures for Haiti, Guatemala, the Ukraine, China, India and Korea. As Katie passed by each table she picked up copies of brochures and printed information sheets. Already several couples, and a few other women who appeared to be by themselves, had scattered throughout the room, reading the materials.

Katie felt a touch on her elbow and turned around to find Aaron smiling at her.

"Where've you been?"

"Come take a look at this," he said.

"First let's find a good seat. It's starting to fill up already."

"Here," Aaron said as he took his jacket off, "give me your coat."

Katie took her coat off and handed it to Aaron. He took the stack of reading material from Katie and walked to two open seats on the near end of the third row. He draped their coats over the back of two seats and laid the materials on them, then walked back to Katie and took her by the hand.

"There," he said. "We've laid our claim, now come on before it starts."

Katie sighed. "Okay," she said, "but let's hurry up and get back."

Aaron grinned at her and began dragging her past the reception desk. Katie didn't find this amusing. She was focused on learning all she could about foreign adoption. She had been checking into domestic adoption and hadn't been too keen on some of the things she'd found out. She'd learned that the domestic adoption laws still favored the birth parents. She had found and read many anecdotes of cases where the birth parent came back to claim the child as much as a year later. Katie knew she wasn't prepared to go there, so foreign adoption was looking more and more appealing.

When they rounded the corner to the hall Aaron had gone down, Katie stopped in her tracks. Covering the walls on either side were pictures of children. Some were Asian, some Hispanic, some black, some white, and some Indian – but all very beautiful.

Many of the pictures included siblings, some of them of the same race, some different. Some of the pictures were of the entire family.

Caucasian parents stood beside Asian or black children, all smiling big for the camera.

"That could be us," Aaron whispered in Katie's ear.

Katie smiled. "Maybe," she said.

They made a pass up and down the hall looking at the pictures. Katie couldn't help but wonder if this was too much to ask for. They all seemed so happy. What were the stories behind the pictures? Were they all as pathetic as hers? Certainly not. Maybe some of them just wanted to adopt instead of have biological children. Perhaps others had biological children but adopted anyway. The stories were all probably as unique as the pictures.

Katie and Aaron made their way back into the conference room and found the seats they'd reserved on the front row. Katie took a seat while Aaron made his way to the refreshment table.

He brought Katie orange juice in a small Styrofoam cup, coffee for himself, and a donut.

"Hey," Katie said, "we've already had breakfast."

"I know, but it's Devils food, my favorite."

"Aptly named, I might add," Katie said as she wiped a chocolate smear off of Aaron's upper lip.

Aaron was about to object when a slightly older woman walked to the front of the room. She appeared to be in her mid to late fifties. She had strawberry blond hair, and was wearing a long, flowing pants and blouse set with flowers of various muted colors on a charcoal grey background.

"Good morning," she said. "I'm Renee Hawkins. I'm the director of the Chinese adoption program I'll get us started, but in a while you'll get to meet the directors of the other five programs we have here at Dickinson." She pointed to the information tables where there were now five other women seated behind them.

"Let me introduce myself," she said as she pressed a button on her computer and a picture appeared with her, and two other young adults. One of them was Asian and the other was black.

"These are my children. Nancy is on my left. She's twenty-two years old, just graduated from OU, and is currently on a mission's trip to her birthplace in Cambodia. The one on my right is Naomi. She's twenty, was born in Haiti, and is in her junior year at OSU. She's the rebel of our family, but we love her anyway."

There was a smattering of laughter throughout the crowd. Katie noticed that some of the crowd seemed relaxed, but many others seemed quite intense, like she felt.

"I like to start off with a picture of my family to let you know that if you decide to adopt through Dickinson, you'll be working with professionals, certainly, but also people who have been there, done that. Many of us have adopted children of our own. I was one of the first to adopt through Dickinson, back when Mr. and Mrs. Dickinson were the case workers, clerical staff and managers themselves."

The idea of working with someone who had been on both sides of the adoption experience appealed to Katie. Renee had a very easy, peaceful air about her that immediately attracted Katie to the director.

Renee went on to talk about the China program. She told of its history, and where it was at now. She conveyed some of the same information the Humphreys had spoken of. Katie learned that there was quite an extensive, daunting application process that was broken into two sections. Like the Humphreys, Renee also spoke of the lengthening waiting period and Katie almost coughed out loud when she heard that the final cost would add up to the twenty to twenty-four thousand dollar range.

The other directors each spoke about their respective programs. The processes were all similar in many ways, but different in others. The expense continued to shock Katie. Some of the programs were as much as twenty-five thousand dollars, while, in comparison, others were a "mere" eighteen thousand.

A moving video was shown, in which an adopted child – now full grown – spoke of her experiences, and the love she felt for her parents. The emotion seemed genuine, and Katie was inspired by it.

After the video, Renee took the floor again. "Now, we always save the best for last." She leaned her head out the conference room door and said, "You all come on in." She held open the door and various families with adopted children filed in. A Caucasian couple with a Chinese baby caught Katie's eye.

"These families are here to talk to you about their experiences," Renee said. "We're just going to have an open question and answer time."

An hour later, Katie and Aaron left the Dickinson's offices. Katie's head was churning with thoughts and emotions. "What did you think?" she asked Aaron.

Aaron whistled. "Seemed great to me, but I don't know how we could pay for adoption. *Twenty-five* thousand dollars?"

Katie nodded, yet couldn't help but feel disappointed. "I guess it's too much."

Aaron shook his head. "I didn't say too much. I mean, how do you put a price tag on a life? I just don't know how we'd swing it."

"Maybe we could pray about it," Katie said as they climbed into Aaron's truck and buckled her safety belt.

Aaron pulled out of the parking lot, going west on 71st Street. "Yes, we should definitely pray. I can't believe how many of the people in attendance already knew which program they wanted. I felt way behind the curve. Did you hear that summary of all of the paperwork, and the things we'd have to do during the application process?"

"Yes, I did," Katie said with a sigh.

"By the time we complete the adoption process I'll be forty."

"I'm trying not to think about it," Katie said. "I've got to believe if others can do it, we can too. Were you leaning towards any program in particular?"

"I don't know," Aaron said as he pulled the truck to a stop at the intersection of 71st Street and Highway 75. "I guess the Haiti program seemed appealing because it was the cheapest. But, it was strange. I felt somehow drawn to the Chinese program."

"I felt compelled toward that program also. All of the directors seemed so nice, but especially Renee."

The traffic light turned green and Aaron turned right onto 75 North. "So it's settled then?"

"What's settled?"

"China?"

"O-kay, I'll go with that. But how do you propose we pay for it?"

"I'm still working on that."

"Let me know when you get it figured out."

"Maybe I could become a male model. I hear they make big bucks. There's bound to be women who like the ruggedly handsome, yet intelligent, sensitive types."

"Let me know when you find one of those, will ya?" Katie said, smiling at Aaron.

"Ouch!"

Katie took Aaron's hand. "Just kidding. God knew what he was doing when he put us together. And I do love you very much."

"Well," Aaron said, "if I can't be ruggedly handsome, intelligent and sensitive, at least there's that."

"What more could you ask for?"

Aaron grinned at Katie. "Well, since you asked…"

* * *

"Hi, Mom."

"Hello Katherine. How's my baby?"

"I'm doing well," Katie said as she sprawled out in her pajamas on the living room couch. Aaron was in bed reading, so Katie took this time to call her parents.

"So you're feeling better about things then?"

"You know, I have my moments, but I'm trying to leave it at the Lord's feet."

"There's a challenge," Margaret said. "But that's always the best place to leave it."

"How's Dad?"

"He's your daddy – still ornerier than ever. He bought a new tractor."

Katie sat up on the couch. "You're kidding. What's he going to do with that old John Deere?"

"He's going to keep it for his brush hogging. You knew we bought a couple hundred acres from the Rankins a few months back. Well, he's decided that he wants to plant all of that with corn. He's thinking that with all the emphasis on alternative fuels and Ethanol, he might want to make a run at it with corn. Two hundred acres isn't much to start, but he figures he can get his feet wet and go from there. But, with all the extra work to do, he decided he needed a bigger tractor. I think he just used it as an excuse to buy one of those new fancy models. It's a lot bigger and it has an enclosed cab with air conditioning."

"I can just see Daddy now. He must be struttin' around like a bandy rooster."

"Oh yes, he definitely thinks he's in high cotton, but what about my Katherine? What's going on in your world?"

"Nothing much, really." Katie paused, wondering whether she should tell her mom about their visit to the adoption agency, but if she planned to adopt she would need her mother's support. "Aaron and I are talking about adopting."

"Oh, really? That surprises me."

Katie frowned at the phone. "I thought you'd be happy for us."

"Well, I don't know, Katherine. I guess it just took me by surprise. I'm not sure how I'm supposed to react."

Katie stood up and began pacing the floor. She could feel her face becoming flush with anger. "Supportive might be a good place to start, Mom."

"Now, Katherine," Margaret said, "don't get sassy with me. You're a grown woman. You can make your own decisions. Your father and I will always stand behind you. But you asked me what I thought about adoption and I was being honest. I don't know. I guess I had settled it in my heart that you and Aaron wouldn't have any kids and that hopefully Janie would some day marry and have some. Maybe that was a conclusion I shouldn't have been so quick to jump to. But your news just came out of left field. I didn't mean anything by it."

Katie took a deep breath. She couldn't see how adoption would be out of "left field," but since she hadn't mentioned it when she was visiting she'd give her mother the benefit of the doubt. "Okay, Mom. I'm sorry. I didn't call you to fight," Katie said as she looked outside to find it snowing.

It usually snowed a handful or fewer times each year in Oklahoma, and almost always one of those instances was in late February or early March – like now. The flakes looked big and wet, as though barely cold enough to form them.

"You're right, honey. You and Aaron will need support if you're going to undertake such a task. We'll help in any way we can, I promise."

Katie smiled to herself. She loved her mother and father, yet it always amazed her how they could love her at any time – be it the good, the bad, or the ugly. *Then again, maybe that's how God the Father loves his children. Maybe, there's a correlation there.* Maybe, just maybe, she'd get to experience that herself.

"Thanks, Mom," Katie said as she walked over to the fireplace mantle and picked up a framed picture of her parents. It was the studio kind, where the photographer used different backdrops to provide a setting. Mom was Mom – as beautiful as ever. But Daddy was dressed in a suit and tie, and looked like he'd rather be anywhere else but there. Katie mused to herself that a more natural backdrop for her father would be a picture of the sun setting on a wheat field.

"So, how does one go about adopting? Are you going to go through DHS or a private agency? I've heard it can be terribly expensive."

"We're actually considering international adoption. We've been looking into domestic adoption, but there are parts of it that leave something to be desired."

"International adoption? My goodness. You mean like England or Germany or someplace like that?"

"Well, Mom, for the most part they're third-world type countries like Guatemala or China. Countries where the governments are less likely to be able to, or be inclined to, provide for orphaned children."

"Of course," Margaret said. "That makes sense – how silly of me. Is foreign adoption more expensive than domestic?"

Katie sighed and began pacing back and forth across the living room again. The conversation was starting to make her nervous. *Where's a money tree when you need one?*

"Generally, yes. We'd probably be looking at anywhere from eighteen to twenty-five grand."

"Good Lord! Where are you and Aaron going to come up with that kind of money, Katherine?"

"You tell me, Mom."

"I don't see how you could swing it."

"Gee, don't you think you're being overly optimistic?"

"Very funny, Katherine Ann. I'm being *realistic*."

"I know, Mom. The cost *is* a slap in the face. Not to mention that it looks like an incredible paper chase as well. I just need to have faith that if this is truly what the Lord wants us to do that He'll provide the means."

"Picture this as another challenge and remember, life's full of challenges, but greater is He that is in you than he that is in the world."

"Thanks, Momma. Tell Daddy hi for me."

"I will. I love you."

"You too, Mom. Bye."

Katie hung up the phone and turned off the lamp. She walked to the window and watched the snow falling.

Spring was coming soon and bringing with it a new hope.

"I won't give up on You this time, Lord."

Chapter 21

Within three weeks Aaron and Katie had submitted their preliminary application for adoption to Dickinson and had received approval. They were now officially working on the long, tedious final adoption application. Although they had a taxing road ahead of them, Katie was excited to have completed the first step, even if it was a preliminary one. She felt hopeful that it was an indicator of things to come.

The preliminary application involved completing a two page questionnaire, writing a motivation for adoption statement, obtaining letters of health from their physicians and the first cash expenditure of $50 for the application fee. The only hitch in the process was Aaron. Much to Katie's displeasure, he couldn't seem to take the motivation statement seriously. After much coaxing he completed it – a full two days after Katie had. It made her wonder if he was really as committed to the adoption as she was. But she chose to remain quiet about her concerns and give him the benefit of the doubt. She knew he was still reeling from the sudden appearance of his father. He hadn't talked about it much, and she hadn't pushed it. He would talk when he was ready.

During that time Katie had also discovered an internet message forum for adoptive parents from the Dickinson agency. Many of the regulars on the message board had adopted before, and some were going through the process again. It appeared to be an invaluable resource for obtaining extra advice for the various steps along the way, as well as meeting people who had or were sharing the same experiences. On the Thursday that Katie and Aaron received approval, she posted the news on the message boards and received several congratulatory replies. Aaron had already started teasing her about becoming a "message board junkie." Katie fired back in a playful manner that it seemed to be the only intellectually stimulating conversation she could find.

One of the regulars on the message boards was a woman by the name of Julie Sanders. Katie had seemed to click with her instantly. She was a Christian, and although she was outspoken about her faith she wasn't obnoxious. Katie had sensed that Julie seemed to have an intense interest in the plight of the orphans in China as a whole, that went beyond her personal interest in adoption.

Late in the evening on the day after they received word on their preliminary application, Katie sat down at their computer to check her email and the boards. Even though it was early March, the temperatures at night were still dipping into the low forties, so Katie dressed warm in red sweatpants, thick tube socks, and one of Aaron's flannel shirts.

She took a sip of lemon zinger tea from her favorite mug as she logged in to the computer and waited for it to finish booting up. She could never understand how computers could do so much, yet be so slow to turn on and prepare for action. She navigated first to email, found a message from Julie and began reading it:

"Hi, Katie! I'm sure you know this already, but now that you've completed your preliminary application you need to start the application with DHS and then begin work on the formal application for adoption. The DHS app is a check to make sure you don't have any previous history of child abuse. Once you get it mailed out it takes the DHS time to process it, so that's when you can start working on the formal application. When we adopted Abby we completed it in about a month."

Katie tucked her right leg under her, took another sip of tea then scrolled down on the page to continue reading. She appreciated all the help she could get.

"I wanted to pass some information along to you. It's supposed to be confidential, for waiting families only – but I have a bad habit of leaking it to others I know who might be interested. There are three special needs babies that Dickinson has posted on their website. By special needs, they are children with some sort of physical deformity or handicap. Cleft lip and palate seems to be a common one, but there are many others, such as blindness, heart conditions, clubbed feet, or even missing fingers on a hand – just to name a few. You may not have discovered all of this yet, but usually the process to adopt one of these children is significantly faster than adopting a healthy child. It could be the difference between you choosing the child, as opposed to a healthy child being chosen for you, but it appears like the Chinese government is much more anxious to be rid of these children."

Katie leaned forward. This was even better.

"Katie, I hurt for these babies. Healthy orphans have a terribly hard time making it in society once they're grown, but handicapped children don't stand a chance. The terrible thing is that many of these 'defects' are very treatable through surgery, but they just don't have the resources over there. I urge you to pray about it and check out the pictures and bios in the attached document. Maybe God's plan for you is different than you ever imagined. Julie."

Katie smiled to herself. *Isn't that the understatement of the year?* She clicked the button to open an attachment, and the document opened up. The first picture was of a little boy named Liang Xioa Bei. A severe cleft lip jumped out at Katie. The bio said he also had a cleft palate. Clothed in a warm looking, royal blue jump suit, he was smiling, which made the cleft lip even more noticeable, but his face had a quality in it that indicated a heart full of life and spirit, and he was still beautiful. His bio also stated that he was found at a train station in Fujian.

Katie moved to the next child. This little girl appeared older. Katie looked at her bio. Her name was Yu Zhou, and she was five years old. The bio also indicated that she too was in an orphanage in Chongqing, and had been blind from birth. Katie looked back at her picture. The blindness explained the blank stare in her eyes. Katie began to choke with tears as she wondered what fate would await this little one, and the others if they weren't adopted. Would they be turned out on the streets, or kept in the orphanage? How could they survive on the streets with no family for support and with such disabilities?

Katie scrolled down in the document to the third and final child and was struck by the picture of an infant girl before her. She was obviously very tiny. Her little head had wisps of black hair that stood up on end. Katie covered her mouth with her left hand. The baby's almond shaped eyes pierced through Katie's heart. Even at such a tender young age, Katie could see that they were the eyes of a fighter – someone who was struggling to overcome adversity. Katie stared at the picture for what seemed like minutes while every detail of the baby's faced burned itself into her heart.

"What could be wrong with this child?" Katie murmured. She looked perfect.

Reading the bio, she learned that this child, named Yu Lin, was an infant found on the steps of an orphanage in Chongqing last December. Her estimated birth date was December 1st. Katie looked up from the monitor, tapping on the keyboard. Last December was when things went downhill for her and Aaron. So much had happened since then. *Surely it's just coincidence.*

There wasn't much detail provided in the bio, but Katie learned that the baby had a heart condition which doctors believed to be treatable with surgery, and that the condition had hindered her development. Katie looked down, running her fingers through her hair. What kind of heart condition, and how treatable was it?

Katie started to move back to the previous child, but hesitated, inexplicably drawn to little Yu Lin. The picture was taken from above the baby, and the camera angle, combined with the position of her arms, made it look like she was reaching out to someone. *Oh Lord, could this be it?*

Looking back at each child again, Katie yearned for any one of the three, but she couldn't help but return to the picture of the infant baby. What was the strong attraction to this one? Could it be the fact that her life began just as Aaron and Katie were coming to this crossroads in their own? Was there really an intersection there?

There was one statement that concerned her, though. It stated that the baby's application would expire in six months, and she would be pulled from consideration if no one expressed intent to adopt her by then. *Six months?* How in the world could they get their dossier ready within six months? Would they have to come up with all of the money by then? The questions were piling up into what seemed like a mountain too steep to climb.

Katie printed the entire document before turning off the computer. She was no longer interested in anything else that might be in her email or on the message boards. Carrying the five pages in her hands, she walked down the hall to the living room, where Aaron was sprawled on the couch, reading his Bible. Looking at her, he sat up and smiled.

"Hey, hot-stuff. What you got there?"

Katie hesitated before sitting down beside Aaron, fidgeting with the diamond solitaire wedding ring on her finger. "Here, look at this."

Aaron glanced at the first page, then back up at Katie with a confused look. "What's this?"

"Julie sent this to me," she said rather impatiently. "It's some information on three children in China who need a family."

Aaron crinkled his forehead. She always hated it when he did that because it usually meant he thought she was being silly.

"Who's Julie?" he asked.

Katie sighed before beginning her explanation. "Julie is someone I met on the Dickinson message boards and she seems to be a good Christian person. She's adopting her second child and she sent this to me so we'd know about these special needs children. I think I want us to adopt one..." She stopped suddenly, realizing that she had been ranting. Her last sentence seemed to hover over the silence like a blimp. Aaron still looked concerned, but there was a hint of amusement at the corners of his mouth.

"Uh...wow. You ever consider a career as an auctioneer? I don't think you could have possibly said that any faster."

"Would you stop, and be serious for a minute?" Katie said. "Just read that over real quick."

Aaron held his amused gaze on Katie for a moment then looked down at the printout again. He read for what seemed like an hour to Katie before looking up.

Katie could tell he was weighing his words. "A son would be cool. But given my past – or lack thereof – with my father, maybe a daughter would be better. But..."

"What about the baby girl?" Katie interrupted.

Aaron rubbed the back of Katie's shoulders with his right hand while holding the papers in his left. His strong hand felt good as it rubbed away some of the tension that had accumulated in her neck and shoulders.

"She looks beautiful, but I don't know. This is all too sudden. There are too many questions. We're still so far away from sending our dossier to China that I don't know how we could even think this far ahead."

"I know, I know. None of this makes sense to me, either. But did you notice her birth date?"

"Yeah, December first. What about it?"

Katie put her hand on Aaron's knee. "Don't you see that she came into this world right as our situation started coming to a head. Think about what we've been through since December."

Aaron looked back down at the picture and back up at Katie. *At least he's being thoughtful, or pretending...*

"Hey, babe, he finally said. I'm not sure you should be doing this to yourself. You're one of the smartest people I know, and you know darned good and well that there are children born every day. I'm sure it's just coincidental. And besides, we're not talking about a puppy; we're talking about another human life, and one with physical issues to boot. Shouldn't we be careful and not make decisions like this on a whim?"

Katie pulled Aaron's hand from around her, and held it in her own hands. "Sure, it could be coincidence, but what if we're wrong? What if this is God's plan? What if he's been piecing this together all along? You remember what Joseph told his brothers in Egypt? What you intended to harm me, God intended for the salvation of many. And this is no whim. I'm sure there've been many babies conceived in the backseats of cars on more of a whim than this. Think about it, honey. We'd be making the choice, as opposed to the Chinese choosing a child for us."

Aaron pursed his lips while nodding his head. "You've got a point there." He wrapped his arms around her and pulled her close. "I don't mean to be negative," he breathed into her ear. "I guess I'm still overly cautious. My head tells me that these kids need a family just like any kid without a disability – maybe even more so. But my heart doesn't want us to step out there onto the firing line. What if this report is wrong and the baby's heart condition isn't treatable? We'd end up dealing with the worst heartache we've faced yet. But…I guess we could face that with a biological child just as well."

Katie looked in Aaron's eyes. Sometimes she could see hints of the old fears and insecurities looming, but she was also beginning to see the foundations of a faith in God that was stronger than either of them had ever known until now. She saw in him a man who could be an incredible father in spite of his doubts and fears. She believed in him. He just needed to believe in himself. "Yes, you're right," she whispered.

"We just need to send our dossier to China, right?" Aaron asked.

"Yes, folks in the biz call it DTC."

"Can we pull it off in six months?"

"I think we can. I hope so," Katie said.

Aaron grinned at her. "Just a minor detail."

Katie nodded her head.

"And twenty thousand dollars."

Katie nodded again.

"And the Lord on our side."

Katie smiled. "I like our odds."

Chapter 22

Wu Chien gagged as she scrubbed vomit out of Lin Lin's mattress. It seemed she and the other workers were dealing with their worst nightmare – a flu epidemic that was running rampant through the orphanage. Many children as well as some of the other workers had fallen ill with it. Chien had been nursing Lin Lin as well as other sick babies for forty-eight hours with only a few hours rest. So besides being exhausted, she was terribly worried about the baby.

The infant had come down with the flu two days ago, and desperate, Chien had been struggling to keep her hydrated. At one point the child had a reoccurrence of one of her episodes. Her lips turned the same dusky blue that they always did when the attacks occurred, but this time, to Chien's horror, the skin around her mouth and nose turned a light shade of blue as well. She was able to give the baby some of the medicine the doctors had provided and by some miracle the baby was able to hold it down. Within thirty minutes her skin had turned normal again.

The old woman grunted as she flipped the mattress over inside the steel crib. She felt her head begin to swim so she raised upright, bracing herself on the edges of the crib. Leaning her head back she took several deep breaths and felt the dizziness subside. She couldn't have one of her own episodes now. Not now. There was too much work to be done.

She looked at her trembling hands, calloused and worn from age and years of work, then at her tattered clothes, spotted and stained from the last two days. Her years of service to Yesu had not been glamorous by any means. Serving Him cost her husband his job, and eventually his life. Turned in by a Communist spy for religious teachings that were against party policy, he wasted away in prison, malnourished and often physically abused. She was never allowed to visit him, but she heard of his death through a fellow believer who worked in the prison. Her husband's death had left her without any family and working seven days a week, for a meager existence at best. There certainly had not been much monetary reward. But she knew she was making a difference. She had privately led several of the children in the orphanage to Yesu. She had even been able to use her connections in the underground church to obtain Bibles for some of them.

But she knew what she had here wasn't all. She believed God's word where it said "store up treasures in heaven." That's what she was doing. Her earthly treasure was the children. Her heavenly reward was to be in the presence of Yesu, and to be reunited with her husband.

She finished making the baby's bed, then wrapped Lin Lin up and put her back into it. The child had barely done more than sleep and be sick. The present epidemic had convinced her that the baby's chances of survival here weren't very good. But the news so far had not been promising. Lin Lin's paperwork had been on file for several weeks, but there had been no word yet of anyone interested in adopting her. She had not checked with the director in several days; they both had been too busy. But she knew that he would tell her if he had heard anything.

She sat down in the rocking chair next to the girl's crib. Her head swam from pure exhaustion, so she closed her eyes. "I love You, Yesu," she mumbled in a fog of weariness. *How long, Father must Your children suffer? I love my homeland, but I can't bear to see what's happening to it. There has always been a remnant of Your followers here. There always will be. Will you not bless Your servants here as well?*

Please Yesu, provide for Lin Lin like only you can. Whatever it takes – even if it means what little life I have left – I'd gladly give anything to see to it that she finds a home. Yesu said that in Your house there are many mansions. Is there not a house here on earth for these precious children of Yours?

Her head swam some more and darkness began to descend upon her. She tried in vain to open her eyes and fight off sleep.

I live in darkness now, but thank You, Yesu, that someday the light of Your glory will prevail.

*   *   *

Ben Phelps pulled into Aaron's and Katie's driveway at precisely seven o'clock on a drizzly Friday evening in late March. He and Aaron had met for lunch once more since there first meeting at the Metro. On Monday Aaron called to invite him over for dinner. Their last lunch meeting had been much like there first – very little talk of substance. As badly as Ben wanted to pursue something deeper, he had restrained himself from taking the initiative. He felt Aaron needed to be the one to make the moves.

Ben checked his hair in the rearview mirror. The salt and pepper mixture served as a constant reminder to him of how quickly life can get away from you if you're not careful. He knew that he could never have the classic father-son relationship with Aaron – he'd blown that long ago. But maybe, just maybe, they could build a lasting relationship of some sort. He wouldn't let *this* opportunity pass by without a fight anyway.

He got out of his old Ford and walked up the drive to their door. It was warm enough that the drizzle was not entirely unpleasant so he didn't rush too much. He rang the doorbell and waited. Turning, he looked out over Aaron's front yard. The grass was still dormant, but he could tell that the lawn was well cared for. The flower bed that ran along the perimeter of the house had large chunks of red pine bark mulch in them. It looked and felt like a home where God's love had a stronghold. *I wonder if we could have… No need to go there.*

There was still no answer at the door, so Ben turned and rang the bell again. Through the windows he could see lights on throughout the house so he knew they must be home.

Finally the door opened and Katie appeared. She looked upset and disheveled. Strands of her long brown hair were hanging out of her ponytail on either side of her face. Her eyes looked red and puffy, and the cuffs of her blue jeans were soaked around her bare feet.

"Oh my gosh," she said. "We were supposed to have dinner tonight!"

Ben frowned. "Is something wrong? If now's not a good time I can come back some other day."

"No, hold on," Katie said as she stood aside. "Please come in. I'm very sorry. Our hot water heater..." She turned and yelled down the hallway. "Aaron!"

Ben stepped inside and Katie shut the door behind him.

Smiling, Katie raked her fingers through her hair and wiped her hands on the back of her pants. "I'm sure I must look horrible."

"No, not at all. Listen, really, I could come back..."

Just then Aaron rounded the corner into the entry hall. He was wearing an old t-shirt and jeans. He was barefoot as well, and his jeans were soaked through on the bottom. He came to a stop, looking somewhat dismayed.

"Your, uh, Ben is here," Katie said.

Aaron glanced at her then shook hands with Ben. "We completely forgot about dinner tonight. We got home from work to find that our hot water heater had ruptured sometime during the day. Parts of the garage, utility room and into the dining room were flooded."

"Oh no," Ben said. "Is there anything I can do to help?"

Aaron shook his head. "Not unless you're a plumber. We called one and he estimated about six hundred dollars to replace the hot water tank. We're trying to save money. This is the last thing we need. So, we borrowed a shop-vac from some friends and we've got most of the water sucked up. I guess I'm going to give it a go myself."

"Actually, I picked up a thing or two about the trade, um, some time back. I'd really like to help."

"Thanks, but I'm going to have to try this on my own. I couldn't pay you for your time."

Ben felt a little stab of guilt. Had he been a father to his son, Aaron wouldn't feel like he should have to pay him to help. "Listen, have you guys eaten?"

"No, not yet," Katie said.

"Why don't you buy us some pizza and we'll call it even. We can have that thing replaced tonight and all it'll cost you is parts and dinner."

Aaron opened his mouth to speak but Katie spoke first. "You've got a deal," she said with a smile.

"Well, alright," Ben said, looking at Aaron.

Aaron glanced back and forth between Katie and Ben.

Ben could see that he wasn't very thrilled about accepting his help, but Katie had put him in a place where he couldn't say no. *I owe you one, sweetie.*

"I guess I'm outnumbered," Aaron said. "But I warn you, I'm not that familiar with the business end of a monkey wrench. Now if you need a strong back and a few brains, I'm your man."

"No sweat," Ben said. "Isn't Home Depot open this time of night?"

"Yeah, I was just about to head that way. Let's take my truck."

* * *

Three hundred and fifty dollars, two pizzas, two trips to Home Depot, six hours, and one hot water heater later, Aaron and Ben sat at the dining room table sipping tea. It was a quarter past one on Saturday morning.

"No, no," Ben said, "Leroy Selmon was the greatest defensive player ever at OU."

Aaron peered over his tea glass at Ben. "I don't know, Tommy Harris was pretty awesome."

Ben looked at Aaron and saw in him what he might've been thirty years ago if he'd stayed. Maybe he would've come to know the Lord sooner, before he messed his – their – lives up. He longed to quit tap dancing around and start for real on building a relationship, but he knew he shouldn't force it. "Both were great," he said. "So I guess we'll have to agree to disagree on this one."

Aaron nodded his head. "Agreed."

There was a long silence. Ben cringed inside. He didn't know if either of them was capable of breaking through. Maybe this was as close to good as it would ever be. Could he live with that? He knew that he didn't deserve *anything*. But he also knew that Jesus had seen to it that he wouldn't get what he deserved. Aaron's voice interrupted his thoughts.

"Did, uh, you ever think of us? I mean after…after you went to prison and met the Lord. Why didn't you contact us then?"

Ben swallowed hard. *At last.* "Yes, I did, Aaron. Prison is such a different world, I can't explain what it's like. But one thing you have plenty of is time. I thought often about your mother and you – even though I didn't know you. I thought about a lot of things. There were many people I hurt along the way." Ben shook his head in disgust.

"Other women?"

"Before prison? Yeah, some, but none that I cared about. Just someone to keep me from being alone."

Aaron's face looked tight. Ben could see that he was clenching his jaws some as he looked down at the table. "Why didn't you make contact sooner?" Aaron asked.

"I wanted to…I don't know. I don't really have a good explanation. I thought maybe your mother had managed to find someone else and build a better life for herself. Maybe if I tried to make contact, it would just screw that up. You know, it's amazing how much the human psyche can learn to tolerate."

"What do you mean?"

"You two were always in the back of my mind, but I learned to block it out. I justified it by saying that you were better off without me – which, quite frankly, before I met Jesus you probably were. I told myself too much time had passed. I built a semi-meaningful existence where I was at. I found a pretty good job. Even worked my way up a little bit. Found a tiny, cheap apartment. Lived like a pauper and actually managed to build up a small savings. I poured myself into serving Christ. I joined a church and worked in it. You know, helping the men's ministry do things for the elderly in the church. Worked vacation bible school carnivals, that sort of thing. I couldn't work in prison ministries because of my record, but I served in homeless shelters. I don't know if it was to earn my salvation – even though I know I can't, or if it was to repay society, or if it was to hide from memories. Maybe it's all of the above."

Aaron abruptly got up from the table walked to the dining room window, where his back was to Ben. Ben turned in his chair where he could look straight at him. Aaron's head was hanging.

"Growing up without a father," Aaron said, "was somewhat of a paradox."

"How so?"

"For one thing, I didn't know different. All I'd ever known was me and Mom. But on the other hand, I knew there was a piece missing. I understand now, that God's plan is one man, one woman, for life. That's the natural order. But back then I didn't comprehend all of that. I just knew mostly from TV and other kids that things weren't exactly 'normal'."

Ben turned his empty tea glass in circles. "I guess in today's world having one parent would almost seem more normal than having both parents."

Aaron was looking up now, out the window and into the darkness of night. "Doesn't make it right."

Ben shook his head in response. "No."

"Seemed the only kids I could relate to were the other misfits. One kid, Bobby Bates, the school bully started calling me a 'bastard'. I found out what that meant and mentioned to him that he was too stupid to know the difference between illegitimate and fatherless. Maybe not in those exact terms, but something like that."

"I'm sure Bobby didn't respond very well to that."

"Bloodied my nose. But I fought back, and learned that fighting was something I could do. And if I wasn't a bully, the other kids thought I was cool because I was tough but I wasn't mean."

"Found a niche."

Sad and regretful, Aaron shook his head and grunted. "So to speak."

They were quiet for a moment. Ben could sense something happening – or maybe he was just being hopeful. It seemed to Ben as if Aaron was deciding if he could make a run at a relationship with him. Ben got up and took his glass to the kitchen and placed it in the sink. He went back into the dining room and stood beside Aaron, looking out the window.

"Thanks for your help," Aaron said.

"Your welcome."

"Saved us a lot of money."

"You mentioned earlier you're trying to save up."

"Yeah, we decided to adopt a child from China. We're both pretty stoked about it, but the cost is astronomical, about twenty grand. We've got to save every penny because I don't really want to go in debt for this."

Ben nodded his head and bit his lip. *I could help. Just ask, kid.* He decided he couldn't bring it up. He couldn't compromise Aaron's pride. "One thing you might think about."

"What's that?"

"People finance cars everyday. They'll finance twenty or thirty thousand for a car or a boat without even blinking. How much more worthwhile is a life?"

Aaron was silent. The only thing breaking the heavy blanket of silence was the hum of the refrigerator in the kitchen. He nodded his head as if deciding something. "That's a thought. Anyway, thanks again," he said after some time. "Not so sure I could've done by myself."

"You would've – maybe not so easy."

"How do you know?"

"You're a survivor. I see it in you. Certainly knowing Jesus and trusting in Him has made the way. But when God knitted you together, he weaved in that instinct to overcome – to rise above."

"I think you give me more credit than I deserve."

"Maybe you don't see it, but I do. And I bet Katie does too."

"Katie has to like me. She lives with me."

Ben laughed softly. "You've got a point there."

When Aaron looked at Ben, Ben could see his shield of distrust dropping. The wall was crumbling. Maybe just one brick at a time, but falling nonetheless.

"What made you decide to come back?" Aaron said.

"Several months ago I ran into someone I used to know before I went to prison. He had managed to get clean and sober. He even had a wife and kid. I tried witnessing to him by telling him how Jesus had changed my life. He wouldn't hear what I was trying to say, but he was still leading a better life. I asked him what convinced him to change. He told me how a girl I, uh, was with before I went to prison had died. Without me there to keep her supplied, she had started turning tricks to support her habit. One night some wacko beat her to death in an alley."

Aaron shook his head. "Wow, lot's of tragedy in your wake."

Ben flinched at the comment, and turned from the window. He walked to the living room and stared into the fireplace. *How long, Lord, must I pay for my past?* He was more hurt than angry. Mostly because he knew the comment was accurate. "I suppose so."

"No offense. I have a tendency at times to be a little ah, tactless."

Ben shook his head once. "Calling a spade a spade."

Aaron walked into the living room and sat down on the sofa. Ben sat down in a side chair across the room from the sofa. The clock chimed the half hour.

"Go on," Aaron said after some time.

"So it occurred to me," Ben continued, "that I never got a chance to make amends to her. Who knows how many people I killed by dealing to them, and I'll never get a chance to tell them I'm sorry. To show them a better way – Him. That's yet another regret I live with. I decided that I couldn't let my regret about your mother and you go on any longer without trying to do something about it – without at least saying I'm sorry, so I came back."

Ben felt weary all of the sudden. The intensity of the conversation was draining his energy. But this was their best meeting yet. He wasn't about to check out now.

"I hated you for a long time," Aaron said after a lengthy silence. "When my life changed, I think I thought I was supposed to just let it all go. But I never dealt with it. I only buried it – hid it away. That day when you first showed up, it reared back up on me." Aaron wasn't looking at Ben now. He was looking off into some faraway space that Ben knew he couldn't get to. "I wasn't a good son. I never told Mom I was sorry. She never got the chance to put closure to her own disappointment and frustrations. By coming back, you've forced me to deal with a lot of this stuff. I guess the shrinks would call it 'repressed anger'."

Ben was silent. He feared speaking for choking up.

"I guess," Aaron said, "I'm trying to say you did the right thing." Aaron looked straight into Ben's eyes. There was softness in Aaron's eyes that Ben hadn't seen before. "Thank you, for coming back."

Ben smiled, but didn't speak. He couldn't. *Prodigal son, meet prodigal father.*

Chapter 23

It was a mild Wednesday afternoon in April as Aaron waited in the reception area of the Dickinson International Adoption Agency to meet Renee Hawkins, their case worker for his one-on-one interview for their home study.

The previous five weeks had been a blur as Aaron and Katie dove headlong into the formal application phase of the adoption journey. They each took a complete physical examination and wrote autobiographies. While Katie breezed through hers, Aaron struggled to complete his, fearing that his family background and past would catch up to him.

The formal application also included a financial statement, copies of tax records and bank statements, birth certificates, marriage licenses and a completed special needs checklist as well as various other forms and schedules. They both found the idea of completing the special needs checklist awkward. To specify which, if any handicaps, deformities or special needs they would accept seemed too finicky. After all, if the Lord had blessed them with a biological child they wouldn't get to choose. Nonetheless, they consulted with their physician and completed the form.

The costs had already begun to mount, and were draining what small savings they had available. They paid $300 when they submitted the application, then $1,500 and $2,500 for home study and program management fees.

Aaron loosened his tie as his stomach churned. Katie had her interview with Renee the previous day and came home raving about how nice she had been and how well the interview had gone. But Aaron wasn't so sure his would go as well. There were many issues from his past that he knew would be touched upon. Many of them he had detailed in his four page autobiography, but he knew that he would have to rehash them again here today. The thought had occurred to him that he could probably lie about much of his past and possibly get away with it. However, there were two flaws in that plan – the first being his past arrest record and the second was that of all the things he was or had been, a liar wasn't one of them. He had decided that he would be truthful in all aspects, but only supply the information that was requested of him.

"Hello, Aaron," Renee Hawkins said as she rounded the reception desk, walking toward him.

Aaron stood up and shook hands with her. "Good to see you again."

"Likewise, come right this way and we'll get started." Renee was wearing a long, red dress made of a lightweight synthetic and cotton blend with a black floral pattern on it. The sleeves were long and flowing as well as the bottom of the dress. She was wearing red and black bead necklaces and bracelets. Her strawberry blonde hair was cut stylishly short. Her smile was bright and her eyes kind, helping to ease the tension he felt.

Aaron followed her down the same hall he had shown Katie on their first visit to the Dickinson offices. She led him into a small conference room where a pre-printed form and two pencils waited on a round table with a white Formica top.

"First I need you to take this personality test," Renee said as she pointed at the table.

"What if I don't have one?"

Renee's laugh was easy. "If that's true, we'll soon find out. My office is next door. Once you finish the test come let me know and we'll talk for a while.

Aaron said "Okay," as he sat down at the table.

Renee left, closing the door behind her. Aaron completed the fifty question test in about fifteen minutes. Carrying the test with him, he knocked on Renee's door.

"Done already?" Renee said as she stood up.

"Yup. I'm quite certain this test will reveal to you that I'm charming, intelligent, witty, and I love puppies."

"Hmm, think so?" Renee said as she squinted at Aaron. She took the form and placed it face down on her desk. "Katie warned me about you."

"In that case I plead innocent," Aaron said as he flashed his sweetest choir-boy smile.

She led them back into the small conference room. Aaron took the seat he had previously been in while Renee sat across the table from him. He felt like his sweat glands were working double time as he wiped the palms of his hands on his pants legs.

"Now I wanted to explain that the purpose of a home study is not to weed people out, but to discover why you would be a good candidate to adopt a child. Of course we're going to make note of any problem areas we find. And, in rare instances we've found reason to reject someone's home study. But first and foremost, we want to have the utmost confidence in the applicants we send to the People's Republic of China, so we focus on the positives. Understand?"

"Sure."

"As you know, I spoke with Katie yesterday. She is such a delightful person."

Aaron crossed his legs and looked at Renee, trying to make good eye contact as they talked. "Yes. I'm very fortunate that I get to be her husband."

"Tell me how you met."

Aaron told her how they met in a college class, and then he started following her to campus Bible fellowship meetings. He also told her how his life had been changed when he met the Lord after one of the Bible study meetings.

Renee finished making notes then looked up at Aaron. "It's amazing how the Lord can work in your life, and the different ways he reveals himself, isn't it?"

"Yes ma'am, it is. I must admit, becoming a Christian was the *last* thing on my mind. I just wanted Katie to go out with me."

"What was it that attracted her to you?"

"This is going to sound awfully shallow, but at first it was simply because I flat thought she was beautiful. Not in the 'Hollywood glamour' way, but outside-in, and inside-out. I think even then, I knew there was something different that attracted me to her. In retrospect I know now that it was the difference God had made in her life that made me really take notice."

Renee made more notes, then looked back at Aaron. "What do you consider some of the strengths of your marriage?"

Aaron sucked on his bottom lip for a moment before responding. He had never really stopped to consider what their strengths were. "I think our mutual faith, and commitment to Jesus Christ is the greatest strength by far. I believe we communicate well. Katie takes very seriously the verse in the Bible that says 'Don't let the sun set on your wrath,' so we've been known to sit up very late until a disagreement is resolved. But more than that – we just talk – about anything and everything. We each have a good sense of humor. And there are enough mutual interests between us that we can almost always find something we both want to do."

"I read in your autobiography that your father left home when you were born. Can you tell me more about your childhood?"

Aaron looked out the window. The traffic on 31st was beginning to pick up for the post-work commute home. As much as he'd dwelt on his past lately he would've thought he could articulate everything with ease. He scratched behind his ear. He'd never liked talking about himself, and lately he'd been doing just that more often than he cared to. He loosened his tie a little more, swallowed hard then told Renee about his childhood, growing up without a father, and many other things he had been talking about with Pastor James, Katie and Ben.

Renee's face had grown serious, and her eyes had a look of concern in them. "You mentioned that you were rowdy in your late teens and early twenties. What exactly do you mean by that?"

Oh boy...

Aaron hesitated. He feared that if he blew their chances it would break Katie's heart – and his. "Let me preface this by saying that everything changed the day I met Jesus. I still had to deal with some of the consequences of my actions, but the desires of my heart changed."

"It's okay, I understand what you're saying," Renee said, taking notes.

"But more to the question, I drank a lot, and fought a lot, and caroused and chased girls." Aaron's voice got progressively softer and less confident as he went through the list.

"I see. The drinking and violence are somewhat of a concern. Have you ever been arrested?"

Aaron put his hands to his temples, closed his eyes, and moaned. The thought of having to rehash his past and possibly pay the price for his mistakes again, made him cringe. *I think maybe I understand a little of what Ben's going through.*

"Yes, twice. Once when I was nineteen and once a year later, when I was twenty."

"Do you recall what for?"

"Yes. In both cases it was for drunk and disorderly conduct, but I really can't emphasize enough that I'm not like that anymore. That was over ten years ago. When I committed my life to Jesus, I changed – almost instantaneously."

"So, you can tell me then that nothing like this has happened since?"

Aaron paused for a minute, trying to make sure he was careful in his answer. "I haven't been arrested since that second time."

Renee's eyes were probing now. They were intent, but not judgmental. Irregardless, Aaron felt as if there was a noose around his neck and it was tightening by the second.

"But have you been involved in any drunk and disorderly conduct recently?" Renee asked.

Aaron hung his head. He wanted to tell her no, but he couldn't – wouldn't – lie. "Yes," he said, in a tone of guilty resolution. "Not drunk, but disorderly."

"I see. I'm really not trying to be mean, but I'm confused. If you've truly changed then how could something similar have happened recently?"

Aaron shrugged his shoulders. "Good question. Katie and I had a bad argument one night." Aaron cringed when he said that. It seemed like he was digging his grave deeper with each word. "It's not that we fight all the time, we rarely fight. But married people *do* fight. I mean…it happens."

Renee smiled at Aaron, reassuring. "I've been married for thirty-five years. Of course they do, I understand that. Go ahead."

"Anyway, we had a bad fight over children. At the time, I was dealing with a lot of uncertainty regarding being a father. I mean, I've always liked kids, but given my childhood, I wasn't sure I had any clue what it meant to be a father. So I guess I was pretty ambivalent about things – at least as far as I was letting on to Katie." Drumming his fingertips on the table, Aaron paused to let his words form. Renee seemed intrigued by his story, but it sounded pathetic to Aaron.

"I guess…I think I didn't trust God to do what He says He'll do or myself to follow through on His word. So Katie jumps my case big time. It was my fault because I couldn't seem to put together a coherent sentence to explain what I was thinking and feeling. We exchanged words, and I left to drive around. I made a stupid decision and decided to go into a bar. I figured I'd *really* give Katie a reason to be steamed at me. I was in there maybe fifteen, minutes. Barely even sipped on the beer I bought, and some gal comes over and tries to talk with me. I show her my wedding ring and tell her I'm not interested so she gets ticked at me – I seem to have a real winning way with the ladies – and two of her friends who were there decide they're gonna let me have it for blowing her off. I tried to leave but they followed me out into the parking lot where we, ah, continued our disagreement."

"You mean you had a physical confrontation?"

"Briefly. A cop car came blasting by with sirens blaring. Didn't stop for us, but kept on going. That scared us all, so we just scattered and I went home."

"So it was self-defense?"

"Pretty much. I was stupid. I had no business being where I was, and maybe I wasn't my usual endearing self either."

Renee chuckled at the last comment. "We can all have our moments." She jotted down a few more notes then laid her pencil down and looked at Aaron. "I'm going to have to review this with the Dickinsons and see what they think. Your arrest record isn't helpful. Neither is this recent incident. However, you were very forthcoming with this information and I respect that. You could've tried to lie your way through all of this. Just out of curiosity, why did you tell me?"

Aaron bit on his bottom lip. His stomach felt queasy. His biggest fears seemed to be coming to fruition. "My arrests probably showed up on the background check anyway. I figure if you found out that I lied about those arrests, then you'd assume I lied about everything else."

"Is that all?"

"I'm not a liar."

"I can't guarantee you anything, but I'm pretty sure that none of this is a show stopper. Your arrests were more than ten years ago, when you were young and stupid. And they weren't for any violent crimes. The incident you described sounds truly like a case of self-defense – stupidity not withstanding. Anything else you want to say, or talk about?"

Aaron smiled. "I think I've said plenty."

The two stood and shook hands. Then Renee escorted him to the reception area. They paused at the door and she smiled at him. "Don't worry," she said. "If the Lord is in this, everything will work out."

Aaron nodded then turned to leave. Halfway out the front door he stopped and looked back at Renee. "I know it will, but if I only knew how…"

*   *   *

Katie was in the smallest bedroom which served as a home office for the two of them when Aaron returned home from his one-on-one interview for the home study. He stopped at the door to their office and found Katie shaking her head in disgust at the computer screen. Aaron was already worried about telling her the not-so-good news from his visit with Renee and seeing Katie so dejected heightened the sense of dread.

"What's wrong?" he asked.

"I was just crunching the numbers on our financial situation and I'm trying not to freak. How are we going to pull this off? We've already racked up $5000 in expenses with much more to go."

Aaron leaned against the doorjamb. "Yeah, I know. It doesn't look pretty. Most of our combined portfolio is in our 401k accounts. We don't have much that's very liquid."

"What are we going to do?" Katie asked. When she looked at Aaron, he could see the worry in her eyes. He couldn't help but feel like he was letting her down again.

"I don't know. We could take out loans on our 401k. But neither of us has enough in it yet to be able to get much of a loan against it. We'd still be at least $8000 short, if not more."

"Besides, Mr. Bean Counter, didn't you tell me once that it's not a good idea to take loans from your 401k?"

Aaron shook his head. He walked behind Katie and began rubbing her shoulders. She leaned her head back as he worked on her neck. "Long term, it's not. You lose interest earned. I've considered getting a loan from the bank."

Katie cocked her head to one side. "I thought you were pretty much dead set against that?"

"Still not crazy about the idea. But something Ben said recently has made me rethink that a little bit."

Craning her head backwards, Katie looked up at him and smiled. "I'm glad you made that breakthrough. I'm proud of you."

"Why?"

Katie spun around in the office chair and faced Aaron. "You showed what kind of character you had by not just being willing to forgive Ben, but actually trying to build some sort of relationship with him. You've shown God-like grace."

Aaron took a deep breath. "Well, while you still like me, I guess I should tell you that it didn't go so well at Dickinson's today."

Katie leaned back with a look of surprise. "Really, didn't you and Renee hit it off?"

Aaron took a few steps back so Katie could look at him without having to tilt her head so far. "No, Renee is a very nice person. I like her. But she started asking questions."

Katie closed her eyes and Aaron could see the realization spread across her face. "She asked about some of your past troubles."

"Yeah."

"What did you tell her?"

"The truth. What could I do?"

"Did you at least try to explain that your life is different now?"

"Of course, but then the incident back in December arose."

"Oh. So how did Renee leave it?"

"She told me she wasn't sure. Said she'd talk to the owners about it."

Katie nodded her head, her eyes concerned but sincere. "Okay, we'll have to take it as it comes."

Aaron squatted down in front of her. "I'm sorry, Katie. It seems like I'm letting you down yet again."

"No. You're never wrong when you're truthful. I wouldn't expect anything less from you."

"But…" Aaron tried to speak but Katie put her index finger to his lips.

"I know it's cliché, but you're still my knight in shining armor."

"Even if the armor's tarnished and dented?"

Katie ran her fingers through his hair. "Battle worn."

Aaron wrapped his arms around her. "Lot's of chinks."

Katie kissed him on the lips then looked at him. "But tried and true."

Chapter 24

Aaron and Katie were giving Renee Hawkins from the Dickinson Adoption Agency a tour of their home as part of the third and final interview during the home study. Katie and Aaron had spent the evening before getting the house prepared for Renee's visit. They were hopeful that they could make a good enough impression to overcome Renee's concerns about Aaron's past and ensure that their home study would be approved. But as Katie and Aaron led her through their home, all Katie could see were little imperfections in each room they walked through. She knew she was probably being hypercritical, but she was praying anyway that Renee would miss the flaws. As they went from room to room Renee was taking pictures with a Polaroid camera, and then making notes on the pictures.

"I love this open area with the kitchen, dining room and living room," Renee said. "It will be great for keeping an eye on children while you're cooking."

"Thank you," said Katie as she wiped off the counter again, hoping that Renee's comment was a good omen. "When we bought the home we loved how it makes this area seem larger than it actually is."

"Let's see the bedrooms."

"Sure, right this way." Katie led Renee down the main hallway and stopped first to show her the smallest of the two rooms, which served as their home office. Before long they took Renee across the hall to the next bedroom. Aaron was silent as he trailed behind. They had prayed together before Renee arrived, but Katie knew his anxiety level must be off the charts.

"This would be the child's room," Katie said as she stepped into the second room.

"Oh yes. This is nice, and bigger than the other one," Renee said with a pleased tone.

Katie pointed out the window and the view to the hills behind the house. "We also liked this one for a child because it doesn't face the street in front of the house. It seems like that might be a little safer for a child."

"Excellent point," Renee said. "Wow, what a nice view! How big is your lot? It seems like there'd be lots of room for a kid to run and play."

"Two acres," Aaron answered.

Renee took some pictures then said, "Very good. Let's go see the rest of the house."

Within five minutes they had completed the tour and moved back into the living room. Aaron and Katie sat side-by-side on the sofa while Renee took a seat in the loveseat, positioned on a wall adjacent to the sofa.

"Well, your house is quite lovely," Renee said.

"Thank you," Katie said, trying to maintain a steady voice. She realized she was holding her breath, so she took a deep one to try and calm her nerves. She felt as if her dream of having a child was riding on this conversation.

Empathetic, Renee smiled as if she could sense their anxiousness. "I've met with each of you separately, then both of you together in our offices. This is the last interview, and at this point I'm just here to make sure your home would be suitable for a child."

Katie reached down and grabbed Aaron's hand and squeezed it. She felt him squeeze back, which gave her some reassurance.

"Let me start," Renee said, "by saying that I think you two are a delightful couple and I have no doubt that you are going to make wonderful parents."

Katie looked at Aaron and smiled. She could tell he was pleased.

Renee continued. "There were, however, two areas of concern we had during the interview process."

Katie tensed. She had tried to prepare herself for this, but still it came as a blow.

"There's always a bit of a red flag when someone seeks adoption after going through fertility issues like you have. The concern being that you need to have settled everything in your mind. You can't hang on to any grief or feelings of loss because adopting a child can be even more challenging than raising biological children – and that's saying something. You've got all of the normal challenges that any child goes through; plus there can often times be attachment or abandonment issues with the adopted children."

Katie realized she had been squeezing Aaron's hand so hard that her knuckles had turned white. She let go and flexed her fingers to get the blood circulating again. She looked apologetically at Aaron who winked back at her.

"Yes," Katie said. "We've already read one of the books on the suggested reading list. I was quite amazed at how traumatic it can sometimes be for children when they learn they've been adopted. But regarding my case, I think it's a little easier because my physical problems have pretty much settled it for us."

"Very true," Renee said. Today she was dressed in a white pant suit with a peach colored jacket. She had a small leather case sitting at her feet. Looking at Renee, Katie thought to herself that her job must be quite rewarding. What a wonderful feeling it must be to help provide families for children who were desperate for one. Then again, what an awesome responsibility to bear. No wonder Renee was so careful and thorough in her evaluations.

"But irregardless, you seem to have responded quite well."

Katie glanced at Aaron and smiled at him. "I have the Lord, and my husband to thank for that. It was pretty ugly for a while."

"Of course it was. There's a certain amount of grieving that comes with your kind of problems. You wouldn't be normal if you didn't grieve."

There was a slight pause in the conversation. Katie wondered if this was the calm before the storm.

Renee looked at Aaron. Katie noticed that he seemed to snap to attention when she looked at him, as if he'd been jolted from his own, private thoughts.

"Aaron, I talked with Mr. Dickinson and we don't see your past arrest record as a significant problem at all. The crimes weren't violent, and maybe you were a troubled youth, but it's been long enough without any other incidents to make us confident there is nothing reoccurring to worry about. Your life has turned around, that's obvious, and sharing the same belief in Jesus that you do makes it obvious to me that He has been at work in your life."

Aaron nodded his head and smiled, but his movements seemed quick and jerky, as if he was on edge, waiting for the other shoe to drop.

"Tell me one thing, Aaron. If I were to ask you to describe your life, what would be the first words that come to mind?"

Aaron spread his hands. "Work in progress."

"Okay, very good. What does that mean to you?"

"In Philippians chapter three, verse twelve Paul says that he hasn't achieved all of his personal goals, and hasn't grown to the point where God wants him to be yet. But he's still striving to become Christ-like in all he does. That's the best way I can describe it. I'm not perfect, about as far as a person can be. But I know where I've been, where I am now, and where I'm going. And I thank God every day for his mercy in me."

Katie welled up with pride. She also knew how far God had taken him – both of them for that matter. She put her arm around his back and squeezed. *Great answer, honey.*

"That works for me, Aaron. I'm still somewhat concerned about your past though," Renee said. Katie tensed up again. Maybe she had let her guard down too soon.

Renee continued. "I feel that you don't yet seem to have resolved all of your guilt issues. You told me how your father has returned and you two are trying to begin a relationship with each other. It seems that will go a long way towards resolving some of that. But I also know you feel like you were a disappointment to your mother before she died. Guilt like that can eat away at a person and wreck havoc in their relationships if you're not careful."

Katie glanced sideways at Aaron. She noticed the muscles in his jaws tightening.

"Have you," Renee said, "considered counseling?"

Aaron paused so long Katie thought he wouldn't answer. Then finally he said, "I always figured after ten minutes the shrink would need therapy more than me."

Everyone laughed, but Katie knew that Aaron often used humor as a self-defense mechanism.

"But I have, in the past counseled with our pastor. I believe I'd mentioned that."

"Yes," Renee said, "I believe so. I just wanted to throw that out as something for you to consider."

"You mean you're not going to require it?" Aaron asked.

Renee laughed. "Oh, heavens no. If I thought you needed counseling enough to require it, I wouldn't approve your home study nor send your dossier to the Chinese government. I have no doubts that both of you are going to make wonderful parents. And I think you particularly, Aaron, have more to offer a child than you realize. I just want you to be as well prepared and as well armed as possible for the challenges that await you."

Katie could see the relief pass through Aaron. He set his jaw, contemplating what she'd just said. "That makes sense. I'll keep it in mind."

"Fine," Renee said. "Do either of you have anything else you'd like to talk about?"

Aaron shook his head as Katie answered "No."

Renee stood and shook hands with Aaron, then hugged Katie. "You should get a formal letter approving your home study within a week," she said. "If not, feel free to call the office and make sure we haven't dropped the ball. The letter will be part of the dossier you send to China."

Aaron and Katie walked Renee to her car and waved at her as she drove off into the fiery red of the sinking sun, underneath a perfect April sky. Katie turned to Aaron, who put his arms around her.

"Another hurdle down," she said.

"Yup. Of course we have to send $2500 more dollars to Dickinson once we get the letter. That'll pretty much tap us out."

"You worried?" she said.

"Honestly, yes."

"Me too."

"But then again, I just keep telling myself, what's a little thing like thousands of dollars when we've got Him on our side?"

Katie kissed him then put her arm through his as they walked back up the drive to the house.

"Well said, my dear, well said."

*　　*　　*

My dear Yesu, I need you now. We need you now. My strength fails me more and more. Her heart weakens more and more. Your word teaches us that You don't always come in the thunder, or the earthquake, or the fire, but in the whisper. Lord, I'm waiting for the whisper.

I cling to the hope I cannot see. I believe in the words I have not yet heard, for me, and for her. My body is weak, but my faith is strong. The days you've granted me are coming to an end, but I don't want to leave here until I know she is where You'd have her to be. My soul longs to go home, where You are – where my family is.

Your glory is unmatched. Even Your word asks who can stand before you. Yet your grace knows the same bounds that you know – which is nothing. Nothing can stop You, or stand before Your will. You created this little one. If she dies, then she has gained You, and You have gained an angel.

But what if she lives, Father? Maybe she's the one. Maybe she can go someplace where she finds Your love. Maybe You will use her to bring this country, my homeland, to You. Maybe she will do great things so that Your name is glorified.

I pray that you be glorified. I ask only one thing of my life – that it may honor You. Thank You, Father, that You hear our prayers – even one as lowly as I. Someday You will come with a trumpet and shouts of glory.

But until then, I'll be waiting for that whisper…

* * *

Easter Sunday dawned sunny and beautiful. Aaron and Katie found their usual spot in the church parking lot, and walked hand-in-hand to the front door. Katie was dressed in a white skirt with matching jacket over a red blouse. Aaron was dressed in a charcoal grey suit with a white oxford shirt, and a red paisley tie. Katie knew there was much to celebrate on this day, but in her heart she felt an almost unbearable sense of sadness and desperation.

Friday they had received official notification that their home study had been approved – news worthy of a celebration. But with the letter came a request for the second half of the home study fee, $2500. Katie had immediately made out and mailed a check, and in doing so, had nearly exhausted all of their savings. After having gone this far, would they now be derailed by financial problems? Katie couldn't help but doubt. And each time she did she felt guilty. How could she doubt the Lord when He had already taken them this far? She felt like the children of Israel in the desert –

never certain where their next meal would come from, even as they stepped on the manna.

Looking up at the steeple on the church, and the cross perched there, she was reminded that Easter represented the resurrection of the eternal and living hope. If the Lord resurrected Christ from the dead, resurrecting their hopes shouldn't be a problem.

As they walked in the front door Pastor James Patterson greeted them. "Good morning. How are Aaron and Katie this morning?"

Aaron shook the Pastor's hand. "We're well," he said.

Katie put her mask in place and screwed a smile on. "We're fine, she said." *I'll ask forgiveness later.*

"Well, that's good to hear," James said. "Hey, step into my office for a minute. I want to hear how the adoption is going."

Oh great!

James walked behind his desk and began thumbing through some papers on top. "So how's it going? Where are we at?"

"We've made it through the home study."

"Really? That's great news. The home study is a pretty big deal isn't it?"

"Yes," Katie said, "if we didn't pass it, our chances would have been shot."

"You couldn't try again with another agency?"

"Yes," Aaron said, "but the chances are that if one agency turns you down, most others would also."

"But you passed, so that's good, right? So why do you look so down in the dumps?"

Katie glanced at Aaron, who gave her hand a squeeze.

"We're about at the end of our resources," Katie said.

James paused and frowned before he resumed rifling through the papers on his desk. "I know that's somewhere on this desk...I can imagine. Aren't the costs outrageous?"

"Yes, they are," Katie said, distracted by James's rifling through his desk. "And I can't get over how it seems like such a racket. I mean, so many people seem to stand to make a lot of money. In some ways it almost seems more like human trade than adopting a baby." Katie couldn't help but feel a little bitter. It seemed as if from fertility right on through to adoption, the whole concept of having and raising children was just another thing humans had screwed up and made more complicated than God had ever intended.

James stopped his search and looked up at Katie with a concerned look on his face. Aaron was looking at her askance as well.

"I'm...I'm sorry," Katie said.

James pulled out his chair and sat down. "Have a seat," he said, gesturing at the chairs in front of Katie and Aaron.

Katie sat down, crossing her ankles in front of her. "That must have sounded harsh. I'm surprised and disappointed in myself. I thought we'd managed to get past all of the doubts and the tragedy. With God's help we were moving forward. I always believed He would provide, but now that we've run out of money and stalled, I guess I'm confused."

"Sometimes things just aren't meant to be easy," James said.

Katie noticed Aaron was unusually silent. He seemed content to be an outsider on their conversation, watching them as if he were watching a tennis match. "No offense, but that seems kind of obvious, doesn't it, Pastor?"

"Ah, here it is," James said as he pulled a white envelope out of his desk drawer. "I'd put it here for safe keeping. Yes, it does. But the flip side to that is for those who've received much grace they're capable of giving grace. Those who've experienced God's love are more capable of giving God's love. When – and I mean 'when', not 'if' – it happens and you get your baby, hasn't it occurred to you how much you will love and appreciate the child because of the struggles and obstacles you've faced? Do you think Abraham offered Isaac on the altar, no big deal? You will never take your child for granted, because you know she will be a gift from the Lord. Don't you think?"

"Yes," Katie said. "It's still not easy, but thanks for the pep talk."

"I'm rooting for you to win. Here," James said as he handed the envelope across his desk to Aaron. "This was brought to the office on Thursday afternoon. It's for you."

"What is it?" Aaron asked.

"I don't know. They didn't say."

"Who gave it to you?"

"I was instructed that the origins of this are to remain anonymous."

"Man or woman?" Katie said.

James shrugged, determined to maintain the person's confidentiality. "Do you want me to leave you alone?"

Aaron shook his head as he tore open the envelope. "No, that's okay," he said.

Aaron looked inside it. Katie could see a look of surprise flash across his face, followed by bewilderment.

"Is this for real?" he said, looking at James.

"Like I said, I don't know what's in it."

Blinking, Aaron handed the envelope to Katie then turned his head to look outside the window.

Katie looked inside and gasped. There was a cashier's check from the Bank of Oklahoma for $10,000. She was speechless. Tears began falling down her cheeks.

This would be just enough to get them by. Whatever the difference at the end, it would be small enough that they could take out a loan, or maybe even save what they needed between now and then. She looked at Aaron. He took her trembling hand in his.

Thoughts and emotions overwhelmed her. Thoughts of gratitude, wonder, awe and guilt all passed through her mind like in a ticker tape parade. How many times would she doubt the Lord? She wanted to say never again. She hoped never again. Her voice thick with emotion, Katie asked Aaron, "Do you realize what this means?"

Aaron ran his hand through her hair. She could see the shock and wonder in his eyes. "Yeah, we've got another chance," he said.

"On Easter."

"Day of miracles."

And hope born anew.

Chapter 25

Aaron and Katie spent the next three weeks finalizing the paperwork for their dossier and now Aaron needed to begin making plans at work as well. They applied for and received passports. Then they took a day and traveled to Oklahoma City where the nearest office for the U.S. Citizenship and Immigration Services was located to have their fingerprints taken. All of which came with fees – fees that they could pay without worry. They had official documents notarized, then had the notary's credentials validated.

Now they waited to receive the magical I-171H document of clearance from the USCIS. Once received, their dossier would be complete and they could send it to the People's Republic of China.

It was a Monday afternoon, and Aaron and Katie had decided it was time to inform their employers of their plans. They had been saving vacation time, and would need to be able to take two weeks at once.

Aaron knocked on the open office door to his supervisor, Chuck Smith.

Chuck looked up from his work and peered at Aaron, cold and distant. He was of medium height and build, but he was soft looking. Not fat, but not toned either. He had brown hair that formed a ring around the base of his balding head, and blue, close set eyes. He had a thick, bushy mustache under his large, sloped nose that evidently hid his smile – because Aaron never saw one.

"What's up, Phelps?" he said with no warmth. Aaron had always treated him with respect as his supervisor, but they had not always seen eye-to-eye on work related issues. Smith was of the "you're either for me or against me" mindset, and distrusted anybody that wasn't a "yes-man" – a category Aaron couldn't fit into even if he tried. Aaron took a calming breath. *Walk before me, Lord.*

"Nothing much," Aaron said as he stepped inside the small office. The office was Spartan, with no decorations to speak of, and had about as much personality as Chuck. Aaron scratched behind his ear as he prepared to talk to him. He was worried that Smith would find, or invent, a reason to deny his vacation and throw a kink into their adoption plans. "I wanted to talk to you about some up-coming vacation I need to take."

Chuck nodded at him to continue.

Aaron cleared his dry throat. "Katie and I have decided to adopt a baby from China."

"China? Why? Why wouldn't you adopt one of our own?"

Aaron did a double-take and stared at Smith. He couldn't believe what his boss had just said. He'd heard and read stories of some of the thoughtless and sometimes even caustic things said to mixed race families, but he wasn't prepared for it right out of the gate like this. For a fleeting moment he thought about slugging him, but decided that losing his job at this juncture wouldn't be in their best interest. But on the other hand, he had no desire or obligation to explain their motivation. "Well, uh, we decided that foreign adoption was a better fit for us."

Smith pursed his lips and stared at Aaron for a moment. Aaron rolled his head a couple of times, trying to loosen the neck muscles that were constricting by the second. He felt as though he was being scrutinized for their decision and he didn't like it.

"To each his own I guess," Smith said with a dismissive tone.

I don't recall asking for your approval in the first place!

"Anyway," Aaron began, "we are almost ready to send our paperwork to China. I will need to be able to take two consecutive weeks vacation for the trip over there."

"They don't bring the kid here?"

"No, other countries do, but China doesn't. We have to go there."

"I don't recall anyone taking two weeks off like that. I'm not sure if it's allowed."

"I checked the company handbook," Aaron said, "and it's allowed with a supervisor's approval."

Smith looked disappointed that he couldn't summarily dismiss Aaron's request. "When would this happen?" he asked.

Aaron paused for a moment, rubbing his chin while he thought. This was the part he dreaded the most. "That's the kicker. I can't give you any exact date, or even a very good time frame just yet."

"What? How do you propose we plan for your absence if we don't know when it will be?"

Aaron plopped down in Smith's guest chair. "The normal process is taking somewhere around nine months right now. But, we're considering applying to adopt a baby from the waiting child list. If we do that and are approved, the process could be much faster."

"What's the difference?"

"The waiting child list is for special needs babies. If you apply for one of the children from the list it bypasses the normal process where the Chinese review our paperwork and match us up to a baby in one of the orphanages." Aaron ran his fingers through his hair. He was growing weary of explaining the situation to someone who made little effort to hide that he cared very little about it, other than how it affected his staff.

Smith snorted. "Well, I'm not crazy about the idea," he said, then paused. "But I don't see any reason why not," he said. Aaron thought he noticed a tone of disappointment.

"Great, thanks!" Aaron said, trying not to sprint out of the office.

"Phelps,"

"Yeah?"

"You need to keep me informed. I want to know as soon as you do."

"Sure thing."

"Okay," Smith said. "Get back to work."

Aaron stopped halfway out the office door. He didn't like to be pushed around by some grumpy old twit. He was about to tell him what part of the human anatomy he reminded him of when Katie's face, and that of Yu Lin's floated through his mind as he remembered the words of Christ who said "Blessed are the peacemakers."

"What?" Smith said dropping his pen, irritated by the prolonged intrusion.

"Nothing. Have a good day."

"Hmmph."

Back at ya.

*　　*　　*

The phone rang, and Katie answered it in the kitchen. It was her mother.

"How are you, Mom?"

"We're fine, dear. Your father has those two hundred acres plowed and planted with corn. I guess we'll wait and see if it gets as high as an elephant's eye. I've started working part-time at the church."

"Really, doing what?"

"Secretarial and clerical work. Doesn't pay much, but I get a little mad money and it gets me away from the farm a few hours a week."

"Wow, good for you," Katie said as she unloaded plates from the dishwasher into a cabinet.

"How are you and Aaron? How's the adoption? I'm still worried about you all adopting a child with a heart condition."

Katie rolled her eyes. "Why, Mom?"

"Well, isn't it obvious, dear? You have no clue what you'd be getting into. Maybe the child has been misdiagnosed and it's worse. I just don't want to see you and Aaron go through any more hurt than you have to. You've already been through enough."

"Thank you, Mother. But whatever happens, it couldn't be any worse than what you and Daddy went through." Katie sighed as she put bowls away. "Besides, I'm not sure we're going to. Aaron hasn't said anything since I first showed him the baby's picture."

"I'm sure he's just taking time to think it through."

"I hope so. But I'm tired of waiting. I've decided I'm going to talk to him about it again. I just feel very strongly that it's what we're supposed to do."

"Well if you're convinced the Lord has called you to this, then you know we'll be behind you all the way, baby."

"Thanks, Mom. I know you will." Katie leaned against the counter and looked out the kitchen window at the oak tree, decked out in a fresh coat of green leaves. It looked healthy and sturdy, like its roots ran deep. She'd learned a thing or two about the value of deep roots through the past five or six months. "Mom, thank you. And tell Daddy thank you."

"Okay, I will. For what?"

"Leaving a legacy. Something I can cling to and pass on to my children. It means even more to me now that we'll be adopting an orphaned child."

"Don't give us too much credit, baby. We're just simple people doing the best we can. The glory belongs to the Lord."

"Yes," Katie said, "it does. I also want to thank you for that money you sent us."

"What are you talking about, Katherine?"

"The ten thousand dollars. I know it was you and Daddy. I guess you figured Aaron would be too proud to take it, so you sent it to the church."

"No, you've got the wrong ones. It wasn't us."

Her eyebrows rose in surprise. Who would have the financial means and the desire to do such a nice thing? "Really, I was so certain it was you. Aaron asked some of our friends and they didn't know anything about it so I figured it had to be you and Daddy."

"Nope. But Frank and I were talking about it the other night and that's why I called. We've decided we want to pay for your airline tickets."

"Oh, Mother, thank you so much, but we can't accept that. We've already been blessed – by *somebody* – beyond what we could've imagined. You don't need to do that."

"Now listen to me, Katherine. You and Aaron can both be too stubborn for your own good. Your father sold the forty acres we owned down around Durant. He's giving some to your sister to help her get into a new house, and we want to do this for you and Aaron. I got together with one of the youth from church and we looked on the internet. We've got just enough for you to get round-trip business class. We know you wouldn't be able to splurge like that, and for a fourteen hour flight we thought business class would be a great gift. Especially when you're coming back with the baby."

"Why don't you all take the money and go on a vacation? Take an Alaskan cruise, or go to Hawaii. Do something for yourselves."

"We are. We'll be helping you bring our grandchild home."

A lump formed in Katie's throat. *Kid, when you come home, you're going to have more family to love you than you could ever dream of.*

"Mom, I don't know what to say."

"You don't have to say a thing. It's settled, and I don't want to hear anymore argument."

Katie turned as Aaron came in through the garage. "Okay, thank you, Mom. Really, I mean it. I'll tell Aaron."

"You're welcome. And don't let him give you any static about it either. Tell him 'Momma says.'"

"Okay, Mom. I love you and Daddy."

"We love you too."

Katie hung up and turned to Aaron, who put his arms around her.

"Was that Mom?"

"Yes."

"How are things?"

Katie smiled and kissed him. "Better and better."

Chapter 26

Wu Chien tapped on the office door of Fu Si Chuan with trembling hands. She wasn't sure of what to expect, but she was fearful of the worst. The continuing deterioration of her health only meant that at some point she would be forced to retire. *Please Yesu, don't let this be the time.*

Chuan looked up from his work and waved her into his office.

"I wanted to let you know," he said without greeting, "that we've received an application from a family in the United States to adopt Yu Lin."

Chien's mouth fell open. She'd been anticipating this news, but to hear it at last seemed almost too good. "That's wonderful news," she said.

"There is still the matter of our government accepting their application, however, so nothing is final yet."

The old woman nodded. She knew he was just covering all bases in case something fell through. He wouldn't want to have to save face if it didn't work out. "Thank you anyway," she said, "for telling me about this news. I will..." She stopped herself in mid-sentence. She almost said she would be praying for everything to work out, but caught herself. She had never been sure about Fu, and she couldn't be too careful, so she had kept her faith a secret in the orphanage. The only ones who ever knew about it were the little ones.

"What?"

"Nothing...I will be anxious to hear the final outcome," she said. She wasn't lying either, she was anxious to hear the good news that somebody was truly going to adopt the baby.

Fu Chuan nodded at her. There seemed to be sadness in his eyes. He took his black reading glasses off and laid them on his desk. "We'll see," he said, and then he frowned and hesitated.

Chien felt her knees buckle so she grabbed the door to steady herself.

"And once the baby is gone, you will need to start planning for retirement. I fear I'm letting you stay here longer than I should, and in doing so I'm putting children at risk due to your health problems."

She swallowed hard and nodded. At least she would get to stay until Lin Lin left.

"But I want you to know," Chuan continued, "that we'll miss you. You've been my best worker. I could always count on you."

The old woman ducked her head and said "Thank you," as she turned to leave.

Battling the cauldron of emotion bubbling up within her, the walk to Lin Lin's room seemed longer than normal. She was happy that the baby would be going someplace where she could receive the medical attention she needed. She would be in a better home and life, but Chien's heart broke at the realization that she would never see her again. This little one who had stolen her heart would soon take it far away.

Turning through the familiar halls of the orphanage, she also felt pangs of loss. She stopped and watched a row of toddlers lined up in wooden highchairs waiting to be fed. Like Chien, the chairs showed the wear and tear from years of use. She was about to be homeless and she didn't know where she'd go. But more than the fear of not having a home, she couldn't face the thought of leaving her current home – such as it was – and her family, who needed her.

She stepped into Lin Lin's room and watched her, as the baby tried to play with a mobile hanging down off the side of the crib. She could see the determination in her eyes as she tried to push herself up and reach for it, even though she didn't have the strength to. Other babies her age were crawling and even in walkers. But her heart condition had kept her in a weakened state where she wasn't developing physically like she should.

As Chien picked her up though, she could see that it hadn't stunted her spirit. A lone tear slid down Chien's cheek as she held the baby close.

"My Yesu is sending a family for you," she whispered to the baby. "You will be going someplace where they can care for your needs better than I can."

Chien's head started spinning and she staggered. Squeezing the baby tight against her, she rocked backwards against the wall. A wave of black passed through her head and she felt herself slide down the wall. The baby whimpered and began to cry.

"Shhh. It's okay," she whispered through the dizziness. She summoned every once of her strength and pushed herself upright and staggered to the crib where she tucked Lin Lin back in.

"Are you okay?" Chien heard someone say. She turned her head enough to see Yu Bao standing in the door. Bao was the one who had nursed her a few weeks back when she had been so ill. She was a beautiful, twenty-year-old woman who had grown up in this orphanage and worked here. She had long black hair that she wore in a ponytail – the preferred hairstyle for the younger workers in the orphanage. Her skin was lighter colored than Chien's, and she was tall, healthy and strong. Chien had taken her under her wing many years ago and had taught her how to care for the children in the orphanage. She had also taught her about Yesu. Bao now carried with her the same secret Chien did.

Chien's smile was half-hearted. "I'm fine," she said, but the waiver in her voice betrayed her.

Bao walked up close to her and put her arm around her. "No you're not. Let me help you back to your room so you can lie down." Her eyes were caring and her voice was full of compassion.

"Just help me get to the chair."

Bao steadied Chien as she staggered to the rocking chair next to Lin Lin's bed. Once she was situated Chien closed her eyes and laid her head back against the chair. "Make me a promise," she said.

Bao knelt down beside her. "What?" she said in a soft voice.

Chien struggled to swallow. Her throat was dry and her breath was short. "If I go home before she does, that you'll take care of the baby."

Bao put her hand on Chien's hand. Chien could feel the youthful strength in it. "I will. But I don't want to lose you, Momma."

Eyes still closed, Chien smiled. Bao had called her momma for years now, but it still made her feel special to hear it. "I know, but my time is coming, my daughter."

Bao looked around. All of the other children were being fed and it was just the three of them in the room. "What will heaven be like?"

"In the presence of Yesu, it will be wonderful."

"I will join you there someday."

Chien smiled and put her hand against Bao's cheek. "Yes, you will. But until then, you must live for Yesu while you're here."

"I will."

"I know."

"You taught me."

Chien smiled again. Her efforts had not been in vain. A life lived for Him is never wasted – no matter how it seems. *Praise You, Yesu.*

*   *   *

Within a week the I-171H form from the USCIS had finally arrived and had been sent with the rest of Aaron's and Katie's dossier to the People's Republic of China. This marked a major milestone in the adoption process and Katie had felt an overwhelming sense of relief once they were officially "DTCd". But this also began the longest, most tedious part of the journey – the wait. From here on out, there was nothing else they could do to move the process forward. Except remain patient, and dream.

In celebration of their newly acquired DTC status, Katie had suggested they go out for Chinese food, and were doing the only other thing left to do – walking through a Babies 'R Us store in south Tulsa.

"So, we can start working on the nursery *now*?" Katie asked with not attempt to hide her impatience. She was wearing a sleeveless royal blue blouse, jeans and sandals.

Aaron grinned, boyish and playful. "Mmmaybe," he said as he tucked his hands into his back pockets. He too was dressed casual, in a black short-sleeve Polo shirt, jeans, and loafers with no socks.

Katie smiled back and bumped him with her hip as they clasped hands and walked through the various aisles of merchandise. She knew why Aaron had urged her to wait to work on the baby's nursery until after they'd been DTCd. It was a good idea. Now that their paperwork had gone out, they could focus their energy on preparing the nursery and getting ready for the trip instead of waiting and worrying.

Katie was twirling her hair around her forefinger as they walked through the store. She was ready to make a move on the little baby girl with the heart condition, but she was trying to wait and let Aaron bring it up.

They stopped in the car seat aisle. The array of choices was staggering.

Aaron was looking at a price tag. "One hundred and fifty dollars! For that much it should rock her to sleep and change her diapers."

"That one's for an older baby. If we're going to adopt the baby on the waiting child list we wouldn't need one that big just yet."

"Good point."

Katie decided to move in on the subject. "Don't you think we should decide? Maybe it would help us know what to buy."

Aaron stepped around Katie to look at an infant carrier. "Yeah, I guess so."

"You don't seem too eager. What's wrong?"

Aaron flipped over the red price tag on the carrier. "Nothing," he said as he raised his eyebrows. "Man, nothing about having a baby is going to be cheap."

Katie put her hands on her hips and stared at him. "Come on, Phelps, I know you better than that. Why don't you want to adopt that baby? I've already checked, and my insurance at work will cover her heart surgery."

Aaron looked at her sideways. "I'm not *that* much of a cheapskate," he said.

"Oh, I wasn't insinuating that you are. I'm just trying to figure out why you're so hesitant."

"Why are you so insistent?"

"I can't explain it. When I saw her, I was just…just drawn to her. Her eyes had so much spirit in them. Didn't you think?"

"Yes, they did."

"Don't you think she deserves to have a shot at life?"

Aaron looked Katie in the eyes. "Yes, of course I do." They left the car seats and started walking through the strollers.

A young couple was checking out the strollers as well. They appeared to be in their mid-twenties, and she was very much pregnant. She was wearing bib overalls that seemed to accentuate the roundness of her abdomen. The young father-to-be stood behind her and wrapped his arms around her midsection and rubbed her tummy. Katie was watching them with sideways glances when she caught Aaron watching her watch them.

She shrugged her shoulders at him and said, "What?"

"Feel like you're missing out?"

Katie bit her lip. "Yeah, some."

"I understand," Aaron said as he put an arm around her shoulders.

"I know you do."

"Do you regret not pursuing the fertility options?"

"No. I don't think so. What about you?"

"About the same."

"But I can't deny that this was God's plan."

"Yeah."

Katie turned to face Aaron. She had to tilt her head back slightly to look into his eyes. "I think Yu Lin is also part of God's plan."

Aaron smiled back at her. She could see the earnest searching in his eyes. "Part of me does also. But she just seems so…so fragile. I've tried telling myself that we should go for a more sure deal. But then again, I know that there's nothing certain about life. Then there's another part of me that thinks maybe this is just another test. Do we have the faith to trust God?"

"Like Abraham and Isaac?"

"Yeah, sorta."

They walked on and started browsing through the clothes. Aaron was following Katie when she stopped in front of a display of onesies. Katie held one up and showed it to Aaron. "Daddy's Little Girl" was embroidered on it in bright red letters.

"Either way," Aaron said as he traced the lettering with his finger, "having a daughter is going to break my heart sooner or later."

Touching her palm to his cheek she said, "I guess it comes with the territory. Just wait until she brings someone like you home to meet us."

Aaron pulled his hands to his heart and staggered backwards. "I'll kill him!"

Katie laughed at her husband – which was what he wanted. He stepped in front of her and put his arms around her waist.

"I don't think I could live with myself," he said, "knowing that we might be her only chance to live and we didn't do something about it."

Katie ran the back of her hand across his cheek. "She has your eyes, you know."

"Except, of course, for the shape and the coloring."

"Better. They have the same kind of life and spirit in them."

"Are you trying to close the deal?"

Katie grinned her special grin at him – the one she knew he couldn't resist. "Did it work?"

Aaron took a deep breath. "Yes, it did."

Katie grabbed him and squeezed tight. She felt him hug her back.

"Do you want to call Renee tomorrow?" he whispered in her ear.

"Yes," Katie said, "I do."

She pulled back from him and tried her best to look stern. "Now can we actually *buy* something while we're here?"

Aaron took the onesie from her hand and held it up. "Let's start with this."

*   *   *

The next day Katie took an early lunch and called Renee Hawkins at the adoption agency on her cell phone.

Katie was sitting in her Ford Escort with the windows rolled down. It was a sunny Friday in May, and as far as Katie could tell, full of promise.

Katie heard the other end of the line click over and then she heard Renee's voice. "This is Renee Hawkins."

"Hi, Renee, it's Katie Phelps."

"Katie! Good to hear from you. Did you and Aaron celebrate your DTC last night?"

Katie smiled. "Of course. We're very excited, and anxious."

"Well, remember what I told you. I want you two to get lots of date nights in between now and the time you travel. You won't get many for quite a while once you get your baby."

"We will."

"So what can I do for you?" Renee asked.

A couple of men who worked in Katie's department walked past her and waved. She waved back at them then turned away. "Aaron and I have decided we want to pursue one of the babies on the waiting child list."

"Oh really," Renee said, "which one?"

"Yu Lin. The one with the heart defect."

"Oh. Uh, have you checked the waiting child page on our website recently?"

Becoming suspicious, Katie bit her lip. "No, not for a week or so."

"I'm so sorry, but we've taken her off the list. We had another couple apply and we've already sent the application letter to the PRC."

Katie closed her eyes and laid her forehead on the steering wheel. She couldn't believe it. How could they have missed God's intentions? Aaron. How would she tell him? Katie blinked away tears as another coworker passed by her car and smiled at her.

"Katie? Are you there?"

"Yes. Sorry. Well, thank you anyway," Katie said. She was trying to be cheerful, but she knew her voice was revealing her disappointment.

"I truly am sorry if you're disappointed," Renee said. "I'm sure you understand that the only fair way for us to deal with the waiting child list is on a first come basis."

"Yes, certainly," Katie said.

"Call me anytime."

"Thank you. Bye." As Katie flipped her cell phone closed, her stomach churned with mixed emotions and her eyes began to well again. She was glad to know that the baby would have the surgery and a family. Since it was through Dickinson, maybe the couple lived in the Tulsa area and they could some day meet. But she felt like her heart had been ripped out of her body. She had been so convinced of God's call on them that she was already beginning to consider the child her own. Would she ever be able to figure out what He wanted from her? Why couldn't she get it right?

She flipped her cell phone open and dialed Aaron's number. After two rings he answered. "Hi, it's me," she said with a small, shaky voice.

"What's wrong?"

"I just talked to Renee."

"Yeah."

"Aaron, they've already taken the baby off the list. Someone else has applied to adopt her."

There was a long silence. Katie knew that Aaron must be wondering why he'd ever listened to her in the first place.

At last Aaron broke the silence. "I'm sorry, babe."

"I'm so sick of this," Katie said as she banged her fist on the steering wheel. "It seems like every step is a struggle."

"It sure seems that way. But the Lord has provided. He had someone finance this for us. That part wasn't as bad as it could've been."

"I know. I know," Katie said as she dabbed at her eyes and checked her makeup in the rearview mirror. "Maybe it's us. We seem to continually miss the mark. I had already picked out a name for her."

"What was it?"

"Hannah Lin," Katie said as she choked up again.

Aaron was silent on the other end. She knew he was waiting for her to get a grip.

"I'm okay," she finally said. "I just need to remind myself that God knows his plans for us, and he's chosen someone for us."

"Or maybe," Aaron said, "he's chosen *us* for her?"

"God help her."

"Hey, speak for yourself."

Though she didn't feel like it, Katie couldn't help but smile. "I am."

Chapter 27

Katie felt conspicuously out of place sitting next to Sherry Cooper in the Crossroads Community Church's Family Life Center during her baby shower on a beautiful Saturday afternoon in early May. Katie had led several members of their Sunday school class in planning the party for Sherry, her best friend, but now as she listened to stories of pregnancy, deliveries and motherhood she wished she weren't there.

Sherry tucked her long blonde hair behind her ears as she rested a large box on her protruding stomach and unwrapped it. "Oh, marvelous!" she said as she held up a Diaper Genie. She read the card. "From the Adult 4 class. Thank you all so much!" she said as she looked around the room.

"Oh, I would've given anything for one of those things when my kids were babies," Helen Jackson said as she pointed her chin at the unwrapped box. She was middle aged, slender and neat as a button with predominantly grey hair. Although she steadfastly refused to be considered an elder within the church, most of the younger women, including Katie, truly admired her and held her in high esteem.

"You didn't have disposable diapers back then did you?" one of the younger women asked.

Helen sat her plastic plate down, brushed a chocolate cake crumb off of her blouse and smoothed out her skirt. "They were around, but no one I knew used them daily because they were too expensive. That was the mid-sixties and they were considered more of a luxury than a staple. We only used them when we took the kids on a trip."

Katie felt like a spectator at a tennis match as she followed the conversations from one person to another. At least the current topic of conversation would have *some* relevance to her.

"So you used cloth diapers most of the time," Sherry said.

"Yes we did, unfortunately," Helen said with a chuckle. "Instead of dropping the diaper into a gadget like that and giving it a couple of twists and a shot of air freshener we shook the diapers out over the toilet and gagged."

Everyone laughed and grimaced at the same time.

"So, Sherry, tell me," another guest said. "Are you going to try natural childbirth or are you going for the drugs?"

As Sherry started to speak Katie checked out. She looked down at her empty plate and wondered if she could sneak another piece of cake without anyone noticing. Where was Aaron when she needed him? He could go get her another and nobody would give it a second thought.

There was a break in the conversation, and Katie leaned over and whispered into Sherry's ear, "I'm going to run down the hall for a bit."

Sherry looked at her and her eyes were immediately full of empathy. "Are you okay? I noticed you've been terribly quiet."

"Yeah, I guess so. I just don't have any first-hand knowledge of some of the topics."

Sherry laid her hand on top of Katie's. "I know. But hang in there."

Katie had just stood up to leave the room when Beth Morris spoke up. "So Katie, when are you going to join your friend in the world of parenthood?"

The room went silent as everyone waited for her to respond. Katie felt as if there were thirty or forty laser beams boring into her from all angles. She hadn't told many people about her infertility problems and the pending adoption yet, and she wasn't prepared to make a grand announcement just yet.

Sherry spoke up, trying to relieve her pressure. "Helen, did you make the cake? It's delicious."

Katie looked at Sherry and rolled her eyes to say thanks. Sherry nodded and Katie quickly left the room. As Katie walked to the nearest restroom she came to the point where the preschool hall intersected with the main hall. She hesitated for a moment, and then turned down the preschool wing. Except for sunlight coming from windows in the hall and rooms it was dark. She stopped in front of the nursery and looked through the big picture window into the room. There were four cribs and four big plantation style rocking chairs. Staring into the dark room at the empty cribs and still rockers, Katie wondered if this was a miniature version of what an orphanage looked like in China, except probably much nicer.

She rarely, if ever had occasion to travel down this hall and even in its current dormant state she was struck with the sense of life and potential that seemed to emanate from the walls. She could picture the scene on a Sunday morning as the church family arrived. It must be something like joyous chaos. Moms and dads taking their kids to the nursery or preschool class. Kids running while their mothers bark at them to walk. Kids laughing. Kids crying.

Pressing her hand to the glass she thought about Yu Lin. Katie hadn't been able to get her out of her mind. She had reasoned, and tried to convince herself, that it was all part of God's plan and she had just misinterpreted the signals. But the more she tried to rationalize the more confused she became. How could she have been so horribly wrong whenever she had rarely been so sure of anything in her life? Was God playing tricks on her, or was she just losing her marbles?

Please Lord, give me a sign.

She turned to resume her trip to the restroom when she saw a poster across the hall. It had a row of boys and girls of various races. The caption above the picture read "Jesus loves the little children, all the children of the world." There was a Chinese girl in the picture with pigtails and a crooked smile that revealed gap in her teeth where the front two were missing. There was a caption below the picture that read, "Red and yellow, black and white, they are precious in His sight. Children are a gift from God."

A calming peace swept through Katie like the ocean's tide rolling onto shore. Maybe Aaron was right. Maybe it was more about God choosing the right family for each child rather than choosing the right child for the family. Maybe the child needed a family that would love and accept the child no matter what and one that would be able to laugh when she laughed and cry when she cried.

You're so cool!

Katie moved on, determined that she would leave it in God's hands. *He knows what's best for each family and each child. Let Him put the pieces of the puzzle together.*

Katie had barely returned to her seat when Beth spoke up again. "Katie, you never answered my question before. When are you and Aaron going to have a little one?"

Katie and Sherry had always treated her with kindness and Christian love, but sometimes it wasn't easy. Between the two of them they referred to her as the "church police" because she always seemed to know who was in attendance in each service and often demanded to know why you were absent.

Katie looked at her and smiled as pleasantly as she could. "Someday soon we hope. When the Lord is ready I'm sure He'll give us the gift."

Beth looked puzzled. "So you want to have children?"

Katie smiled and nodded.

"And you are trying?"

Smile and nod.

"But you're having trouble?"

"Not so far," Katie said from behind her smile. She heard Sherry choke as she suppressed a laugh.

Beth looked puzzled again and much to Katie's relief she changed the subject.

Sherry giggled, elbowed Katie playfully in the ribs and whispered, "Not so far?"

Katie shrugged her shoulders. "Well, she didn't specify *what*."

*   *   *

A week later Aaron pulled his truck into a parking spot next to Ben Phelps' car in the Crossroads Community Church parking lot, and he and Katie got out. Ben had agreed to attend the Sunday morning service with them.

During the past months Aaron and Ben had been meeting regularly for lunches and the threesome had gone to dinner a time or two. Aaron looked around for anyone who might spot them as he got out of the truck and greeted Ben. He wasn't sure why, but he was a little nervous. This was the first time he and Ben had met in a place where Aaron knew many, if not most of the people. He had told himself he didn't want to cause any kind of distraction. But in reality, he knew of at least three people to whom he had revealed a certain amount of contempt for Ben – before he knew him. He felt somewhat two-faced to come strolling in side by side with him.

"How are you two holding up with the wait?" Ben asked.

"Terrible," Katie said with a laugh. "But thanks for asking."

"It's only been a few weeks since you sent your paperwork in hasn't it?"

"Yeah, I know. Wait until it's been months. You'll be peeling me off the walls."

"Well, hey, let's go in," Aaron said.

Pastor James Patterson was at his customary greeting post as they walked into the church building. He smiled at Katie and Aaron, and then nodded at Ben who nodded back. Aaron thought it was odd that there wasn't more of a surprised reaction from the pastor, and that they would exchange nods as if they knew each other.

"Pastor, this is my...uh, this is Ben Phelps."

James shook his hand and said, "Nice to meet you."

"You too," Ben said.

Aaron again thought he picked up on a vibe that they knew each other but he decided it was just his nervousness making him paranoid.

They entered the auditorium and found three open seats on the same pew Mark and Sherry Cooper were sitting in. When Aaron introduced them to Ben he noted more of a surprised reaction.

Before long the service began with upbeat choruses. Aaron watched Ben peripherally throughout the song service and noticed the way he individually worshipped God. There was nothing outward in his worship, but the air of humble adoration in his expression caught Aaron's eye.

The song service ended with a pre sermon ballad called *Tender Mercy* by the band *Come To Pass* who was home on hiatus from their touring schedule. Crossroads was their home church so they sang there often.

The pastor then began his sermon. As Ben flipped his Bible to the key passage Aaron noticed how faded and worn the pages were from years of constant use. He also spotted handwritten notes in the margins and various passages highlighted or underlined. Through their frequent meetings Aaron had managed to move beyond his initial feelings about Ben and was discovering that he was a man of depth, understanding and faith. He had a humble, peaceful spirit that had been very calming for Aaron – even when Aaron wasn't looking for calm. Plus it didn't hurt that Katie had grown to like him as well.

Aaron found himself thumbing through his own Bible and noticing fewer signs of wear and tear on it. He always had his daily quiet time, but the past several months, and his growing knowledge of Ben were showing him how much more depth there should be in his relationship with Christ. Could he someday bring himself to ask Ben for help in his own personal walk?

The service ended and they shook hands with James Patterson again. Aaron and Katie thanked him for the inspiring message and Ben, who was behind them, thanked him as well.

As they left the building James said, "Good to see you again."

Aaron looked at Katie and raised an eyebrow. Katie just shrugged her shoulders. Once in the parking lot they stopped in front of Ben's Ford.

"How about Tuesday for lunch," Ben said.

"Sounds fine. Did you enjoy the service?"

"Very much. I really like this church. I'd like to come back if that's okay with you."

"Sure," Aaron said. "I couldn't prevent it even if I wanted to. Hey, you and Pastor James acted like you knew each other."

Ben scratched behind his ear. "Yeah, we've uh, met a time or two."

Aaron noticed a look in his eye that indicated Ben knew something that he wasn't about to tell.

Aaron decided not to press him. He shook hands with Ben and said, "See you around."

Katie hugged Aaron's father and they started to get into their vehicles.

Ben stopped with one foot inside his car. "Keep me posted on the adoption."

Aaron locked eyes with him for a minute. For one of the few times since they'd met he noticed something other than sadness in Ben's eyes – instead there was a small twinkle. "We will."

Chapter 28

"It just seems awfully strange to me," Aaron said as he followed Katie up the produce aisle pushing a grocery cart, "that Pastor James and Ben acted like they knew each other. I mean, you even heard James say 'good to see you again,' didn't you?" It was Tuesday evening and they were doing their weekly grocery shopping at the Wal-Mart Superstore in Sand Springs.

"Yes, I did," Katie said as she inspected a cantaloupe. "But I'm sure he was just referring to meeting him before the service."

Aaron frowned as he leaned over the cart, steering it more with his forearms than with his hands. "I doubt that. There was something there, but I'm not sure what."

Katie placed the cantaloupe in the buggy and moved to the bananas. She stopped and looked at Aaron as if she were inspecting him. "I'm curious Mr. Holmes, why make it a big mystery? What does it matter if they've met?"

Aaron picked up the cantaloupe and looked at it. Its rough outer layer still had the slightest hint of green coloring in it. He didn't like it when he was wound up about something and Katie was calm and practical. The role reversal seemed peculiar. "I don't know," he said with a shrug. "I guess I figure they're talking about me, or us, and I'm not sure I like it."

Katie rolled her eyes. "What makes you think it's about you? And besides, you've never given a rat's rear-end if other people talk about you." She looked him up and down. "You're hiding something, mister. I can read you like a book."

Katie pointed further down on the other side of the aisle. "Go pick out a green, yellow, and red bell pepper please."

Aaron snapped to attention and saluted her. "Yes, ma'am," he said, making his voice as deep as he could.

As Aaron began picking through the peppers he wondered. *Why does it bug me?* Katie was right, what *did* it matter if they were talking, and even becoming best friends for that matter? He found a nice green one that didn't have any yellow spots in it and dropped it in a clear plastic bag.

Now that he and Aaron were developing a decent relationship, maybe Ben was just trying to get settled in and make a better life for himself. He couldn't find a finer man to get to know than the pastor. It just seemed weird that he would show up out of the blue and then start spending time with the preacher at their church. Aaron found a good red and yellow pepper and put them in the bag with the green one, grabbed the open end in one hand and gave the bottom a spin with the other. After it quit spinning he put a twist tie around the wound-up end and met back up with Katie as she was leaving the produce section.

"You're right," Aaron said.

"Of course," Katie said grinning at him. "I'm always right. Haven't you figured that out by now?"

"I thought it was more like I'm always wrong."

"That too."

"But," Aaron said, unable to let it go, "I guess it seems strange that he would show up unannounced and suddenly start hangin' with our pastor. And, in the meantime a boat-load of money falls out of the sky and lands in our laps."

Katie stopped and looked at Aaron. Her head was tilted to the side the way it did when she'd just had a sudden revelation. Aaron had always found that adorable. "You don't think *he's* our benefactor do you?" she said.

"I don't know. It would be an awfully big coincidence, don't you think?"

"Wow! You know what?"

"What?"

"When we went out to eat with Ben a couple weeks ago a piece of paper fell out of his wallet when he opened it up to pay for his dinner. I leaned down and picked it up for him. You know what it was?"

"Do tell, Mrs. Holmes?"

"Oh hush. You know it makes me crazy when you turn my words on me."

"So what was it?"

"It was a receipt from the Bank of Oklahoma."

Aaron stared at Katie as he tried to recall why that might be significant. Then it hit him. "Wasn't the cashier's check from BOK?"

Katie nodded her head.

"And James gave it to us."

Katie looked puzzled again. "But, on the other hand, I wouldn't think he'd have those kind of resources."

"He told me once he'd managed to accumulate some savings over the years since he got out of the pen."

Katie giggled and shook her head. "Isn't that just like the Lord?"

"What's so funny?"

"Our angel, the ex-con."

Aaron pushed the cart silently behind Katie as they went up and down aisles, skipping some and turning down others. Aaron was confused. He didn't know whether to be grateful or angry.

He watched Katie as she picked out a box of all-bran cereal and put it in the cart.

"Ughh. I like Cap'n Crunch better."

"I know you do little boy, but this is what we're getting," she said as she started walking again.

Aaron felt his pride kicking up inside. He wanted to give the money back, but he knew Katie wouldn't go for that. Was Ben trying to buy his way into Aaron's and Katie's life? No, he wouldn't have given the gift anonymously if that were the case. Besides, Aaron had become well enough acquainted with him over the last months to know that wasn't his style. If anything, Ben was a humble man and wouldn't want any undo attention or fuss.

They turned down an aisle with various frozen foods in it. While Katie wasn't looking Aaron grabbed a half-gallon of ice cream and hid it in the cart under some other items.

Maybe Ben thought he was paying a debt, but Aaron didn't want that for a couple of reasons. One, he didn't want to feel like he owed Ben. And two, Aaron didn't want Ben to think they were a charity case. But again, Ben wouldn't be condescending and he would know that Aaron wouldn't accept a gift like that from a sense of debt or pity.

Then again, maybe Katie had touched upon it earlier. Maybe for Ben the money wasn't about Aaron at all. Maybe it was something he felt God was leading him to do. Ben would do it if he thought it was a calling. Aaron made up his mind that he would swallow his pride. Let it lie. That was the best answer. Maybe somehow, he could repay him some day.

They finally made their way to the checkout and waited in line. Aaron was still mulling everything over when Katie looped her arm through his.

"Is it hard for you?" she asked looking up at him. Aaron peered into her deep blue eyes and was reminded once again of the ocean.

"What?"

"Taking so much money from someone. Especially in a scenario like this."

Aaron bit his lip for a moment while he thought. "Maybe a little. But there are things in this world that are bigger than me and my pride. I choose to accept the offering for what it is."

"Are you going to say anything to him?"

"Naw."

"Why not?"

Aaron shrugged his shoulders as he pushed the cart to the front of the checkout line and began unloading its contents onto the conveyer belt. "It doesn't feel right. I wouldn't like it. He wouldn't like it. It's best to just leave it alone."

Katie shook her head. "It's a guy thing, isn't it?"

"I prefer not to generalize, but yeah, I guess so."

Katie picked up the half-gallon of ice cream and looked suspiciously at Aaron. "And how did this get in here?"

"I don't know. It must have jumped in while we weren't looking."

"That's funny, it's always chocolate chip that jumps in."

Aaron looked innocently at the girl checking their groceries who was giggling as she rang the items up.

"Maybe there are some things in this world that are irresistibly attracted to me."

Katie grinned, and nodded her head knowingly. "You mean like trouble?"

"Well, yeah, among others."

Katie patted him on the rear as she squeezed by him to pay the bill. "And me," she said with a wink.

"Chocolate chip ice cream and thou. At least I've got that going for me."

*   *   *

A little more than a week later, Katie was unloading dishes from the washer into the cabinets when the phone rang. It was about five-thirty on

Thursday evening and Aaron was outside mowing the lawn, so Katie dried her hands on a red checkered dish towel and answered it.

"Hello, Katie?" She recognized the voice of Renee Hawkins.

"Yes, hi Renee, this is Katie."

"Katie, I apologize for calling so late in the day. Am I interrupting anything?"

"No, not at all. What can I do for you?" Katie said as she began unloading glasses. She wondered what was up with a call at this time of night – and Renee's voice sounded especially chipper.

"You called me a few weeks ago expressing an interest in adopting the baby girl, Yu Lin, who is on the waiting child list, correct?"

Katie stopped with a glass still in her hand and rested her backside against the counter. Her heart began to pound as a million thoughts filled her head. Surely nothing bad had happened to her. "Yes, that's correct."

"Well, something's happened..." Katie held her breath. "There has been a change in the situation and the couple who had first committed has had to back out."

Katie shook her head as she tried to wrap her mind around what she had just heard. "And that means?"

"It means that if you and Aaron are still interested you are next in line to apply for adopting the child."

The glass she was holding slipped out of her hand, bounced off the door to the dishwasher and landed on the floor with a crash. Katie's mind raced as her excitement began to grow. She had just recently made peace with it by turning it over to God. She closed her eyes as they began to well with tears. *Thank you, Lord.*

"Katie, are you there? Did I hear something crash?"

Renee's voice startled Katie back into the moment. Staring at the broken glass a few feet from her she said, "Oh, uh, it's okay. I just dropped a glass."

Renee laughed and her voice sounded relieved. "I guess I should've had you sit down first."

As the initial shock passed Katie's mind began to refocus on the sudden new reality. "No, that's okay. Yes, we're still interested. What do we need to do?"

"Excellent," Renee said. Her voice sounded as energized as Katie felt. "You two will need to come in and fill out some more forms. I know that's your favorite thing..."

Katie could hardly contain the excitement in her voice as she laughed. "No, that's okay. Whatever it takes. Aaron and I will be there tomorrow afternoon."

"Great, I'll be looking for you. Any other questions?"

"Yeah, just one. I'm dying to know, what changed with the other couple?"

Renee laughed. "You're not going to believe this, but they found out early last week that she's pregnant. They're going to have to put the adoption off for at least another year."

"No! You're kidding me! Is that like a first or something?"

"No, it's rare, but that's actually happened a couple times before."

Katie shook her head. She still couldn't believe what she had just heard. "Thank you very much for calling, Renee."

"It's always my pleasure."

Katie said thank you and hung up. She turned and rushed barefoot out of the house and sprinted toward Aaron.

Aaron must have seen her coming because he let go of the handle to the mower so it would turn off. As Katie neared him still running full speed, his eyes got big and he said, "Hold up honey, I'm all sweaty and gross."

Katie didn't care. She was elated beyond description. As she reached him she jumped into his arms and wrapped her legs around his waist. Katie squealed in excitement as she kissed him all over his face.

Aaron swayed, then righted himself. "Wow, I think I'll get sweaty and gross more often."

"I can't believe it," Katie said, half laughing and half crying now. "We get to adopt her! We get to be her parents."

Still holding Katie, Aaron leaned back so he could look at her. "Who? What are you talking about?"

"Yu Lin! That baby on the waiting child list."

"But I thought…"

"No the other couple had to back out. It's our turn," Katie said, closing her eyes and pressing her cheek against his.

"Really?"

"Really."

Aaron looked at her as if she were crazy. "That's nuts. Who would back out on a commitment like that? You didn't hear this from one of your message board pals, did you?"

"No. Renee just called. The other couple is pregnant! Can you believe it?"

A broad smile swept across Aaron's face as sweat trickled down it. "Yes, I think I can."

Katie rested her forehead against his. At long last her dream of having a baby was taking shape, and it was the child of her dreams. The Lord had once again moved in a way like only He could.

"Yeah," she said. "Me too."

When You Come Home

Chapter 29

Three months later Katie and Aaron were seated in the business class section of a United Airlines 777. They were somewhere over Siberia on their way to Beijing, the capital city of the People's Republic of China.

"I don't really want to go to Beijing," Katie said.

"This sure beats flying coach, don't you think?" Aaron said in a vain attempt to change the subject and help Katie get her mind off of their worries – at least temporarily – but she just looked at him and frowned.

Much had happened since they had received the phone call from Renee. They applied for and received permission to adopt Yu Lin. Then, after an interminably long wait they received travel approval.

But then Renee called the day before they were set to leave with news that tempered their enthusiasm for the trip. "We've received word from the orphanage that Yu Lin's heart condition is gradually deteriorating and she's going to need advanced medical attention as soon as possible."

No one knew the full extent of what that meant, but it was enough that it had sent Katie into a panic induced tailspin. Aaron had tried to play it down by telling her it was probably nothing, but she wouldn't take the bait. She had asked him if he truly believed that, and he couldn't meet her eyes as she looked at him. He had finally told her that he believed God had it under control and all the worry in the world wasn't going to help it. He truly believed what he'd said, but the words sounded hollow and trite, so he didn't put much conviction behind them.

Aaron ran his fingers through her hair and smiled at her with as much reassurance as he could muster. "Hey, babe, keep your head up. We've got the surgeons waiting for us, and just two days after we're back home Hannah will have her surgery and her heart will be like new." They had decided they would name her Hannah Lin, keeping her given name as her new middle name in deference to her heritage.

"I know, but I just want to get her, do what we have to do to finalize the adoption and get back home where I know we'll...*she'll* be alright."

Aaron sighed and looked at the screen in the seat in front of him. He didn't have it tuned to any of the in-flight programming – he'd grown tired of that rather quickly. He currently had it on the map which showed their present location. It said there was only about three hours left in their flight. "Look, let's get some rest. We're going to need it."

Katie nodded her head and closed her eyes. "Okay. I'll try."

Aaron closed his own tired eyes and quickly drifted off into a semi-sleep state – the best he could do on a plane. He dreamed he'd been exiled into Siberia, like one of the many Russians who were sent there to die during Stalin's reign of terror. He was alone, dragging a sled weighted down with rocks into deeper and deeper snow. Soon he found himself imprisoned in an icy tomb of snow, with no hope of making it out alive.

Sometime later Aaron was awakened with a start as a flight attendant gently nudged him. She was a pretty woman who looked several years younger than Aaron. She had on the same standard attire as the rest of the crew.

"Mr. Phelps?"

Aaron sat his chair upright and wiped his eyes to try and focus on her. "Uh, yeah."

"We had a call from the terminal in Beijing. I was told to let you know that once we land you and your wife will be the first to deplane and you will be escorted to the security offices in the airport."

Aaron looked at the screen in front of him. It showed only thirty minutes left until they landed. He looked at Katie who shrugged her shoulders. "Okay. May I ask what this pertains to?"

The attendant smiled without any warmth. "I'm sorry, sir. That's all I know. I'm sure it's just a paperwork problem of some sort. Those things happen from time to time."

Aaron shook his head and scratched behind his ear. "Yeah, thanks," he said.

The attendant moved back to the front of the plane and Aaron leaned over to Katie.

"What do you think it is?" Katie asked.

Aaron rubbed his face. "I haven't a clue. But isn't that part of what we pay the adoption agency for is to help prevent foul-ups from happening?"

"Yes, but I'm sure it's nothing. Don't get worked up just yet."

Aaron stood up and stretched. "Yeah, I suppose you're right."

He went to the phone booth sized restroom and splashed water on his face and combed his hair. If he was going to have to smooth out a problem he wanted to be as presentable as he could after nearly twenty-four hours of travel from Tulsa to Chicago and now to Beijing. Of course a day's growth of beard wouldn't help much.

As promised, Aaron and Katie exited first, but Aaron was shocked to be met just outside of the plane by a uniformed Chinese police officer carrying a compact assault rifle. Aaron's heart began to race. *What the heck!*

"What's going on?" Aaron asked the officer who shook his head without answering. Aaron decided he probably didn't understand much English so there was no point in pressing it.

He looked at Katie and could see fear in her eyes. But to her credit, that was the only sign, and probably only he would notice it. He took her hand as they were escorted up the runway that led from the plane to the terminal gate. Once inside they were met by another policeman driving a cart and then transported to the administrative section of the airport where they were escorted to one of the inner offices.

By now Katie was squeezing his hand harder and harder, and Aaron himself was beginning to freak, but he was trying his best to contain it. Now was the time to be as cool as possible.

On the office door was a sign in Chinese lettering with no English translation. One of the police officers opened the door and Aaron saw a metal office desk and two metal-framed guest chairs. A Chinese man was seated behind the desk. He was wearing a suit and tie, and looked to be a little smaller than Aaron. There was a Chinese woman wearing a long sleeved shirt un-tucked from her blue jeans standing along the wall to Aaron's left and a Caucasian male in khaki trousers and a navy blue Polo shirt standing along the wall to his right. The man behind the desk waved them in, so Aaron and Katie slowly walked in and the officer shut the door behind them.

The Chinese woman spoke first. "Hello, my name is Xiang. I'll be your guide in Beijing. You can call me 'Christy'," she said nervously as she shook hands with Aaron.

"What's going on?" Katie asked.

Christy's eyes darted across the room to the other man who was standing. He cleared his throat and stepped forward to shake Katie's and Aaron's hands.

"I'm Dean Phillips. I work in the U.S. Embassy here in Beijing. We were phoned regarding a problem with your Visa, Mr. Phelps."

Aaron's shoulders relaxed slightly, relieved that there was an American present who could talk with him, but now his fear was slowly turning to frustration. He didn't have the time or inclination for dealing with problems at this point. They just wanted to get their baby before it was too late for her.

"What's the problem, did we miss a signature someplace? Lord knows, we probably forgot to have the notary's notary authenticated or something."

"No, I wish it were that simple, Mr. Phelps. It seems someone in the FBI discovered a mistake they made."

"What mistake?"

"Apparently, they overlooked your previous police record."

"Two arrests when I was a teenager? Our caseworker said this wouldn't be a problem."

"No, that's not it. The FBI is concerned that they cleared an ex-convict with a prison record to leave the country and adopt a baby. I'm sorry to be the one to tell you this, Mr. Phelps, but you will not be allowed to enter China."

Aaron was speechless – searching his mind for some clue as to what might have gone wrong.

Katie spread her hands out in front of her. "Ex-convict? Prison record? What are you talking about?"

Phillips shrugged his shoulders. "The FBI has record of an Aaron Phelps serving time in California. That's all I really know. They contacted the Chinese Consulate in Houston and your Visa has been suspended pending further review."

Aaron looked at Katie and back at the others. Christy was nervously taking it all in. It was obvious that her training as a guide for adoptive families had never prepared her for a situation like this. The other man behind the desk was picking at his nails, seemingly disinterested in their conversation. Aaron figured him for head of airport security.

He looked back at Phillips and pointed his finger. "Mr. Phillips, there's been some mistake. I've never spent time in prison…"

Phillips took Aaron behind the arm at his elbow. "I'm sorry, Mr. Phelps. Those are the orders I've got. If you will hand over your return ticket we will have it exchanged for you for the soonest available flight back to the states."

Aaron jerked his arm away from Phillips causing him to stumble backwards. Christy gasped and the man behind the desk jumped to his feet and reached for a drawer while Aaron quickly held up his hands.

Everyone froze for a split second then Katie put her hands to her head. Aaron could see she was losing it, and so was he for that matter. Then it dawned on him.

"I'm sorry, Mr. Phillips, this is just so sudden…"

Phillips nodded his head as he straightened his clothes. The Chinese man behind the desk slid a shiny nightstick back into the desk drawer, closed it, then sat back down and resumed his disinterest. Christy breathed out audibly, as if she'd been holding her breath.

"But listen to me, please," Aaron said. "Aaron Joseph Phelps doesn't have a prison record, but Benjamin Aaron Phelps does."

Katie's eyes widened in surprise. "You mean your dad's middle name is…"

Aaron nodded.

"Who? What are you talking about?" Phillips asked. His eyebrows were crinkled in confusion.

"Benjamin Aaron Phelps is my father. He served time in California, many years ago." Aaron added the "many years ago" hoping it would sound less condemning. "I've never been in prison and have no record."

"Okay," Phillips said. "That makes sense. I'll do all I possibly can to help, but we still have a problem because, right or wrong, your Visa has been suspended. You're still going to have to leave the country immediately."

"Whoa, wait a minute," Aaron said. "This is the government's mistake, not ours. Can't you give us some time to straighten this out, or at least figure out what we're going to do?"

Phillips thought for a moment. Aaron could tell he didn't like to be put in this kind of situation where he had to make a command decision.

"Fair enough," he finally said. "I'm going to step out for a minute. I'll be right back," he said as he started for the door.

"Before you go, is there a phone available where we can make international calls?"

Phillips pulled a cell phone from a holder clipped onto his belt and tossed it to Aaron. "Here, use this. It's got full international connectivity. Government issue."

Aaron took the phone and Phillips left the room. He looked at Katie in exasperation. "I'm sorry."

Katie's face was flush, and her eyes were still very wide. "You didn't cause this," she said. "It was probably some pin-headed, pencil-pushing, over-zealous bureaucrat in the FBI with nothing better to do. What are we going to do?"

"First we call Renee. Maybe if I have to go home you can stay here and complete the adoption."

Katie held her hands up in frustration and let them flop down to her side. "I don't want to do this without you. And I don't want you to miss out on it."

"Well, I don't either. I know it's not ideal, but maybe it's our best choice – our only choice. When it's all said and done we'd still have Hannah. It's the end result that's the most important."

Katie took Aaron's hand. "I can't believe this is happening," she said.

Aaron shook his head. "Same here."

"Why?"

Aaron shrugged. "Beats me."

"Kinda makes you wonder what God's up to."

Aaron put his right hand around the back of Katie's neck. "But we're not going to go there."

"No."

"We've learned our lesson about having faith in God. Right?"

"Right…I guess."

Aaron nodded his head in agreement and took a steadying breath. "Yeah."

*   *   *

Three hours later, and several calls to Renee Hawkins, Ben Phelps, and the U.S. Embassy in Beijing Aaron and Katie had formulated a plan. Katie was standing with Aaron outside the administrative offices in the airport. He would soon be transported back to the departures terminal while Christy would take her to check in at the Grand Hotel in Beijing. She was trying hard to keep a brave face, but as Aaron prepared to leave she felt her resolve beginning to evaporate.

They had kept his return ticket and purchased another set of tickets that would take him from Beijing to Chicago and Tulsa and back to Chongqing via San Francisco and Hong Kong.

"This is a mess. I almost think it would be simpler if you could just handle it yourself," Aaron said as he hugged Katie.

Katie only nodded her head as she fought back tears. They had learned that since they were joint petitioners for the adoption they would both have to be present for the adoption to be finalized. Their plan – such as it was – was for Aaron to return home and clear things up, then meet up with Katie in Chongqing. Katie held no hope of the plan working, outside of another miracle from God, but like Aaron had said, they simply had no other choice.

"How are you going to hold up with all of this traveling?" Katie asked in a tiny voice.

Aaron pulled away to look at her and she could see in his eyes that he, like she, was already tired.

"I don't know," he said. "Hopefully, well." Then he took her hands in his and smiled at her. It looked somewhat forced, but she smiled back with all she could muster.

"Remember," he said, "what's impossible for man..."

Katie nodded her head. "Aint nothin' but a thang for God."

Aaron kissed Katie. "Now I don't want to find out you and Christy have been hitting all the clubs while I'm gone."

"Then don't ask when you get back."

Aaron grinned and nodded his head. "Either way, I'll see you soon."

"Okay."

"I love you."

A tear slid down Katie's cheek. "I love you too."

Aaron climbed back on one of the transport carts, and one of the uniformed policemen drove off with him.

Katie looked at Christy, whose smile was full of empathy.

"I hope it works out for you," Christy said as she stepped onto another transport cart with Katie.

Please...Lord...me too.

*   *   *

It was Saturday night in Beijing and Katie was packing her bags, preparing to leave for Chongqing the next morning. She hadn't heard from Aaron since he'd left and panic was overwhelming her thoughts and reasoning. *What is Aaron going through right now? Is he making any progress? Why hasn't he called?*

Aside from the uncertainty, the worry, and the crushing fear that their dream had died, Katie had managed to survive the days by numbing herself to almost everything. In a group with three other adoptive families from Dickinson they spent the days visiting many of the incredible attractions in Beijing. Even in her present, almost zombie-like state Katie had observed in Beijing a world shockingly different from anything she'd ever known in Oklahoma. Although the city was brimming with promise as it prepared for the 2008 Olympic Games, she had seen enough of Beijing to realize that what passed as a moderate lifestyle in Tulsa, Oklahoma would be seen as living like royalty any place over here.

But there was no doubting that China was far richer in history. Katie saw many historical wonders they'd only read about, including the Great Wall, the Summer Palace, the Forbidden City and Tiananmen Square. She had noticed a sense of contact with ancient history and the spectacular view around her when she followed the rest of the group as they hiked up a restored portion of the Great Wall. Walking into the giant, concrete courtyard of Tiananmen Square gave her chills. As she looked up at the portrait of Mao Zedong, Katie thought she could almost hear the whispers of the students who had died during the tragic events in 1989. As they toured each sight she wondered how Aaron would react if he were there. He'd been looking forward to seeing these incredible places even more than she had.

But when the daily activites were over it was the evenings that haunted her. She had never liked being away from Aaron, but with him halfway around the world she had never felt so alone while in the middle of a city with millions of people in it. Thursday and Friday night she had eaten in, hoping to hear from Aaron but with each passing hour her desperation grew until she cried herself to sleep somewhere around midnight.

Katie finished packing her main bag and sat it next to the baby's by the door. Everything else she would need in the morning so she left it out. She plopped down on the bed and took a cookie from the mini package of Oreos she had bought at a small market down the street during one of their daytime excursions. She separated the cookie and began to eat the filling off one of the sides. The sight of Aaron's bag, and the one they'd packed for the baby, were like reminders of what they were about to lose and made her heart ache even more than the previous two nights.

Once she finally did see Aaron, she wasn't sure if she'd kiss him or punch him first. How could he go so long without contacting her – especially with so much at stake? But then again, Aaron probably hadn't slept the whole time he'd been away, so she was continually worried about him as well. The constant flip-flopping of emotions kept her stomach in knots. That, combined with the new smells and foods, diminished her appetite to the point where she was eating very little. She felt tired and sick and weak.

Katie set the alarm clock for 7 A.M., even though she was pretty certain she wouldn't need it. Then, for the first time since she'd been in China, Katie picked up her Bible. Seeking refuge within, she saw that it had fallen open to Romans chapter eight, verse fifteen where she read: "Who shall separate us from the love of Christ? Shall trouble or hardship or persecution or famine or nakedness or danger or sword? No, in all these things we are more than conquerors through him who loved us." Katie closed her Bible and wrapped her arms around it. A peace settled over her, the words a balm to her wounded spirit.

How can I doubt you Lord, when you've given us such a wonderful promise? I believe Father, but please help me with my unbelief...

Chapter 30

Katie's China Southern flight landed in Chongqing at 1 P.M. Sunday afternoon. Carrying a backpack stuffed full of a complete copy of their dossier and other official paperwork over her shoulder she slipped a pair of sunglasses on to hide her red, puffy eyes. Despite several desperate messages for Aaron to call, another morning had passed without word from him and she had cried, alone and silent, for the entire flight. She had even thought about changing her itinerary and going home, but something made her come to Chongqing anyway.

She was wearing blue jeans and one of Aaron's black golf shirts she had procured for the trip, hanging to mid-thigh outside her faded jeans. She had also donned a teal-colored baseball cap which she wore on bad hair days, and had her hair in a haphazard ponytail, hanging out of the hole in the back of the cap. She was certain she looked as bad as she felt, which was saying a lot.

Resigned now that her dream was dead, Katie trudged slowly up the runway. She knew what she would do. She would wait it out one more day then get up Monday morning, the day they were supposed to get Hannah, and go home – alone.

As Katie transitioned from the runway into the airport terminal she was immediately overwhelmed by the mass of humanity she saw scurrying in every direction. This had to be the busiest airport she'd ever seen.

Katie located a sign in English that directed her to the right for the terminal exit and baggage claim. She picked her way through the crowd and finally reached the exit. Once through, the mob wasn't nearly as thick and she felt like she could breathe again so she stopped and quickly scanned the area, but she didn't see anyone who looked like they'd be searching for her. She was supposed to meet Mona, their guide for this leg of the trip.

She heard a honk behind her and barely dodged an airport maintenance cart that was traveling way too fast. She glared at the driver as he sped by to her left and mumbled a choice word under her breath then looked to her right and saw him.

Aaron was trotting toward her, coming from the entrance to the airport. When she saw him she started running and stumbling in his direction. Her legs had suddenly gone limp and she was gasping through her tears. Aaron broke into a sprint and quickly covered the last of the gap between them. As he reached her Katie fell into him and he lifted her off the ground in a hug.

Katie couldn't catch her breath enough to talk so she just cried as Aaron cried with her. They kissed and Katie looked at him. His eyes were red and his nose was running. He was wearing jeans, a plain blue t-shirt, his OU cap and he looked haggard with several days' growth on his beard and big, dark circles under his eyes.

"You look like crap," Katie said as she rubbed his face. After going through several days of such turmoil her emotions were raw and completely exposed so there was no filter on her thoughts anymore.

"Gee, thanks. I thought you were going to say I look bad."

Katie banged her fist against his chest. "What happened? Where've you been? Why didn't you call?"

Aaron looked around then picked up the backpack Katie had dropped and pulled her over to the side, against a wall. He ran his hands up and down her arms and shoulders. She could see a light in his eye that wasn't there when he left. "I never got a chance to call. My cell phone battery gave out over the Rockies and I've been traveling literally nonstop since I left you. Hence the crappy appearance."

Katie took a deep breath, trying to compose herself, refusing to believe anything other than the worst. "So what happened?"

"It's a go!"

"What?"

Aaron looked her squarely in the eye. "We got the Visa problems cleared up. We're going to get Hannah!"

Katie stared at Aaron as she tried to compute what she had just heard. A smile crept across her face and she felt instantly energized. "How in the world? I thought there was no chance."

Aaron shrugged his shoulders. "All I can tell you is that it was a God thing. I arrived back in Tulsa late Thursday afternoon and went straight to the Dickinson offices. Renee and Ben met me there. You're going to love this part."

Katie nodded for him to continue.

"A couple of weeks ago Renee had run into an old friend of hers that used to work at Dickinson."

"Okay, but how does that matter?"

"If you'll be patient I'll tell you."

"Listen, buster, I just spent three days thousands of miles from home. In a foreign country. Alone. Don't even mention the word patient."

"Okay, okay. It just so happens that Renee's friend now works at the Chinese Consulate in Houston."

"Oh my gosh," Katie said, making one word out of the three. "What are the chances?"

"I know," Aaron said, pointing to the sky. "Anyway, Renee called her and told her our situation and she talked to some people and got us an appointment. So Ben and I drove ten hours straight through to Houston and the Chinese Consulate."

Katie shook her head in disbelief. "No wonder."

"That's not all. When we got there, we couldn't find anyone who knew of our appointment. After a lot of sweet talk and flirting with the receptionist I finally got her to call Renee's friend."

"I'm over here in anguish and you're back home making eyes at some young bimbo?"

"Yeah, I really had to butter her up to get her help. I think I'm going to have to marry her when we get back. So finally we get to talk to a couple of Chinese officials. We show them our birth certificates, and Ben shows some of his paperwork. They didn't seem overly eager to help so it didn't seem very promising. They finally took our info away and were gone for a long time. I bet we waited for two or three hours. I don't guess I'll ever know what actually happened, but finally, at about five Friday evening they issued me a new Visa."

Katie smiled. "You're right. What other explanation could there be except that God did his thing?"

Aaron suddenly looked exhausted, as if recounting the past seventy-two hours had zapped him of what energy he had left. "So," he said with a big sigh, "we drove all the way back to Tulsa. I dropped Ben back off at the Dickinson offices and drove straight to the airport. Almost missed my flight. Had to run to my gate. Arrived just an hour ago."

"How are you still standing?"

Aaron tried to look sincere. "I have the strength of many, my dear, because I'm pure of heart."

"Whatever."

"Met Mona," Aaron said as he turned and waved a Chinese woman over to them. "She says most English speaking people can't pronounce her Chinese name so she adopted Mona as her English name."

Mona's face was kind and sincere. She had a genuine warmth about her that made Katie instantly at ease with her.

"What an ordeal you two have been through!" Mona said as she smiled at Katie. "I'm so sorry to hear about your trouble. I promise you I will do all I can to make your stay here in Chongqing as pleasant and easy as possible. Honestly, when I heard what was happening I was told you probably wouldn't be coming. I can't believe it worked out."

Katie looked at Aaron and smiled. "I can."

*   *   *

Aaron sat with pounding head and heavy, scratchy eyes in a steamy, darkened room on the twenty-fifth floor of the Chongqing Hilton. It was 5 A.M. and he had been awake since three, unable to sleep for the nervousness and excitement he felt. He had slept nearly nine hours Sunday night but he was still very fatigued from four days of constant travel. He was counting on adrenaline to get him through the day.

The evening before, he and Katie had a wonderful dinner at a restaurant across the street from the hotel called *Cheers*. Nobody there knew their name, and the menu was written entirely in Chinese, but they were very friendly and the host ordered for them. They enjoyed cashew chicken, steamed rice, and broccoli with oyster sauce. It was the first decent meal he'd had in three days so it seemed like a feast to Aaron. When they left, Aaron was certain he was too full to ever eat again so they started out for a walk. The air pollution hung in the sky like a think blanket, burning their already weary eyes, so they cut their walk short, returned to their room and were in bed by six.

Aaron rubbed his eyes. *Great way to start one of the most important days of your life. But then again, at least we're here.*

Aaron reached out and pulled the covers back over Katie where they had slid off one of her legs. She didn't look like she'd budged since they went to bed and he was glad she was sleeping well. Later today they would both need all of the energy they could muster. Aaron laced his fingers behind his head and pulled it forward, trying to release some of the tension he felt in his neck. Later today…their lives would change forever. He had been praying nonstop for the last three days, and he still felt the need to pray, knowing they were facing an imminent challenge once they got Hannah.

A horn honking on the street below jerked Aaron back to the present. Their joy in having the Visa situation resolved was soon tempered by a mixed bag of anticipation and anxiety.

Aaron didn't know what to expect. Those who were "veterans" in the adoption process – including the Humphreys – had cautioned them to expect some inaccuracies in some of the information coming from the orphanage. It was doubtful that any of it was intentional. Some of the discrepancies were likely a result of errors in translation, while others could probably be attributed to generalized statements regarding the diet and activities for all of the children who lived in the orphanage. Irregardless, the fact remained that Aaron and Katie had no way of knowing exactly what to expect when they finally received their baby.

Aaron walked quietly across the room and pulled a twenty ounce bottle of water from a case they had purchased yesterday afternoon at a small grocery store a few blocks down the street from the Hilton. Drinking water was another oddity of traveling abroad. They had to use bottled water, or boil tap water for everything, including brushing their teeth. Katie had even tied a ribbon around the faucet in their bathroom as a reminder not to drink from the tap.

Aaron located the small bag where his toiletries and their medicines were kept and took it and the water into the bathroom and closed the door. He dug around in the bag until he found a bottle of ibuprofen. His trembling hands caused him to fumble with the child-proof lid. Once he finally removed the lid he shook three tablets into his hand and downed them with one big gulp of water. He looked at himself in the mirror and rubbed his hand over his five-day beard. *Katie's right, I do look like crap.* He secured the lid back onto the plastic bottle and left it in the bathroom as he carried his water back into the main room.

He walked to the bedroom window, partially pulled one side of the curtain back and rested his forehead against the glass as he looked down at the lights, the buildings, and the street below him.

His biggest fear was that Hannah would be far worse than they were told. What if she couldn't fly for thirteen hours? What if something happened where they couldn't get her medical attention? What if... A shiver ran up his spine and he stopped short.

Father, we've placed our trust and our lives in your hands. Only you could've taken us this far. Lead us through this safely. And if not safely, give us the strength to accept your good and perfect will.

Aaron had been thinking a lot about the hands of Christ lately. They were hands of a carpenter. They were meant for working. Looking back on the events in their lives during the last nine months, and especially the past three or four days, Aaron could see unmistakably that Jesus' hands were in all of this as well. He had been working within each scene of their life, and as it unfolded he put the pieces into place so that they would form a glorious picture of His love for them and a grace that could only come from above. Indeed, it seemed no coincidence that it had been just over nine months since all of this began.

The pain, disappointment, fights and trials he and Katie had gone through pulled them closer together than ever before. Even during these past few days when they were a world apart there was still a palpable connection between them. Aaron could feel her prayers for him. This bond was something they would need as they stepped into the role of parenting Hannah.

The arrival of Ben had forced Aaron to come to terms with unresolved issues about his own past and Ben's abandonment of him and his mother. Aaron had managed to come to terms with the guilt he was carrying from how he had lived his life before his mother died. And he understood too, that Ben was the one meant to help pay their way. Aaron couldn't be mad at Ben when he was just fulfilling God's purpose.

Even during the drive to Houston, the Lord made a way for Ben and Aaron to overcome the awkward silence between them. Aaron had fought with resentment, and the urge to blame him for the fiasco. And he was sure Ben struggled with guilt. But in the end, Aaron realized that Ben had once again been there for him. He had stepped up and done whatever he needed to. Maybe Ben was an ex-con, but Jesus had released him from his chains long ago, and Ben had helped Aaron look to the Lord to rid himself of his own shackles.

Aaron watched two taxis nearly collide on the street below as they both ran through red lights. The drivers honked at each other, waved their fists out the window and moved on. Inside of one day in China he had already made the observation that traffic laws seemed to be merely a suggestion, not actual *laws*. Aaron shook his head at the humorous sight then walked back to the recliner he had been sitting in, plopped down, and laid his head back.

The irony of it all was that as they approached the hour when they would greet their new child, Katie became more and more anxious and unsettled about becoming a parent while Aaron found himself swept up in an unexplainable calm and peace. Maybe Katie was still unnerved by all they had been through, but for Aaron it was as if the Lord was telling him he had formed him for this. And it made sense. Who better to relate to an orphan than someone who knew what it was like to be abandoned as a baby? Even though he was blessed to have his mother in his life for the first nineteen years, Aaron could still understand feelings of rejection and loss, and of incompleteness that haunted a child who had been abandoned. Yes, he had never before felt more in the center of God's will.

The tension and pain in his head and neck was finally beginning to dissipate so Aaron pushed himself up from the chair and crawled back into bed, pulling the covers up to his waist. He leaned over and kissed Katie on the cheek.

"I love you," he whispered in her ear.

Katie squirmed and mumbled something unintelligible.

Aaron wrapped his arm around Katie and thanked God for this life he'd lived where nothing added up without the presence of the Lord in the equation.

* * *

Katie paced the floor as she waited for the call from downstairs. It was 10:30 a.m. and there was still no word regarding the arrival of her daughter who was supposed to be there thirty minutes earlier.

Had something happened to her? Was there a last minute glitch in the plans? A million questions rolled through her mind. After having their hope resurrected from ashes, she couldn't stand waiting any more. She looked at Aaron, who was sitting in the recliner in the tiny "living" area of their room. He was stretched out with his hands folded over his stomach and his eyes closed. The only sign of consciousness was his wiggling left foot and the occasional grunts he made in response to her questions.

She stopped in front of him. "How can you just lie around like that?"

Aaron opened one eye and looked at her. "Easy. Just pull back this lever on the side of the chair, and the foot rest kicks out."

"Very funny smarty pants. Aren't you nervous?"

"Suppose so."

Katie shook her head in frustration and stomped to the other side of the room. On her way back across she stopped for at least the tenth time in front of the small crib the hotel had provided. When they walked into the room upon arrival and turned on the lights the blue crib was the first thing she saw. Seeing it yesterday and the promise of what was to come made her heart jump, and it still did today. She picked up the baby blanket her mother had made for Hannah. It was bright red with ladybugs of various sizes and colors stitched into it. It had a one inch denim border around it, and down the middle was her name in big block letters made from the same denim as the border. She couldn't believe that yesterday morning she had planned to pack it away in the attic and forget about it.

Katie looked at her watch again. Ten thirty-three. Their guide, Mona, was supposed to call from the hotel lobby once Hannah arrived. She didn't know firsthand, but Katie had been told that the children would be delivered to the hotel if the Chinese officials felt like the orphanage conditions weren't up to par.

"Do you think I should call Mona?" Katie asked as she folded the blanket and laid it flat on the baby's bed.

"No. I don't see any need to pester her. She said she'll call us when they're here."

"I know. I just can't stand the wait; it's making me crazy."

Aaron folded in the recliner, took hold of Katie's hand and pulled her down onto his lap. Katie laid her head on his shoulder, closed her eyes and sighed deeply. His calm demeanor helped to settle her nerves.

"I'm so afraid I won't know how to take care of her."

"As far as I recall from anatomy class, an instruction manual doesn't come tied to a baby's toe. No one does, but they all get by."

"I know, but what if she's sicker than we knew?"

Aaron started to stroke her hair but Katie pulled away.

"You're going to mess my hair up," she said without moving.

"Oh yeah, you're right. I'm sure that's the first thing Hannah will notice. Probably blow the deal right off the bat."

"There will be pictures you know."

"True, but by then I'm sure your eyes will be red and puffy anyway. Might as well have frizzy hair to complete the look."

"Gee, thanks for the encouragement."

They sat together in silence. Katie knew Aaron was just trying to help her relax by teasing her like he was and she appreciated it. Katie pressed her cheek against his. He had shaved earlier, and it felt soft and smooth once again. But in the peaceful silence, doubts began to rise like flood waters from the Yangtze, and Katie wondered if this was just the calm before the storm. They had received information telling them about how the baby's tet spells came on and how it was treated. She was worried that she wouldn't give her the right amount of meds, or that she couldn't get to them in time. But then as if through divine guidance, she recalled the first part of Psalms chapter forty-six verse ten: "Be still and know that I am God..."

Then the phone rang. Katie sprang from Aaron's lap and stood in front of him with wide eyes, staring at the phone.

"Aren't you going to answer it?" Aaron asked.

Katie nodded her head but didn't budge. She couldn't seem to make her mind engage. A mix of excitement and fear flooded her thoughts and paralyzed her.

After the third ring Aaron cleared his throat and answered the phone. "Hi, Mona," he said while smiling at Katie. "They're here? Terrific. We'll be down shortly."

Aaron stood up from his chair and wrapped his arms around Katie. "Ready?" His voice trembled, betraying his emotion.

Katie couldn't speak. He wasn't asking in the rhetorical sense. Aaron was asking in the here and now. Her dream of having a child was just minutes away from becoming reality. She nodded her head again.

"Okay. Take a deep breath. You're going to be fine."

Nod.

"You can do this."

Nod.

Aaron closed his eyes. "Thank you, Father, for taking us to this point. We ask for you to lead us in your will. Amen."

Katie could feel her heart rate begin to settle. Not a lot, but enough. She took a deep breath and looked at Aaron. "Thank you."

Aaron grinned at her. "C'mon. Let's go."

Not knowing what to take, Katie looked around quickly and grabbed the brand new diaper bag Mark and Sherry had bought them, Hannah's baby blanket and a handful of tissues. Aaron picked up the gift bags they had brought for the orphanage director and the baby's nanny, and took Katie by the hand and led her out of the room and down the hall to the elevators where they waited for one to stop on their floor.

Aaron squeezed her hand, and she squeezed back.

After what seemed like forever, an elevator finally stopped. Another couple got off carrying a Chinese baby that looked to be about a year old. She wasn't very happy and being very vocal about it. Her new parents looked frazzled and scared.

Katie swallowed hard and took more deep breaths, trying to remain calm.

"How can such a big sound come from such a little body?" Aaron asked once they were alone on the elevator and moving down.

She just smiled at him. It was taking every ounce of her concentration to keep from hyperventilating.

The ride down was agonizingly long for Katie as the elevator car made several stops along the way. By the time they reached the first floor it was crowded and hot.

Once they finally stepped out of the elevator into the ornate hotel lobby they immediately saw Mona waiting for them, standing in the little sitting area to the left of the reception desk. They had met her there earlier in the morning to fill out yet more paperwork.

Mona had long, thick black hair and her almond shaped eyes were kind and expressive. It was late August in Chongqing and sweltering. But while Aaron and Katie were wearing shorts and short-sleeved shirts, she was wearing long pants and a lightweight long-sleeved shirt. Her face lit up in a big grin when she saw them and she met them halfway between the elevators and the sitting area.

"Do you have the envelope with the money?" she asked. Her voice seemed calm and reassuring.

Aaron pulled a white envelope from his back pocket and handed it to her. As part of their fees they had to provide three thousand dollars to the orphanage in crisp, one hundred dollar bills. To keep them crisp, Aaron had cut out two pieces of cardboard that were slightly bigger than the bills, placed the bills between them and secured them with rubber bands before putting them in the envelope. Aaron had mentioned to Katie that he thought this smacked of bribery. Katie had urged him not to mention a word to anyone and he had begrudgingly agreed to it.

Mona put the money in her satchel then took Katie by the hands and smiled at her. "Ready?"

"Yes," Katie said, her voice already shaking.

"Okay then. Follow me."

Aaron and Katie trailed her quietly as she walked around the elevators and down a long hall on the other side of the hotel lobby. She stopped at a door and said, "Here we are." She took the camera Aaron was holding and said, "I will take the pictures for you," as she opened the door.

Katie's mouth was dry and she could barely hear for the sound of her heart pounding in her chest. As the door swung open she saw a medium-sized Chinese man in khaki pants and a white, long-sleeved dress shirt. To his left and just behind him was an old woman wearing black pants and a grey, long-sleeved blouse. She was holding a baby wrapped snugly in a blanket. The old woman was smiling, and her eyes had a twinkle in them that felt almost familiar and inviting.

Katie put her hand to her mouth. She felt her knees begin to tremble as tears immediately filled her eyes. She walked toward the old lady who looked her in the eyes and smiled. As Katie got closer she could see wisps of black hair and the most beautiful face she had ever seen.

Hannah Lin was awake and seemed to be studying her intently. Her almond shaped eyes had the same intensity in them that drew Katie to her initially. Her little lips formed a perfect Cupid's bow and her cheeks were soft and smooth looking. Katie vaguely noticed a camera flash off to her left as she reached for the baby.

The old woman carefully placed her in Katie's arms and at that moment her heart exploded with a fountain of love and joy. Everything they had been through – even the last few days – seemed to point to this very moment. Month after month of disappointment vanished instantly. God had answered "yes" to her heart's desire and the bitter pill of infertility seemed to vanish in His grace. She was now a mother. Tears flooded her eyes and streamed down her cheeks as she laughed and cried all at once.

"Hi, baby," she said with a small voice as she looked deep into her daughter's eyes. She laid her cheek against the baby's and felt the warmth from her tiny face.

"I'm Mommy, and this is your daddy."

Katie looked up at Aaron who was smiling from ear to ear. He wiped his eyes with the heel of his hand as tears streamed down from their corners. He put one arm around Katie and brushed the baby's cheek with the back of his forefinger.

Hannah looked up at them with a blank gaze, as if she were unsure what to make of these crazy strangers who were crying and carrying on for no good reason.

Katie wiped her eyes and nose with a tissue that was wadded up in her hand. She was struck at how tiny the baby was, even after a little more than nine months. And this led to a realization of just how sick the child had become.

But none of that mattered at the moment. She would worry about that when the time came. For now she was going to revel in this beautiful gift God had given to them. She suddenly became aware of the steady stream of camera flashes going off in the room.

She looked up and Mona said, "Okay, you two, look at me and smile."

They did and Mona snapped the shutter on their first family portrait.

Hannah whimpered, and shifted in her arms. Katie thought she noticed a bluish tinge around her lips, but she looked again and it was gone. Still, just the thought reminded her that they weren't out of the woods yet. They had to get Hannah home, where they had surgery scheduled for her the Monday after their return. Until then, Katie would have to live with the fear of what might happen.

To the right-hand side of the room was a conference table and chairs. Katie took a seat in one as Mona began making introductions.

"This is Mr. Fu, the orphanage director," she said.

He stepped forward, smiled at Katie and shook her hand in a polite, formal manner. Aaron then shook hands with him and handed him the gift bag they had brought for him. They had found out from Renee that the orphanage director was a man so they purchased him a red ball cap with the University of Oklahoma's "OU" symbol on it, some chocolates from a candy store in downtown Sand Springs and a nice ink pen with a pine wood casing.

"And this is Chien," Mona said as she smiled toward the old woman. Chien nodded and shook Katie's and Aaron's hands. Aaron handed her a gift bag with more chocolate from the same store, and a small wicker basket containing a few nice smelling soaps.

"*Xie xie,*" she said quietly. Her voice sounded tired.

Mona and Mr. Fu left the room, and Katie looked at Chien and noticed tears in the corner of her eyes.

"Lucky baby," she said in English.

Aaron shook his head and patted himself and Katie. "Lucky *mamma* and *ba ba.*"

The old woman smiled again. Katie looked closely at her. There seemed to be a light in her eyes that she had recognized in only a few of the other Chinese people they had been around.

Katie stood up. "Do you want to hold her?" she asked as she held Hannah out to Chien. The old woman looked confused, so Katie said, "Say goodbye?"

Chien seemed to understand and smiled at them. Her chin quivered as she took the baby from Katie's arms. She whispered softly in her ears using her native Mandarin dialect. Katie couldn't make out anything, except for one word – *Yesu* – the word for Jesus.

Katie stepped closer to her and whispered "*Yesu,*" to her, and put her hand over her heart and over Aaron's. Chien smiled with obvious delight and handed Hannah back to Katie. She looked at the family of three and smiled. "*Yesu,*" she said, looking at them.

Katie handed Hannah to Aaron, who took her cautiously. He seemed nervous, but eager to learn. He looked down at Hannah with a smile as wide as the Oklahoma plains.

"When you get big enough," he said, "I'm going to teach you how to play golf with me."

The sight of Aaron holding their daughter brought tears to her eyes again. Here was the man who had run from fatherhood, so fearful from his own childhood. Now he stood by her side and embraced their daughter with her.

The warmth of gratitude spread through her.

Thank you, Jesus. Thank you, Yesu.

Chapter 31

The following week, on Tuesday, Katie and Aaron boarded a United Airlines 777 in Hong Kong, China. As Katie found her seat and pulled Hannah from the snugly she had carried her in and slipped out of it, she couldn't stop thinking about home. The next time they touched down it would be on American soil, in Chicago. She could picture the scene in her mind's eye. They would exit the plane and probably stand in line at the customs gate. But once they passed through the gate at customs Hannah Lin Phelps would become an official citizen of the United States of America. The thought sent goose bumps traveling up Katie's arms. Hannah, of course, would be oblivious to the moment. In fact, she may never really appreciate its significance. But after a week and a half in China, it was not lost on Katie and Aaron.

Katie settled into her seat, buckled the belt, and thanked God for her parents and their insistence on paying for an upgrade on their flights to and from China. Even Aaron, who stubbornly refused most help, had mentioned how nice it was. After flying coach on the unexpected flights home and back he fully appreciated what a treat it was – especially with a baby.

After receiving Hannah last Monday, they had gone to the civil affairs office in Chongqing that afternoon to finalize the adoption in China. They had to sign an oath saying they would never harm or abandon their baby. Katie remembered having to bite her tongue to keep from making a wisecrack about the irony of signing such an oath for a government that forces its people to abandon or abort their children.

They then spent Tuesday and Wednesday sightseeing while they waited for Hannah's passport to be completed. They received their passport from Mona on Wednesday afternoon then flew to Guangzhou on Thursday.

In Guangzhou they stayed in the opulent White Swan Hotel on the Shamian Island, a small strip of land in the Pearl River that bisects

Guangzhou. The island, which was connected to the rest of the city via many bridges, was a welcomed oasis for Katie in the middle of yet another large city, full of millions of people who were battling through life at a breakneck speed. Friday, Saturday and Sunday they toured the city and shopped in various street front stores that had sprung up all over the island.

The White Swan Hotel had been the standard location for adoptive families for many years due to its proximity to the U.S. Consulate. And even though the consulate had moved forty minutes away, it was still the place to go for adoptive families and Katie could understand why. The pace of life around the hotel was much more akin to what Katie was accustomed to back home, and given all they had been through, it was much needed.

For at least the sixth or seventh time since they had left Guangzhou that morning Katie checked her fanny-pack for their passports. Early Monday morning their guide, William, delivered their paperwork to the consulate then escorted Katie, Aaron, and Hannah to the consulate where they went through a semi-formal ceremony with several other families to complete the U.S. part of the adoption. Cameras flashed and popped all around the room as families captured the moment. At one point the flashes were coming at such a pace that Aaron had likened it to a Tiger Woods press conference.

Katie studied Hannah with concern. Her color didn't look good today. They had a scare Sunday night and ended up at an emergency room across town when Hannah had one of her tet spells. It was the first time it had occurred since they had received her, but Katie panicked when it didn't seem like the medicine was helping as much as it should have.

Aaron leaned over and kissed Hannah and Katie each on the forehead. "Everything okay?"

"Look at Hannah. Doesn't her color seem off today?"

"Yes, it does," Aaron said. "I noticed it during the flight to Hong Kong but didn't want to say anything."

Katie nodded and looked back at her baby who had cried every night since they received her. During the day she seemed okay, but at night she cried, soft and mournful. They had been warned during one of the adoption seminars they attended that if the baby had been well cared for there would be a grieving period for her. In the long run, those babies seemed more likely to form closer, lasting bonds with their parents, but in the short run it was certainly tougher. Only when Katie or Aaron held her and rocked her did she quiet down so they had each taken shifts during the nights holding and loving on the child while the other slept.

Katie thanked God for the old woman, Chien, who obviously loved Hannah and had taken great care of her. It comforted her to know that Hannah had received such care while Aaron and Katie dreamed of her every night. She wondered what would become of the old woman. Hannah certainly wasn't just another child to her, but there were many more that relied on her care. Chien also served to highlight the Lord's provision though, that in a country that was "officially" atheistic, there would be a lone woman who served God by serving his children, and Hannah was one of them.

The giant plane taxied to the runway then began accelerating for takeoff. The force of it pushed Katie's shoulders back against her seat. While holding Hannah Katie closed her eyes. *Thank you God, for all you've done. Please see us home, and make us well.*

After several hours spent talking with Aaron, eating dinner and watching a movie, the plane had been darkened and Hannah and Aaron were both asleep. Katie was still holding Hannah and could barely keep her own eyes open so she slid her arms through the straps of the snuggly, transferring the baby from one arm to the other as she worked to slip it on. When Hannah did sleep it was very deep and sound – probably a result of living the first nine months of her life in an orphanage. This made it easier for Katie to slip her back into the snuggly and secure all the straps without awakening her.

Katie settled back into her chair and was soon deep into sleep herself. She dreamed of her home in Oklahoma, and all its green grass and trees. She dreamed of the wheat fields of Central and Western Oklahoma that seemed to spread out into the horizon as far as the eye could see. She then dreamed of vacationing in Florida where the tide bounced her about as it rolled in and out on the shore and the wind of the ocean seemed to whistle at her.

Suddenly she was startled awake by Aaron, who was shaking her forcefully.

"Katie, wake up!" he said loudly.

Katie squinted at him. "What?" she said, but just as she said that she heard Hannah wheezing loudly and struggling for air. She quickly checked the straps on the snuggly, but none of them were around her neck.

Aaron was already up, digging through the overhead compartment for their backpack and Hannah's medicine.

A flight attendant approached Aaron, frowning at him. "Sir," she said, "the seatbelt light is on. That means you need to stay buckled in your seat until we pass through this turbulence."

Aaron just ignored her as he pulled the backpack out of the compartment and began sifting through it.

"Sir!"

Aaron appeared as close to panicked as Katie had ever seen him. "I can't find her medicine!"

The attendant looked from Aaron to Katie, then at the baby. Once she saw the baby and the bluish hue that was spreading on her face her expression instantly changed from anger to worry.

Katie's heart sank as fear gripped her once again. "The medicine! I forgot to take it out of the suitcase before I checked it!"

Aaron's eyes darted back and forth. Katie could see the wheels in his mind turning as he tried to think of a solution.

Katie felt like crying, and only the panic within her stopped the tears. She couldn't believe she'd been so stupid!

"What do we do?" she said to Aaron.

Aaron looked at the flight attendant. "Ma'am, do you know if there are any doctors or nurses on board?"

"We'll check the roster," she said as she hustled back towards the cockpit.

Katie could feel all the eyes in the business class section resting on her as they watched. Some of the people were obviously annoyed that their tranquil sleep had been disturbed. Others seemed genuinely concerned, while others looked on in morbid curiosity.

Oh my God! Father, please don't punish her because of my mistake!

Katie helplessly watched as her baby struggled for life. She stared up at Aaron. She could feel herself crumbling within. "I'm sorry," she said before she choked up.

Aaron glanced down, then back at her. She could see the strain in his face. "It's not your fault," he said. "You're tired. The airlines are so freaky with their regulations these days..."

Katie knew he meant it, but it didn't ease her pain or guilt. Just then the baby stopped wheezing. Katie didn't see her chest or stomach rising. She looked up at Aaron who was also watching the baby.

Oh God, no...

Just then, Katie began to recall the infant CPR class they were required to take. She searched for a pulse and couldn't find one. She jumped to her feet and snatched Hannah from the snuggly. She laid Hannah on her back across the airplane seat and tilted her head backward with her left hand under her chin and her right hand on her forehead. She gave her two gentle breaths, covering her mouth and nose with her mouth.

Right on cue, Aaron dropped to his knees beside her and performed five chest compressions just above her sternum with the index and middle fingers of his right hand.

Oblivious to all around them, Katie and Aaron continued this rotation for what seemed like hours but was only a minute or so, stopping at times to check for a pulse, before the flight attendant returned with a nurse.

"This is Georgia," she said. Katie glanced up from her breaths to find an older woman peering down at them with concern. She had thick brown hair pulled back into a bun. Her mouth was wide and her large brown eyes showed years of experience.

"Let me in there," she said. Her tone was serious, but not panicked. Aaron moved to let her next to Katie. Georgia checked her for a pulse again.

"Still no pulse," she said as she stood up and Aaron moved back into his spot. Katie and Aaron glanced at each other as they resumed CPR. Katie could see the panic in his eyes.

"How long have you been performing CPR?"

Aaron looked at his watch. "No more than three minutes."

"Is there a portable defibrillator on board?" Georgia asked the flight attendant.

The attendant began moving off in the direction of the cockpit. "Yes," she said as she hurried away. Within seconds she returned with a small red case.

Georgia took the case and waved her head at Aaron who quietly moved over. She rummaged through the box then emptied it. Suddenly her head snapped up and she stared at the flight attendant, concern filling her eyes. "There are no pediatric pads in this kit," she said.

"We've got some," Katie answered hurriedly. Their doctor had recommended that they verify that the plane carried a portable defibrillator, and that they purchase their own set of pediatric pads for use with it before they left home – just in case.

"Get them out, quickly," Georgia said. "We can't use these pads, they're meant for adults."

Katie took over compressions while Aaron dumped the contents of the backpack into the aisle and sifted through it until he found them. They looked like EKG pads, except bigger.

Georgia took the pediatric pads out of their wrappers, stuck them on the baby and hooked them to the battery as Aaron ripped the blue dress they'd brought for Hannah to come home in down the middle to get it off of her.

Katie and Aaron continued CPR until Georgia brought the battery up to charge and placed the pads on Hannah's tiny chest.

"Back," she said and Katie and Aaron removed their hands from Hannah.

Katie winced and jumped as Georgia shocked her baby. Then she and Aaron resumed CPR.

Georgia checked for a pulse again and shook her head when she didn't find it. She shocked Hannah again and checked for a pulse a second time. Nothing. She tried it one last time. She raised her arm and looked at her watch. "Got it," she said.

Katie's head sunk to her chest as a wave of relief washed over her. She placed her hand over Hannah's small chest. When she felt it rise slightly, she nodded her head at Aaron.

"We've got her back," Georgia said, "but just barely. Her pulse is still weak and slow. We need to divert to the nearest hospital."

"The captain has already been in contact with San Francisco International Airport. We are diverting there and should land within a few hours."

Katie began to tremble uncontrollably. Aaron took her hand in his shaking hand and she felt her eyes filling with tears. "I can't believe I've done this. I almost killed my baby."

"No, you didn't," Aaron said. "Don't say that!"

"But…"

"No!" Aaron interrupted. "You didn't do anything wrong. It's a mistake anyone could make. You don't even know that the medicine would've helped this time."

"He's right," Georgia said.

"Will she make it four or five hours longer?" Katie asked Georgia.

She placed her hand over Katie's. "I don't know, dear. All we can do is pray and hope."

Katie took Aaron's hand. "All we can do…"

Aaron shook his head, his brown eyes were big. "No," he said softly. "It's not *all* we can do. It's the *best* thing to do."

*   *   *

The plane landed in San Francisco four hours and forty-five minutes later. Katie had kept her hand on the baby's chest for the rest of the flight while Georgia stayed close and checked her pulse periodically. The runways had been cleared and the plane made it to the gate quickly after landing. Paramedics met them just outside the gate and immediately took over, placing electrodes on her chest and hooking her to a heart monitor.

Katie took Georgia by the hand. "I don't know what to say but thank you."

"I hope everything turns out okay."

Katie smiled at Georgia, and for a brief moment, they shared a palpable connection that strangers rarely experience. There was no need for words. She would never see Georgia again – she didn't even know her last name. But she would never forget her.

Aaron took Katie by the hand and they followed the paramedics to the waiting ambulance where they loaded Hannah into the ambulance and instructed Aaron and Katie to follow in a waiting taxi. They were taking her to Saint Francis Memorial Hospital where a team was waiting to perform the surgery Hannah needed on her heart.

As the ambulance pulled away from the curb Katie leaned up from the back seat and stared at it. She memorized the license plate number and the ambulance number. Her heart ached like never before. This was the first time she'd been separated from her daughter since they got her.

Katie closed her eyes and tried to pray, but she didn't know what to say. She wanted to find the words powerful enough to make God understand how desperate she was but instead she could only picture Hannah's face and that torn blue dress and the red whelps on her ribs.

Lord God, I'd give up my life right now...

Chapter 32

She passed peacefully in the night. There were no press releases, or parades in her honor. In the eyes of the world her life had been inconsequential and of little value. But in the eyes of Yu Bao, her life had significance and importance beyond description.

As Bao sorted through Wu Chien's belongings she came across the thing she was looking for the most – her Bible. Chien had hidden it underneath the lining in her old, torn up suitcase.

It wasn't like the gleaming, leather-bound Bibles she had seen some foreigners carry. It was pieced together with photocopies, handwritten transcriptions and portions of published translations.

Bao thumbed through it in reverence, because despite its outward appearance, she knew it contained something more precious than gold – the good news of Jesus Christ.

The last page said "My Children" at the top, written in Chien's handwriting. Below it was a list of fifteen to twenty names with dates by them. Bao scanned the list until she found her name, and the date – "6/13/2005." She smiled as a lone tear slid down her cheek. It was her birthday. Not the day they *thought* she was born onto this earth, but the one they *knew* about – the day she'd accepted Christ.

No, there wasn't much commotion when Wu Chien left this earth. But Yu Bao was certain there was thunderous applause in heaven as she was born into the waiting arms of Jesus.

I will do my best to honor your memory. I love you, Momma...

* * *

Aaron and Katie Phelps walked up the long runway that connected the arrivals terminal to the baggage claim and airport entrance in Tulsa International Airport. Katie was proudly carrying Hannah – a triumphant smile on her face. Aaron trailed a step behind, dutifully carrying Katie's purse, the backpack, Hannah's diaper bag and one small suitcase – and loving every minute of it.

Hannah had gained half a pound in the week since the heart surgery, a sure sign that it had been a success. She was more active, energetic and louder than ever before.

Aaron could see the sun, red and brilliant sinking into the western horizon through the smoky tinted windows. Approaching the end of the runway, he could see Katie's parents, and her sister Janie. They were smiling and waving happily. Margaret was dabbing at her eyes with a tissue and Frank was holding his cap in his hands and smiling proudly in his own dignified way. Janie held up a big, colorful bouquet of balloons with "Welcome Home" and "It's a Girl!" printed on them.

Aaron waved and gave a thumbs up to Mark and Sherry Cooper, and their son Ryan, born the day Katie and Aaron left for China. And behind all of them were some friends and employees from Dickinson. Someone was holding an American flag high into the air.

When they reached the mob of friends and family they were instantly surrounded in a raucous sea of love and joy. The hugs and tears and laughter didn't even register with Hannah, who was sleeping soundly in Katie's arms.

Frank took some of the baggage Aaron was carrying and Mark took the rest. Aaron stood on his toes looking around, over, and through the happy mob.

Finally, off to the side Aaron spotted Ben Phelps, standing quietly in his own unassuming manner. Ben smiled and waved. Aaron left the crowd and walked toward his father. Ben stuck out his hand but Aaron ignored it as he embraced his dad in a hug for the first time in his life. It was clumsy and awkward, but it counted.

"Thanks for calling," Ben said as he looked over at Hannah.

Aaron watched Ben watching his granddaughter and shrugged. "I figure she's got a lot of life ahead of her. She's going to need all the family she can get."